Yahoo!® For Dummies®, 2nd Edition

W9-CFC-633

Major Destinations in Yahoo!

Yahoo! Finance

finance.yahoo.com

An incredible range of investment news, plus personalized portfolios.

Yahoo! Sports

sports.yahoo.com

A data-rich compendium of current sports news and stats.

Yahoo! Chat

chat.yahoo.com

A continual global party! Create your own room and search for friends.

My Yahoo!

my.yahoo.com

Customize the Yahoo! experience.

Yahoo! News

dailynews.yahoo.com

Exhaustive (and exhausting) coverage of current events.

Yahoo! Games

games.yahoo.com

Play cards and board games with other Yahoo! members.

Yahoo! Clubs

clubs.yahoo.com

Mini-societies of folks who share an interest.

Yahoo! Companion

companion.yahoo.com

A customizable destination bar for your browser. Portable bookmarks!

Yahoo! Personals

personals.yahoo.com

Find a pen-pal or a soulmate.

Yahoo! Photos

photos.yahoo.com

A personal online photo album. Share with selected friends or the whole world.

Yahoo! Briefcase

briefcase.yahoo.com

Upload valuable files to your own storage area, and share them with associates.

Yahoo! GeoCities

geocities.yahoo.com

Join a bustling, dynamic Web-page community. PageBuilder is free and easy.

Yahoo! Radio

radio.yahoo.com

Listen to Internet radio from your computer desktop — it's free.

Yahoo! Greetings

greetings.yahoo.com

Send online greeting cards for free, through e-mail.

For Dummies®: Bestselling Book Series for Beginners

Yahoo! For Dummies, 2nd Edition

Make the Most of Messenger

Chat with friends voice-to-voice free of charge.

Receive e-mail alerts.

Follow your local (or non-local) sports teams.

Read your customized news.

Track your stock portfolio.

See which friends are online at any time.

Look up profiles of other Yahoo! members.

Set up group charts.

Search Yahoo! with keywords.

Meet People

Join the party at Yahoo! Chat.

Develop groups of friends with Yahoo! Messenger.

Join in the discussion on Yahoo! message boards.

Join a Yahoo! Club or start your own.

Meet other gamers at Yahoo! Games.

Post an ad at Yahoo! Personals or respond to one.

Find other Yahoo! members at the Yahoo! Member Directory.

Exercise Your Right to Buy

Fill your shopping cart from Yahoo! stores.

Bid on stuff at Yahoo! Auctions.

Browse the "used" marketplace at Yahoo! Classifieds.

Comparison-shop the Internet at Yahoo! Shopping.

Put These Features on My Yahoo!

Your horoscope

Local sports scores

Your TV or cable listings

Selected stocks

Movie times at local theaters

Best airline fares to selected cities

E-mail and friend alerts

News, news, and more news

Health tips

Get Organized with Yahoo!

Save files at Yahoo! Briefcase.

Keep your shopping info in Yahoo! Wallet.

Stay informed with Yahoo! Alerts.

Be on time using Yahoo! Calendar.

For Dummies®: Bestselling Book Series for Beginners

Yahoo!® FOR DUMMIES® 2ND EDITION

Yahoo!® FOR DUMMIES® 2ND EDITION

by Brad Hill

IDG Books Worldwide, Inc.
An International Data Group Company

Foster City, CA ◆ Chicago, IL ◆ Indianapolis, IN ◆ New York, NY

Yahoo!® For Dummies® 2nd Edition

Published by
IDG Books Worldwide, Inc.
An International Data Group Company
919 E. Hillsdale Blvd.
Suite 400
Foster City, CA 94404
www.idgbooks.com (IDG Books Worldwide Web Site)
www.dummies.com (Dummies Press Web Site)

Library of Congress Control Number: 00-103654

ISBN: 0-7645-0762-1

Printed in the United States of America

10 9 8 7 6 5 4 3 2 1

2B/RQ/RQ/QQ/IN

Distributed in the United States by IDG Books Worldwide, Inc.

Distributed by CDG Books Canada Inc. for Canada; by Transworld Publishers Limited in the United Kingdom; by IDG Norge Books for Norway; by IDG Sweden Books for Sweden; by IDG Books Australia Publishing Corporation Pty. Ltd. for Australia and New Zealand; by TransQuest Publishers Pte Ltd. for Singapore, Malaysia, Thailand, Indonesia, and Hong Kong; by Gotop Information Inc. for Taiwan; by ICG Muse, Inc. for Japan; by Intersoft for South Africa; by Eyrolles for France; by International Thomson Publishing for Germany, Austria and Switzerland; by Distribuidora Cuspide for Argentina; by LR International for Brazil; by Galileo Libros for Chile; by Ediciones ZETA S.C.R. Ltda. for Peru; by WS Computer Publishing Corporation, Inc., for the Philippines; by Contemporanea de Ediciones for Venezuela; by Express Computer Distributors for the Caribbean and West Indies; by Micronesia Media Distributor, Inc. for Micronesia; by Chips Computadoras S.A. de C.V. for Mexico; by Editorial Norma de Panama S.A. for Panama; by American Bookshops for Finland.

For general information on IDG Books Worldwide's books in the U.S., please call our Consumer Customer Service department at 800-762-2974. For reseller information, including discounts and premium sales, please call our Reseller Customer Service department at 800-434-3422.

For information on where to purchase IDG Books Worldwide's books outside the U.S., please contact our International Sales department at 317-572-3993 or fax 317-572-4002.

For consumer information on foreign language translations, please contact our Customer Service department at 1-800-434-3422, fax 317-572-4002, or e-mail rights@idgbooks.com.

For information on licensing foreign or domestic rights, please phone +1-650-653-7098.

For sales inquiries and special prices for bulk quantities, please contact our Order Services department at 800-434-3422 or write to the address above.

For information on using IDG Books Worldwide's books in the classroom or for ordering examination copies, please contact our Educational Sales department at 800-434-2086 or fax 317-572-4005.

For press review copies, author interviews, or other publicity information, please contact our Public Relations department at 650-653-7000 or fax 650-653-7500.

For authorization to photocopy items for corporate, personal, or educational use, please contact Copyright Clearance Center, 222 Rosewood Drive, Danvers, MA 01923, or fax 978-750-4470.

About the Author

Brad Hill has worked in the online field since 1992, and is a preeminent advocate of the online experience. As a bestselling author of many books and columns, Brad reaches a global audience of consumers who rely on his writings to help determine their Internet service choices.

Brad's twelve books include a Publishers Weekly bestseller and a Book of the Month catalog selection. Brad's titles in the "...*For Dummies*" series include *Internet Searching For Dummies*, *The Internet Directory For Dummies*, and *WebTV For Dummies*, 3rd Edition. As a columnist, Brad writes about cyber-cultural trends and online destinations. His work appears regularly in *ComputorEdge Magazine, Online Investor Magazine,* Raging Bull, and TipWorld.

Brad is often consulted in the media's coverage of the Internet, and appears often on television, radio, Webcasts, and as quoted in publications such as *Business Week, The New York Times,* and *PC World.*

Brad doesn't get outdoors much. As compensation, he is listed in Who's Who and is a member of The Author's Guild.

ABOUT IDG BOOKS WORLDWIDE

Welcome to the world of IDG Books Worldwide.

IDG Books Worldwide, Inc., is a subsidiary of International Data Group, the world's largest publisher of computer-related information and the leading global provider of information services on information technology. IDG was founded more than 30 years ago by Patrick J. McGovern and now employs more than 9,000 people worldwide. IDG publishes more than 290 computer publications in over 75 countries. More than 90 million people read one or more IDG publications each month.

Launched in 1990, IDG Books Worldwide is today the #1 publisher of best-selling computer books in the United States. We are proud to have received eight awards from the Computer Press Association in recognition of editorial excellence and three from Computer Currents' First Annual Readers' Choice Awards. Our best-selling ...*For Dummies*® series has more than 50 million copies in print with translations in 31 languages. IDG Books Worldwide, through a joint venture with IDG's Hi-Tech Beijing, became the first U.S. publisher to publish a computer book in the People's Republic of China. In record time, IDG Books Worldwide has become the first choice for millions of readers around the world who want to learn how to better manage their businesses.

Our mission is simple: Every one of our books is designed to bring extra value and skill-building instructions to the reader. Our books are written by experts who understand and care about our readers. The knowledge base of our editorial staff comes from years of experience in publishing, education, and journalism — experience we use to produce books to carry us into the new millennium. In short, we care about books, so we attract the best people. We devote special attention to details such as audience, interior design, use of icons, and illustrations. And because we use an efficient process of authoring, editing, and desktop publishing our books electronically, we can spend more time ensuring superior content and less time on the technicalities of making books.

You can count on our commitment to deliver high-quality books at competitive prices on topics you want to read about. At IDG Books Worldwide, we continue in the IDG tradition of delivering quality for more than 30 years. You'll find no better book on a subject than one from IDG Books Worldwide.

John Kilcullen
Chairman and CEO
IDG Books Worldwide, Inc.

Eighth Annual Computer Press Awards ≥ 1992

Ninth Annual Computer Press Awards ≥ 1993

Tenth Annual Computer Press Awards ≥ 1994

Eleventh Annual Computer Press Awards ≥ 1995

Dedication

This book is dedicated to Susan Pink, its editor and my collaborator on many projects. Susan's humor and expertise lighten the stresses of a book's many deadlines, and she is a joy to work with.

Author's Acknowledgments

Mary Bednarek and Steve Hayes engaged in a flattering conspiracy to involve me in this project. Many thanks to them both for their confidence.

Mary Corder got me writing these bright yellow books in the first place, for which I'll always be grateful.

Allen Wyatt's contributions to this book are essential.

Many thanks to Nicholas Smith.

Publisher's Acknowledgments

We're proud of this book; please register your comments through our IDG Books Worldwide Online Registration Form located at http://my2cents.dummies.com.

Some of the people who helped bring this book to market include the following:

Acquisitions, Editorial, and Media Development

Project Editors: Susan Pink

Acquisitions Editor: Steve Hayes

Proof Editor:

Technical Editor: Allen Wyatt, Discovery Computing, Inc.

Editorial Manager: Constance Carlisle

Editorial Assistant: Beth Parlon, Candace Nicholson

Production

Project Coordinator: Dale White

Layout and Graphics: LeAndra Johnson, Tracy K. Oliver, Jeremey Unger, Erin Zeltner

Proofreaders: Laura Albert, Corey Bowen, David Faust, York Production Services, Inc.

Indexer: York Production Services, Inc.

Special Help
Amanda Foxworth

General and Administrative

IDG Books Worldwide, Inc.: John Kilcullen, CEO; Bill Barry, President and COO; John Ball, Executive VP, Operations & Administration; John Harris, CFO

IDG Books Technology Publishing Group: Richard Swadley, Senior Vice President and Publisher; Mary Bednarek, Vice President and Publisher; Walter R. Bruce III, Vice President and Publisher; Joseph Wikert, Vice President and Publisher; Mary C. Corder, Editorial Director; Andy Cummings, Publishing Director, General User Group; Barry Pruett, Publishing Director

IDG Books Manufacturing: Ivor Parker, Vice President, Manufacturing

IDG Books Marketing: John Helmus, Assistant Vice President, Director of Marketing

IDG Books Online Management: Brenda McLaughlin, Executive Vice President, Chief Internet Officer; Gary Millrood, Executive Vice President of Business Development, Sales and Marketing

IDG Books Packaging: Marc J. Mikulich, Vice President, Brand Strategy and Research

IDG Books Production for Branded Press: Debbie Stailey, Production Director

IDG Books Sales: Roland Elgey, Senior Vice President, Sales and Marketing; Michael Violano, Vice President, International Sales and Sub Rights

◆

The publisher would like to give special thanks to Patrick J. McGovern, without whom this book would not have been possible.

◆

Contents at a Glance

Cartoons at a Glance

By Rich Tennant

"Face it Vinnie— you're gonna have a hard time getting people to subscribe online with a credit card to a newsletter called 'Felons Interactive!'"

page 9

"Children- it is not necessary to whisper while we're visiting the Vatican Library Web site."

page 103

"No, Thomas Jefferson never did 'the Grind,' however, this does show how animation can be used to illustrate American history on the Web."

page 193

"It's a letter from the company that installed our in-ground sprinkler system. They're offering Internet access now."

page 55

"NOW, THAT WOULD SHOW HOW IMPORTANT IT IS TO DISTINGUISH 'FERTILIZING PRACTICES' FROM 'FERTILITY PRACTICES' WHEN DOWNLOADING A VIDEO FILE FROM THE INTERNET."

page 277

"SINCE WE BEGAN ON-LINE SHOPPING, I JUST DON'T KNOW WHERE THE MONEY'S GOING."

page 307

"IT'S JUST UNTIL WE GET BACK UP ON THE INTERNET."

page 337

Fax: 978-546-7747
E-mail: richtennant@the5thwave.com
World Wide Web: www.the5thwave.com

Table of Contents

Introduction

● ●

I know what you're thinking. A whole book about a Web site? If that question crossed your mind, a major surprise is headed your way.

Yahoo! began as a mere Web site, though an important one. Yahoo! was one of the first attempts to index the Web when the Web was little more than a small, quirky, mostly noncommercial network of personal pages. Because you could search Yahoo!'s index, the site was everyone's favorite launching point for a night of Web surfing.

That was then. Yahoo! grew, adding features to its core index and search service. In time, Yahoo! began to resemble a distinct network of sites: sports, finances, communities, entertainment, chat. Like planets orbiting a sun, these discrete destinations made up a self-contained system of impressive dimensions.

The growth and evolution continued. When certain Internet measuring firms began keeping track, they found that the vast and burgeoning Yahoo! was one of the most popular destinations on the entire Web. Now, with many millions of registered users and an astonishing number of Web pages displayed each day, Yahoo! is clearly a full-fledged online service. Great content and a vibrant community add up to one of the dominant and most-used domains in cyberspace.

Yahoo! still has its index and its search engine. Those features retain their high status among experienced and new Internet users. But Yahoo! has evolved light-years beyond its roots. This book takes you on a tour of unexpected depth and breadth. Do you think you know Yahoo!? Prepare to be amazed.

About This Book

This book is your companion to the Yahoo! experience. It exposes you to information and introduces you to communities. It makes your life easier by explaining Yahoo!'s sources of free e-mail, free stock portfolios, free interactive gaming, free sports coverage, free clubs, free auctions — in fact, the money you spent for this book might be the cheapest introduction you ever bought to one heck of a lot of free services and content.

You might be familiar already with some Yahoo! services. If you've been around the Web for a while, you almost certainly have used Yahoo! in some capacity. So don't read this book like a novel. I'll tell you right now, the butler committed the crime and the guy gets the girl. So feel free to skip around or even read the book backwards. (Sense make will that sentence only the is this, backwards it read do you if.)

This book is best used as a reference and a companion to your on-screen explorations. The book isn't going anywhere. (Unless you let your dog have it, in which case it will soon be buried under the geraniums.)

What's New in the Second Edition

It has been almost a year since I completed the first edition of this book, and in that short time Yahoo! has continued its explosive growth in both popularity and services. The service gets better and more comprehensive all the time. And certainly bigger! This book is longer than the first edition, yet the challenge to squeeze everything in is more daunting than ever.

Yahoo! has made cosmetic changes, of course, as all Web services frequently do. But Yahoo! has maintained its basic page design with greater continuity than most sites. The real changes are substantive — the additional services Yahoo! has acquired or created from scratch. Yahoo! seeks to provide a complete, rounded online lifestyle experience, and at this point has nearly attained that goal. The addition of Web hosting services and the slick evolution of the Yahoo! Briefcase and Photos sections make it easier than ever to build a complete (and free!) homestead on the Net. This edition also covers Yahoo!'s gradual positioning as a mobile-computing service, so get your connected cell phones and PDAs ready.

Every chapter of this book has been updated to the latest Yahoo! realities, and I added six entirely new chapters. It's a Pulitzer-worthy effort, I tell you. Soon to be a major motion picture, without doubt.

Foolish Assumptions

Some of my assumptions about you, the reader, might be mistaken. For example, I assume I'll get a holiday greeting card from you. That might be merely a vain hope. Chocolate in the mail? Wishful thinking for sure.

In the area of reasonable assumptions, I have a few. This book doesn't require very much Internet or Web experience. But I do assume you have online access. I don't describe how to get on the Internet, but if you are on, I take it from there and guide you to the splendor of Yahoo!. It doesn't matter to me *how* you get to the Net — through an ISP, or America Online, or a connection from work, or WebTV. Yahoo! is open to every online citizen.

I also assume you know how to operate a Web browser in the most basic way. This book doesn't explain how to click a link, for example, though it does tell you *which* link to click. You should know how to use the Back button — click it once, you'll find out.

Conventions Used in This Book

Being the conventional type, I thought I'd put some conventional conventions in this book. I've use different typefaces to help you pick up certain on-screen elements, as they are presented on the page, in a glance.

URLs (Uniform Resource Locators), which are Web addresses, are indicated in this kind of type:

```
chat.yahoo.com
```

When I introduce a term for the first time, I *italicize* it to get your attention and notify you that there's no reason for you to know what it means.

Often I point out hyperlinks to look for, and they appear <u>underlined</u> in the text.

How This Book Is Organized

This book uses a radical and innovative organization system. Text is printed on pages, and pages are bound into a portable folio! And that's not the half of it. The book's content is divided into distinct parts called . . . well, they're just called *parts,* a term that might not win any prizes for originality. What's amazing is that each part has chapters! I feel confident that this startling idea will spread to other books, revolutionizing the entire publishing industry. Either that, or the sun will rise tomorrow. Place your bets.

This section tells you what's in each part. Here goes.

Part I: Starting the Yahoo! Experience

Part I explains how to join Yahoo!. Joining costs nothing and is not necessary if you use the service casually. But if you hang around Yahoo! enough, you inevitably find a good reason to get a Yahoo! ID, and Chapter 1 describes what that gets you and how to do it. Chapter 2 details how to set up a personalized My Yahoo! page — one of Yahoo!'s most valuable features, in my opinion. The final chapter in this part is devoted to Yahoo! Mail, a free and sophisticated Web-based e-mail system.

Part II: Building Your Yahoo! Nest

This entire part contains new information that wasn't in the first edition. Chapter 4 details the Web hosting community Yahoo! GeoCities and explains how to build a home page using either of the two page-building programs. The next chapter is for folks ready to take their Web site to the next level by hosting it at Yahoo! Website Services — the professional-level hosting service of Yahoo!. Finally, Chapter 6 describes how to build an online file repository using Yahoo! Briefcase and its sister service, Yahoo! Photos. The latter provides a great (free) way to share family albums.

Part III: Knowledge and Fun

Yahoo!'s traditional services of indexing and searching the Web are intact and thriving. The first chapter in Part III instructs you in using the Yahoo! directory and search engine. More than that, it offers little-known tips from my Bag of Tips (which is kept in my Tip Vault, located in my Secret Fortress of Tips) on how to maximize your use of these features.

When it comes to raw information, nobody beats Yahoo!. Cooked information is available, too. Chapter 8 walks you through Yahoo! News, and Chapter 9 runs you through Yahoo! Sports. Yahoo! Finance, one of the must-use sites for wired investors, is taken apart and then put back together again in Chapter 10. Online music is a hot topic, and I explain the several ways that Yahoo! dishes up the tunes in Chapter 11. Finally, the fun moves into high gear in Chapter 11, which takes you on a trip through Yahoo! Games.

Part IV: Meeting the Yahoo! Community

Yahoo! goes way beyond information. In and around the millions of information pages served up every day, a community lurks restlessly, emerging into the forefront in the chat, message-board, and club domains of the Yahoo! service. The chapters in Part IV get specific about how to meet people and how to operate the slick Yahoo! community features. Yahoo! Chat is an extraordinary, Java-powered chatting empire. Yahoo! Messenger is an incredible free gadget that allows you to talk — really talk, with your voice — to any other user, anywhere in the world, free of charge. Yahoo! Clubs are wonderful prefab Web sites that anyone can easily build and share. All these wonders and more are divulged in these chapters.

Part V: At Your Service, Yahoo! Style

Information, community, and services: the three parts of any complete online service. Part V steps you through travel planning, car buying, job hunting, reservation making, ticket purchasing, game playing, and real estate hunting. In addition, a separate chapter explains the excellent Yahoo! Companion, a little-known feature for your browser that I think is the cat's meow (without those annoying claws digging affectionately into your skin).

Part VI: Buying and Selling

Ah, shopping. Isn't that the point of life, when you get right down to it? Even if you're less superficial than I, you might find some use and a lot of fun in this part. The three chapters in Part VI describe not only shopping in the Yahoo! online mall, but also how to set up your own virtual auction and run a classified ad. Did you know you can comparison-shop the entire Internet with a click of the mouse in Yahoo!? Chapter 21 tells you how.

Part VII: The Part of Tens

Part VII is where I share my laundry and shopping lists. No, wait — that's another book. The two chapters in this part are lists of a sort. They point you to Yahoo! services that don't fit in the rest of the book. Book-size limitations notwithstanding, all the Yahoo! destinations covered in the two Part of Tens chapters are important aspects of the overall service, and many would be worthy of an entire chapter if there were room.

What You're Not to Read

Hey, this book isn't a novel. It doesn't even have an exciting ending. (No butler whatsoever.) You shouldn't feel like you must read the whole book straight through. In fact, there's no need to read even a single chapter straight through. For that matter, think twice before reading an entire paragraph. Don't finish this sentence! Okay, I'm getting carried away. My point is that you can find out a lot, and probably have more fun, by choosing what to read from the Table of Contents. This isn't school.

Occasionally, I can't resist explaining a particular point in technical terms. Just ignore me — I always return to normal quickly. As a public service, the reader-friendly editors of this book have marked all geekish paragraphs with the Technical Stuff icon. You're at liberty to read those paragraphs or not; nothing in them is necessary to have a good Yahoo! experience.

Icons Used in This Book

This book wouldn't be a ...*For Dummies* book without goofy pictures in the margins. Those little designs are called *icons,* and each one signals something different. Here's the rundown.

The Tip icon flags a nugget of wisdom that you'll remember for a lifetime (or at least until your next snack). These tips are worth their weight in gold. Needless to say, they don't weigh anything.

This icon, if recollection serves, reminds you of something you shouldn't forget. Like turning off the oven before the muffins burn. Or more likely, some on-screen item that's easily forgotten.

I don't devolve into my innate geekhood very often, at least not publicly. When I do, it isn't a pretty sight. Accordingly, the editors of this book have placed this warning icon next to such paragraphs to warn you away. Heed the warning.

Occasionally, if you do something wrong on the Web, your computer liquefies into a steaming puddle. Just kidding. It's hard to do any damage on the Net. Still, my sense of drama prompted me to include a few dire warnings in the text.

Where to Go from Here

If you're an occasional Yahoo! user but not a registered member, I recommend starting with Chapter 1. Get yourself a Yahoo! ID — you'll be using it plenty as you browse through this book. If you already have the ID but haven't customized Yahoo! to your preferences, you might want to start with Chapter 2.

Besides the first two chapters, your best bet is to examine the Table of Contents, choose a chapter that looks interesting, and start exploring. Remember, this book doesn't have to be read page by page. Dart in and out according to your interest at any moment.

At some point in your surfing, visit me at my site and drop me a line. I'm always home at

```
www.bradhill.com
```

And now . . . let the fun begin. Yahoo! awaits. It's better than you imagined.

Part I

Starting the Yahoo! Experience

The 5th Wave   By Rich Tennant

"Face it Vinnie— you're gonna have a hard time getting people to subscribe online with a credit card to a newsletter called 'Felons Interactive.'"

In this part . . .

You might think Yahoo! is just another Web site, but in this part I describe how to register in the Yahoo! community, get an ID, create a My Yahoo! personalized page, and begin using Yahoo!'s free e-mail system. The complete, integrated awesome Yahoo! experience begins here.

Chapter 1

Making a Name for Yourself

*B*ecause Yahoo! is a Web-based service equally available to all Internet users, it doesn't require membership, but it does encourage it. In fact, Yahoo! withholds certain functions from nonmembers. Getting a Yahoo! membership is simple and free. The process amounts to filling in a few bits of information and clicking an on-screen button. Yahoo! members are defined by their Yahoo! IDs, which are like on-screen membership badges that I refer to repeatedly throughout this book. Your ID is your screen name when using any of Yahoo!'s many community and interactive features.

I encourage you to create a Yahoo! ID. Doing so is the first step in making the most of the service. With a Yahoo! ID, you can mold the service around your information needs and tastes. Each Yahoo! ID, if taken advantage of to the max, can create an entire customized service, especially through the use of Yahoo! Messenger, Yahoo! Companion, Yahoo! GeoCities, My Yahoo!, and Yahoo! Mail.

This chapter explains how to make your ID (it takes only a minute or so); how to create a public profile; and how to search for other member profiles.

Finding Yourself

Frequent Yahoo! users almost always end up establishing a Yahoo! identity (ID). Each Yahoo! ID is paired with a password, and you must know both to sign in and view your personalized settings. Many services are available only to people with Yahoo! IDs — in particular, the interactive services that allow you to create something within Yahoo!.

You need a Yahoo! ID to buy something in a Yahoo! store; make travel reservations; build a Web site at GeoCities, place a Yahoo! Classifieds or Yahoo! Personals ad; chat; play games; open a Yahoo! Mail account; use Yahoo! Messenger; personalize the service with My Yahoo!; create a stock portfolio; post a message; use the calendar; make a Yahoo! profile; and take advantage of other functions and services.

It's important to emphasize that joining Yahoo! with an ID and a password is entirely free. Your membership gives you access to many interactive portions of Yahoo! and doesn't cost a dime, ever. You have no limit on how much you can use your ID. Everyone in your family can have his or her own Yahoo! ID, with its own set of personalized features, and never incur charges.

If you explore Yahoo! enough, you're bound to encounter invitations to join. The following steps work no matter where you start from:

1. **Type the following URL in your browser:**

   ```
   login.yahoo.com
   ```

   The Welcome to Yahoo! page appears.

   Surprisingly, the Yahoo! home page doesn't have a Create a New Account button. When wandering around the service, however, you are repeatedly prompted to sign in or create a Yahoo! ID. So you can start your free account from many places, but one of those places isn't necessarily on your screen when you want it to be. Use the preceding URL.

2. **Click the <u>Sign me up!</u> link.**

   The sign-up page appears, as shown in Figure 1-1.

3. **Under the Create Your Yahoo! ID heading, fill in the fields.**

   You choose your own user name (Yahoo! ID) and password. If you choose an ID name already in use, Yahoo! prompts you to choose another after you submit the form. You must complete all the fields in this section.

4. **Under the In case you forget your password heading, fill in all fields.**

   You can choose from a selection of questions Yahoo! will ask if you ever forget your password. This section is important, especially for those who keep multiple IDs.

5. **In the Personal Account Information section, complete all fields.**

   This information helps Yahoo! provide relevant information to various customizable pages of the service.

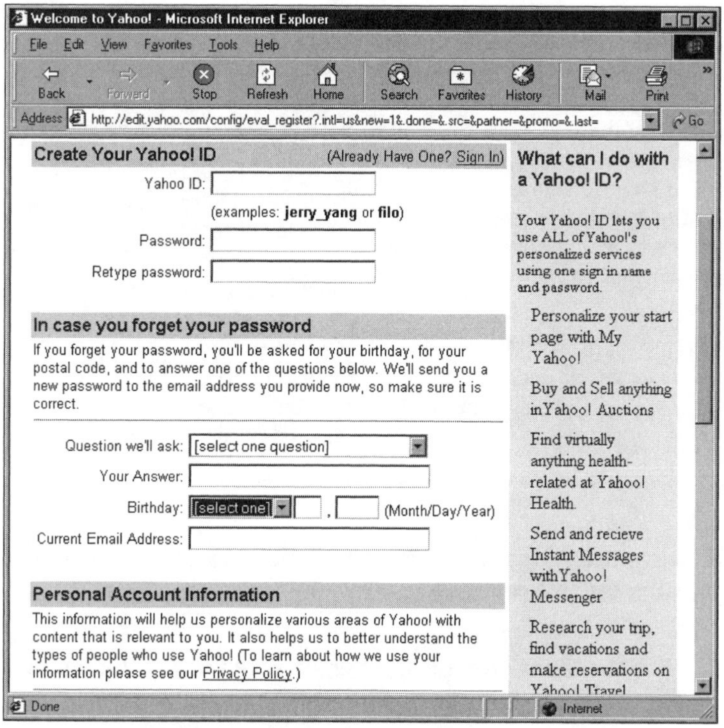

Welcome to Yahoo! - Microsoft Internet Explorer

File   Edit   View   Favorites   Tools   Help

Back   Forward   Stop   Refresh   Home   Search   Favorites   History   Mail   Print

Address   http://edit.yahoo.com/config/eval_register?.intl=us&new=1&.done=&.src=&partner=&promo=&.last=

Create Your Yahoo! ID   (Already Have One? Sign In)

Yahoo ID:

(examples: **jerry_yang** or **filo**)

Password:

Retype password:

In case you forget your password

If you forget your password, you'll be asked for your birthday, for your postal code, and to answer one of the questions below. We'll send you a new password to the email address you provide now, so make sure it is correct.

Question we'll ask: [select one question]

Your Answer:

Birthday: [select one]   ,   (Month/Day/Year)

Current Email Address:

Personal Account Information

This information will help us personalize various areas of Yahoo! with content that is relevant to you. It also helps us to better understand the types of people who use Yahoo! (To learn about how we use your information please see our Privacy Policy.)

What can I do with a Yahoo! ID?

Your Yahoo! ID lets you use ALL of Yahoo!'s personalized services using one sign in name and password.

Personalize your start page with My Yahoo!

Buy and Sell anything in Yahoo! Auctions

Find virtually anything health-related at Yahoo! Health.

Send and recieve Instant Messages with Yahoo! Messenger

Research your trip, find vacations and make reservations on Yahoo! Travel

Done   Internet

Figure 1-1:
The sign-up page for creating a Yahoo! ID and password.

6. In the Tell Us About Your Interests section, check any boxes that apply.

This section is optional and important only if you don't personalize the service manually. Chapter 2 describes how to create a My Yahoo! page, which I recommend for getting the most out of the service. If you do get involved with My Yahoo!, these check boxes are irrelevant.

7. Click the Submit this form button.

That's it! You now have a Yahoo! ID and password. A page appears with those two crucial bits of information — it's a good idea to write them down some-where or commit them to your flawless photographic memory.

After you have a Yahoo! ID, you can sign in to Yahoo! in a number of ways. Booting Yahoo! Messenger logs you on automatically (see Chapter 15), and the Yahoo! Companion (Chapter 20) has a dedicated Sign In button. Any number of Yahoo! services request a sign-in before letting you see that por-tion of the service. Other than these methods, the best way to sign on is to follow these steps:

Signing in and out

When you sign in to Yahoo! with your ID and password, you stay signed in for the duration of your session. You have to sign out manually (using a Sign Out link, which appears on almost every page of the service) or shut down your browser to end your session.

However, there's no harm in remaining signed in, even if you're elsewhere on the Web and not using Yahoo!. You're not incurring any charges by being signed in. Normally, signing into Yahoo! is the first thing I do when I go online, and I never have a reason to sign out.

The Sign Out links are useful if your computer lives in a household with more than one Yahoo! user, each with an individual Yahoo! ID. (Because the service is free and Yahoo! is not your Internet service provider, there's no limit to how many IDs can be initiated from a single computer.) Every Yahoo! ID in your household can have its own identity, e-mail account, Personals mailbox, My Yahoo! pages, and so on.

1. **Go to the Yahoo! home page by following a browser bookmark or using the following URL:**

   ```
   www.yahoo.com
   ```

2. **Click the My button (or the Personalize link) at the top of the page.**

   The Welcome to My Yahoo! page appears. On the Yahoo! home page, the My Yahoo! link leads to the same place.

3. **Enter your Yahoo! ID and password and then click the Sign in button.**

   If you check the Remember my ID & Password box, Yahoo! places your sign-in information on your computer's hard drive, where Yahoo! can find it. From then on, clicking the My button in Step 2 signs you in and takes you to your My Yahoo! page.

Creating a Profile

The Yahoo! profile tells other Yahoo! members a bit about you. How much you reveal is up to you. Every Yahoo! ID has a corresponding profile that's created automatically when you establish the ID. These default profiles contain nothing more than the basic information you supply when creating your ID. You can elaborate on that stripped-down profile or not, as you choose.

Many user-enhanced profiles remain basic, including the member's name, perhaps a general location, and nothing else. But if you really get motivated, you can put in your gender, location, age, marital status, real name (not your

ID name), occupation, e-mail address (different from your Yahoo! e-mail), a statement of your interests, personal news, a favorite quote, a home page URL, and other Web links you enjoy visiting. Oh — and a picture, if you have one scanned.

You must have a Yahoo! ID to create a profile. After you've established your ID, follow these steps:

1. **When signed in with your Yahoo! ID, go to the Member Directory page at the following URL:**

   ```
   profiles.yahoo.com
   ```

2. **Click the <u>My Profiles</u> link at the top of the page.**

   The Public Profiles for *YourID* page is displayed.

3. **Click the <u>Edit</u> link next to the Yahoo! profile you want to adjust.**

   If you have more than one Yahoo! ID assigned to a single password, choose from the list of profiles. You can start from scratch with a new profile by clicking the Create New Public Profile button. Creating a new profile adds it to the list shown on this page. The check box turns off the I'm Online! Status icon that appears on some profiles. That icon alerts visitors to your profile of your online/offline status — it lights up with a smiling face when you are available through Yahoo! Messenger (Chapter 15) or Yahoo! Chat (Chapter 13). Check the box to disable the status icon.

4. **On your Profile page, click the link representing the portion of the page you want to change.**

   As you can see in Figure 1-2, you can edit your basic profile information, your picture, your voice greeting, and your page colors.

Yahoo! profiles have expanded considerably since the last edition of this book. You can now change the way your profile page looks and sounds to visitors. The following sections describe how to adjust the four main portions of your Yahoo! profile.

The basic you

Your most essential information is displayed in the central portion of your Yahoo! profile. On your Profile page, click the <u>Edit Profile Information</u> link to add, remove, or alter this information.

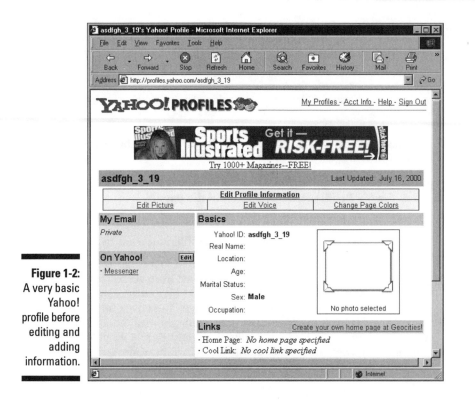

Figure 1-2:
A very basic Yahoo! profile before editing and adding information.

The Edit Public Profile page (Figure 1-3) presents several information fields, each of which is optional. Fill in only what you want to fill in. Some people display their name but not their gender or age. Others, perhaps trying to meet a significant other, include age, marital status, and gender. You might not want to display your non-Yahoo! e-mail address — visitors can always write you easily enough at your Yahoo! ID address. (See Chapter 3 for a thrilling, play-by-play account of Yahoo! Mail.)

Near the bottom of the page is a check box for adding your profile to the Member Directory. Doing so allows other Yahoo! members to find your profile by matching keyword or interest. Leave the box unchecked if you don't want to be found.

The photogenic you

Any profile can contain a photo of you or some other picture. If you don't select or upload a picture for display, the photo space of your profile remains blank with a "No photo selected" caption. Most people either upload a photo or leave the space blank, but you can also place a Yahoo!-provided drawing in that space.

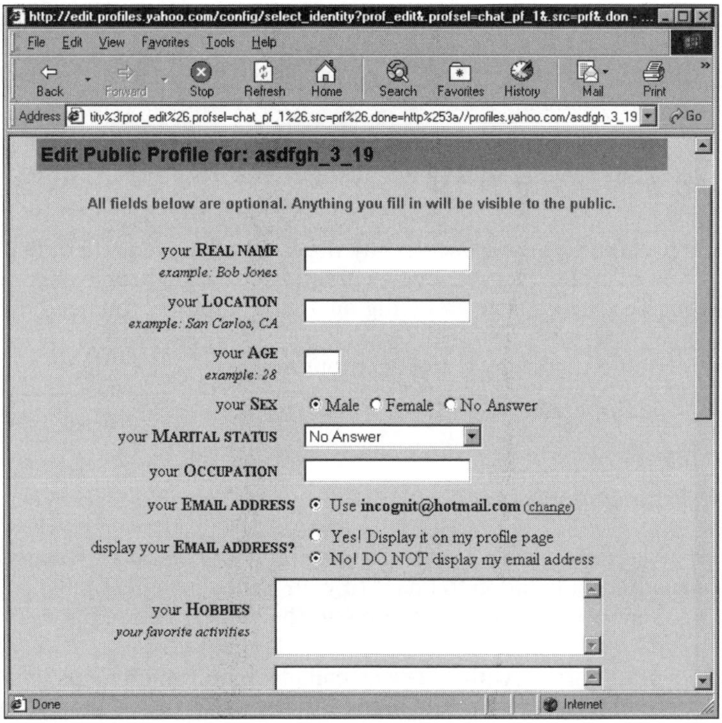

Figure 1-3:
Use this
page to
supply your
profile with
basic
personal
information.
All fields
are optional.

If you have a photo of yourself scanned and residing in your computer, and you'd like to show the world what you look like, follow these steps:

1. **On your Profile page, click the <u>Edit Picture</u> link.**

2. **On the Add Picture page, click the Browse button.**

   You can link also to a photo of yourself that currently resides at a Web location — for example, in your server space at Yahoo! GeoCities (a great service described glowingly in Chapter 4). Quite possibly, you have photos of yourself stored in Yahoo! Photos, and you can link your profile's photo to that space also. If you decide to pursue one of these options, click the appropriate link on this page.

3. **In the Choose file dialog box, double-click a photo file from your hard drive's folders.**

4. **Click the Upload button.**

   It may take a minute or two for your photo to upload, depending on its size and your connection speed. After the upload is complete, your Profile page is displayed with the photo in place. Every photo is compressed into the available space on the Profile page, which is not large. You can see a full-sized version of the photo (and anyone else's photo on other profiles) by clicking the photo itself.

The voluble you

Adding a voice greeting is certainly the most advanced and difficult aspect of a Yahoo! profile. Very few voice greetings exist on profile pages as of this writing. To create a voice greeting on your computer, you need the following:

- ✔ A sound card, which most computers have
- ✔ A microphone
- ✔ Speakers
- ✔ Recording software

If you manage to record a voice greeting on your computer, you need to upload it to an Internet location to link it to your Yahoo! profile. Unlike adding a photo, Yahoo! does not offer to upload the voice greeting for you.

Yahoo! does partner with a service called Pagoo, which helps you record a voice greeting using your telephone. After you do that, Pagoo stores the file for you at a linkable location, and you're in business. This service takes much of the hassle out of adding a voice greeting to a profile.

Pagoo is a fine service, but it does not provide a toll-free number when recording over the telephone. So you may incur a charge on your phone bill — non-American users should be especially cautious. The Pagoo dial-up number is in the United States, in northern California.

To try Pagoo, follow these steps:

1. **On your Profile page, click the <u>Edit Voice</u> link.**

2. **On the Edit Voice for *YourID* page, click the <u>Use your telephone to record a voice message!</u> link.**

3. **Enter your e-mail address and then click the Start! Button.**

    The next page provides instructions, including a phone number and access code. The Pagoo service is free except for possible phone service charges. You must enter your e-mail address to complete the process, because some instructions arrive through e-mail.

The colorful you

Yahoo! Profile pages are simple and rather sparse in design, like every Yahoo! page. There is some choice, however, in the color scheme of headings, subheadings, and the background. Click the <u>Change Page Colors</u> link on your Profile page and then select the color scheme you prefer. When you click the Finished button, your Profile page appears with the new colors. You can change them as often as you like.

Cruising the Profiles

You can become acquainted with other Yahoo! members in several ways — chatting is perhaps the most obvious (see Chapter 13). Searching for public profiles that meet certain criteria can give you some ideas of who to look for in those chat rooms. It's also a way to get ideas for your own profile. Here's what to do:

1. **Enter the following URL in your browser:**

   ```
   profiles.yahoo.com
   ```

   The Yahoo! Member Directory page appears.

2. **Use the keyword field and radio buttons to search for public profiles.**

   If you know a person's Yahoo! ID, use that radio button. The Real Name button is an excellent way to search for a person by his or her real name, which may or may not be entered in that person's profile inform ation. Use the Keyword selection to locate people who may match your interest. Yahoo! compares your keyword(s) to every word in every profile.

3. **Click the Find button.**

   The Profile Search Results page appears.

4. **Click any Yahoo! ID to see that profile.**

   If you get too many search results, you might want to try a power version of the profile's search engine. Use your browser's Back button to return to the Member Directory Search page and then click the <u>Advanced Search</u> link. The page that appears gives you several more searching options, including the capability to search for only profiles with pictures, profiles indicating one gender, or profiles within a certain age range.

Every search results page in the Member Directory comes with its own search form. This duplication is handy, because you can initiate a new search without backtracking to the original Member Directory page from which you started. In fact, the persistent search form is a better way to search because it lets you specify that you want only profiles with pictures.

Adding Interest

You can add interest to your Yahoo! profile — literally. Yahoo! has added a My Interests section since the last edition of this book. My Interests operates as a self-contained feature, but you can also link your interests to your Yahoo! profile. Here's how to proceed:

1. **On the Member Directory page, click any topic link under the Browse Interests heading.**

   You begin drilling into the Interests directory.

2. **On any Interests directory page, click the <u>Add this interest</u> link to put that interest on your Yahoo! profile.**

   When you take this step, your profile shows the interest as a link, directing visitors to the directory page.

Each directory page of the My Interests section contains a list of every Yahoo! member who has added that interest. Figure 1-4 shows the My Interests page for Internet Business. Click any member name to see that person's profile.

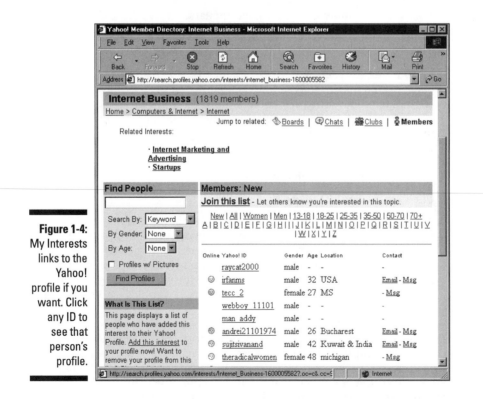

Figure 1-4:
My Interests links to the Yahoo! profile if you want. Click any ID to see that person's profile.

Using My Interests is a superb way to meet people with shared interests and find their profiles. This service is far more effective than roaming around chat rooms or message boards hoping to find somebody with whom you have common ground.

Chapter 2

It's Yours! Customizing the Experience

I like an accommodating online service, don't you? One that takes an interest in my needs and preferences — and doesn't make it hard to find them. Yahoo! is so accommodating that it devotes a substantial part of its service to something called My Yahoo! — but for the purposes of this chapter we'll pretend it's yours. (But it's mine! All mine!) In fact, My Yahoo! belongs to anybody who cares to personalize it, which is pretty easy to do.

Yahoo! places a great deal of its content into the personalization basket. That means you have a grand array of choices to make when customizing your Yahoo! experience. Fortunately, you need never etch a choice in stone (in fact you can't, and I discourage using chisels near computers); you can change your personal settings as often as you please. I tweak mine almost daily.

This chapter instructs you in choosing and configuring your personal Yahoo! choices. In addition, I recommend certain choices as good starting points. That doesn't mean I discourage you from making any of the available selections — I just like to see people getting started on the right foot. Feel free to ignore my advice and explore on your own.

If I were to create detailed explanations of every feature available in My Yahoo!, this book would deal with nothing else and a scandal would ensue. (Ha! Wishful thinking from someone who has never been pictured in a tabloid.) So instead, I offer a quick rundown of all the features, pointing you to other parts of this book if I explain them in detail elsewhere.

Some users ignore My Yahoo!, and indeed, you don't have to use it. The design of Yahoo! makes it pretty easy to click your way anywhere you want without much delay. But I feel certain that any Yahoo! user who creates a My Yahoo! page (or two) will quickly become dependent on it (or them). It's a great way to consolidate the Yahoo! experience, which can be overwhelming in its vastness, and put frequently visited parts of the service within easy reach. Give it a try.

Explaining the Not-So-Obvious

Right about here, you might be thinking, "What the heck is personalization, anyway? And what's in it for me?"

Good questions. Every online service presents its members with content — lots and lots of content in big services such as Yahoo!. *Content* is simply stuff that appears on your screen — information, forums, entertainment, and various services. There can be so much of this content, in so many categories, that grappling with it all is daunting. You might find a great feature one day and then forget how you got to it the next day. You need some way of customizing the experience to suit your taste, needs, and discoveries.

On the Web, the most common customization feature is the Bookmarks or Favorites list in your Web browser. America Online users have used Favorites for years to keep track of online destinations worthy of repeat visits. Internet Explorer also has a Favorites feature, and the Navigator browser offers a customizable list called Bookmarks. In all these cases, the lists enable you to assemble pointers to favorite virtual places, but they don't change the basic interface of the online service or Internet browser you're using.

Yahoo! goes a step further, thanks to its convenient Web-based foundation. Because every Web browser on the planet understands HTML, the software language that Yahoo! (and every other Web site) is built on, My Yahoo! can let you change the actual interface — in other words, the way Yahoo! looks on your screen. You do have limits to how you can change its appearance, and some large portions of Yahoo! are off-limits to customization, but the important point is that through My Yahoo! you are empowered to create your own custom Web pages of Yahoo! features. That's far more control than you have in America Online or any other non-Web service.

Customizing This and That

Yahoo! is vast. It's enormous. The service is massive, prodigious, and colossal. I hope I'm conveying the impression that Yahoo! is big. It has features within features, and still more features within those. You might compare it to a planetary system, with several large bodies orbiting the home page, each of which contains its own atmosphere, topographical features, and society. If you ever make such a comparison aloud, don't be surprised if people edge away from you at parties.

Untangling a few terms

In television ads, you hear phrases like "Internet online service." In this chapter, I refer to online services and Web-based online services. It's a good idea to clarify these everyday terms because they can cause so much confusion about what online services are and how they differ from each other.

An *online service,* speaking in the most general way, is any collection of information and interactive features that you view and use by logging your computer into a network. Whether you use a phone-line modem, a cable modem, a wireless connection through a handheld device, or a network connection from an office is immaterial. The important thing is that you connect a personal computing device to another computer, and view something on your screen that was designed to be accessed by you and others. Generally, online services present pages of information, interactive features such as message boards and chat rooms, entertainment such as streaming music, and services such as e-mail and shopping. An online service can be large or small, public or private, free or subscription based, on a private network or on the Internet.

The phrase *Internet online service* is a marketing buzzword that traditional online services began using when the Internet became popular. It indicates that the online service has the capacity to connect you to the Internet. Thousands of online services, large and small, were around before the Web brought the Internet into the mainstream. Each one was a little network of features unto itself, providing members with phone numbers for their modems to dial in to so that members could see stuff and talk to other members.

The Internet is like an ocean surrounding each of these online service islands. When the Web made that ocean a popular place to swim, some of the larger online services started offering their members virtual surfboards (by which I mean Web browsers and connections to the Internet). As people began valuing Web content more highly than private online service content, companies such as America Online and CompuServe started calling themselves Internet online services to show how cool they were.

The important thing to remember is that an Internet online service such as America Online is not really located on the Internet — it's still an independent network. It offers its members a gateway to and from the Internet, like a revolving door. On the other hand, a service such as Yahoo! is truly an Internet online service because it started on the Web and uses the Web's natural language (HTML) in all its features. It is, basically, a gigantic Web site — and by *gigantic* I mean that it consists of millions of Web pages. A *Web-based online service,* then, is any collection of features that exists on the Web, not on a private computer network.

Using a Web-based online service has several advantages. The biggest is that you don't need special software (besides your Web browser) to see its content. America Online members must download or acquire new software to view overhauls to the AOL service, whereas Yahoo! is always redesigning portions of its service and you don't need anything more than your good ol' Web browser to be up to date.

The sheer magnitude of Yahoo! is what makes the My Yahoo! feature so useful in getting a grip on it all. At the same time, you can't possibly squeeze the whole shebang onto a few customized pages. Yahoo! doesn't even let you try. My Yahoo! touches on many main-feature satellites and some little-feature asteroids and lets you consolidate them onto screen pages formatted to your taste. But in almost every case, you're customizing just the tip of an iceberg, with plenty of depth waiting to be explored. This book covers the depth in other chapters.

Following are the main types of content you can gather together using My Yahoo! and the instructions in this chapter:

- ✔ **Web searching.** Mapping the Internet is Yahoo!'s traditional function — the service started as a simple directory and search engine. (See Chapter 7 for an explanation of these terms and a guide to using the features.) In My Yahoo!, you can place the Yahoo! directory or a variation of it on your personal page. You may also place the Yahoo! keyword-entry form on your page for searching by word, phrase, or name.

- ✔ **Finances.** Yahoo! Finance is a major realm unto itself — one of the most popular and trafficked money sites on the Web. (Chapter 10 gets deep into the heady atmosphere of high finance.)

- ✔ **News.** News headlines can take up a major portion of your personalized page. My Yahoo! offers all kinds of news categories, and you can even set up clipping folders (a service called News Clipper) based on keywords, names, or places.

- ✔ **TV and movies.** If you're willing to part with a bit of personal information — namely, the ZIP code of your residence — you can get some real-time, local entertainment information.

- ✔ **Sports.** Yahoo! delivers sports news with the same attention to detail that you find in *USA Today* and other information-rich publications.

- ✔ **Community.** My Yahoo! lets you position a hook into the vast community features of the service by placing links to favorite message boards, clubs, and chat rooms on your personalized page.

- ✔ **Tips and tidbits.** There's no reason your personal page shouldn't be fun. You can sprinkle lottery results, recipes, and other nuggets through your My Yahoo! design.

- ✔ **Weather.** I read recently that America is the only country whose citizens take weather beyond mere small talk and establish it as an important news topic in daily life. Yahoo!, being an American company, must resonate with this priority, because it puts the weather on My Yahoo! as a default item.

- ✔ **Travel.** Yahoo! runs an online travel agency whose reservation pages (for flights, hotels, and rental cars) can be linked to your My Yahoo! page.

- ✔ **Organization.** Keeping your feet on the ground and your mind neatly compartmentalized is part of the value in personalizing Yahoo!. You can keep your e-mail address book and interactive calendar on your page. The calendar is especially useful and flexible.

- ✔ **Daily features.** Like a newspaper, My Yahoo! can enliven your page with an array of items whose content changes daily.

Much of Yahoo! is left untouched by My Yahoo! — in other words, plenty of features and reams of content can't be placed on your personalized page. For example, the digital music content in Yahoo!'s Broadcast.com is unavailable as My Yahoo! links. Likewise, the stock quotes are good to have in a glance, but they represent the riches of Yahoo! Finance in only the most meager way. Yahooligans! and Internet Life, two major portions of the service, are not available as links on a My Yahoo! page.

Even those portions of Yahoo! that can be placed on your personal page are reduced, in most cases, to simple links that lead to the full features. The value of My Yahoo! is in providing shortcuts to areas of the service that you use over and over, and in highlighting a few tidbits (such as horoscopes and the Daily Tips) that you might otherwise find once and never again.

Have It Your Way

Although you can customize the look and content of My Yahoo! pages, they all have the same fundamental design. Figure 2-1 shows a My Yahoo! page as it appears before customization. Notice that it has two columns of features. All the features you select for your page (or pages) are either left-side features or right-side features.

My Yahoo! features are modules that you plug into and out of your page and arrange in whatever order you please — except that you can't move a right-side module to the left side, or vice versa. Each column (left side and right side) can be extended as far as you like down the page. A page can be as long as you want, though at some point it makes more sense to create another page.

You may have more than one Yahoo! ID, but you can make only one My Yahoo! page per account. A Yahoo! account is defined by an ID and that ID's password.

Every content module has a main headline banner, and some have secondary headline banners. Look at Figure 2-1, and you can see that the Message Center, a left-side module, is a main headline. My Front Page Headlines, a right-side feature, has several secondary headline banners for different types of news. When designing your page, you decide which modules (main banners) you want and, whenever applicable, which secondary features within those modules you want to appear.

Left-side features   Right-side features

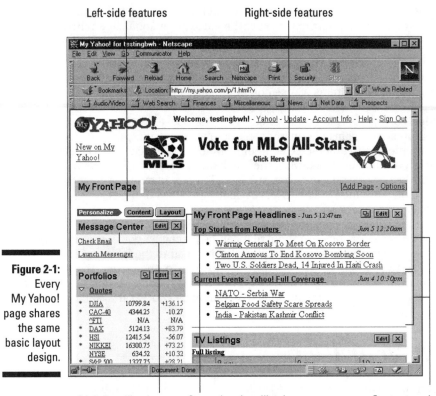

Figure 2-1:
Every
My Yahoo!
page shares
the same
basic layout
design.

Main headline banner   Secondary headline banner   Content modules

My Yahoo! always starts out with preselected content modules in place. You may keep them, edit them, or discard them. Then, you may move around what remains to the order you prefer. The following sections walk you through the details of setting up your page's substance and appearance.

Making basic settings

The basic settings of any My Yahoo! page include a short greeting that appears at the very top of the page, your color scheme, and the refresh rate. You can set and change the name of the page as well.

The best place to begin making your basic settings is on the Options page. Let's go through the steps:

1. **On your My Yahoo! page, click the <u>Options</u> link.**

   The Options page appears (see Figure 2-2).

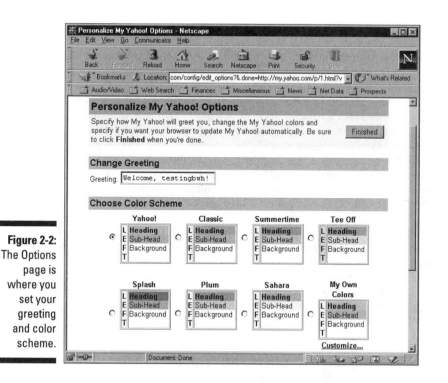

Figure 2-2:
The Options
page is
where you
set your
greeting
and color
scheme.

2. **In the Greeting field, type a greeting.**

   Keep it short, or it won't fit on your page. Two or three words, at most. Mine says "Back again, eh?" just to remind myself that I spend too much time online. The greeting appears at the very top of the My Yahoo! page associated with my ID.

3. **Select your color scheme by clicking the radio button next to your choice.**

   Figure 2-2 doesn't show the colors and makes each selection look pretty much like every other. Check it out on screen, however, and you'll get the picture. Each preset color scheme sets a hue for the left column, the background of the whole page, the main headings, and the subheadings. You can test one by choosing it and clicking the Finished button.

4. **Scroll down the page and set the refresh rate for the page using the drop-down menu.**

   My Yahoo! can be set to automatically reload itself into your browser at a preset interval. It's a good way to make sure your news headlines, stock quotes, and e-mail alerts are current. Because the reload takes only a few seconds in most cases (a little longer for content-packed pages), there's no reason to set the time interval for anything longer than fifteen minutes, the shortest setting. You can, however, extend the refresh period to as long as four hours.

5. Click the Finished button.

When it comes to setting your page's color scheme, you have more choices than the presets would indicate. To design a custom color scheme, click the Customize link on the Options page. Figure 2-3 shows the Custom Colors page. (It's a much more colorful experience on the screen.) On this page, you may choose from a wider selection of hues for the left side of your page, the main heading, the subheading, and the page background. Notice the distinction between 256 Color Mode and High Color Mode. You should use the High Color Mode selections only if your computer is set for color resolution greater than 256 colors. How can you tell? If the color samples on the High Color Mode part of the Custom Colors page look good to you, go ahead and select them. After all, no one is going to look at your My Yahoo! page except you.

Under each of the four page elements for which you may select a custom color, you can find a My Own Color radio button with a text-entry field. If you're familiar with HTML color codes, you may select a hue that isn't sampled on the page. Every color on a Web page is represented in HTML code by a six-character identifier. You can't effectively guess these identifiers because they're a mix of numbers and letters. This option is for experienced HTML coders.

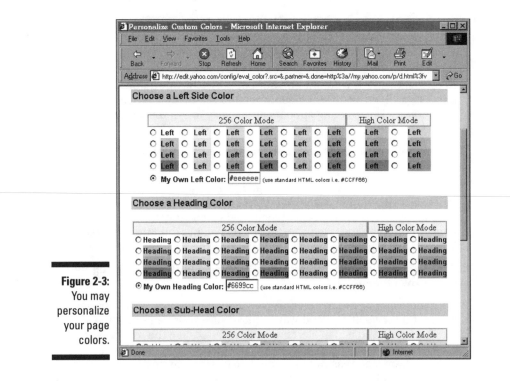

Figure 2-3:
You may personalize your page colors.

The next step in making basic settings occurs in the Personalize Page Content page. Here's how to make a name for your page:

1. **On your My Yahoo! page, click the Content button.**

   The Content button is located above the left column of your page. When you click it, the Personalize Page Content page appears, as shown in Figure 2-4.

2. **In the Page Name field, type a name for your page.**

   Your page name may be 20 characters long (including spaces between words). In general, shorter looks better.

3. **Click the Finished button.**

Before clicking the Finished button in Step 3, you might want to look over the content selections on the Personalize Page Content page. Notice that each selection is marked N or W, indicating whether it is a narrow (right-side) or wide (left-side) feature. Just click the box next to any feature you want to include. Prechecked boxes currently exist as default content on your page — click to uncheck them and remove them from the page. You can add content here too, but in the next section I describe an easier way to do it. Nevertheless, feel free to experiment here. (Like you need my permission.)

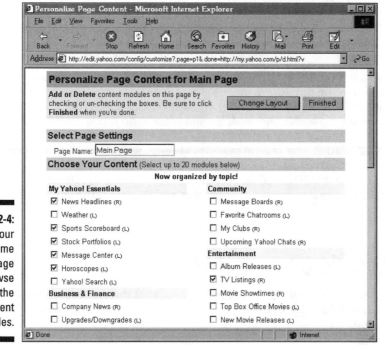

Figure 2-4:
Set your
Page Name
on this page
and browse
among the
content
modules.

Plugging in some content

Adding content is where the fun really begins. (Assuming you're as easily entertained as I am.) Placing content modules on your page shapes it into something useful. It's best to select features first and arrange them second. Content precedes layout. For the time being, you might want to leave all the default features on the page — I describe how to get rid of them in the next section.

Using the Personalize Page Content page, described in the preceding section, is one way to add content modules. But I prefer using the drop-down content menus at the bottom of My Yahoo! (see Figure 2-5). Scroll down to see them, under the Personalize This Page banner.

Here are the basic facts about adding content using the drop-down menus:

✔ You have two drop-down menus, for left-side and right-side features.

✔ The two sets of features do not overlap, and you can't make any of them switch sides.

✔ Each menu has a scroll bar for browsing the entire list of features.

✔ You may add 20 features to your page but only 1 feature at a time. Click the Add button after selecting a module from either drop-down list. After the page reloads, add another feature to either side.

✔ You may stack features on either side of the page, up to the limit of 20 overall.

As your modules get plugged into your page, you get a better sense of what they are. The drop-down menus give you only a broad clue; you need to see the modules to decide whether you want them. Keep reading to find out how to customize within the modules and what to do if you don't want them.

 If you'd rather add several modules at once, without waiting for your page to reload between each addition, use the Personalize Page Content page described in the preceding section. There, you may use the check boxes to make wholesale changes to your page and then view the entire alteration at once.

Editing your content

If you look back at Figure 2-1, you can see that the content modules include some combination of editing buttons in the main heading banner. The three buttons are:

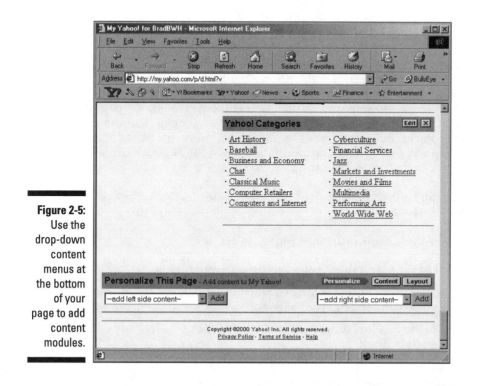

Figure 2-5:
Use the drop-down content menus at the bottom of your page to add content modules.

✔ **Edit button.** The function of the Edit button varies depending on the module. Click it to discover what specific content features are available for that module and to choose among them. I describe the Edit selections of a few major content modules in a later section.

✔ **Remove button.** The button with an X in it deletes the module from your page.

✔ **Detach button.** The button with little squares in it whisks the content module right off your page and establishes it in a new, small browser window. You may resize the window to whatever dimensions are best.

When you detach a content module into its own window, it remains on your main My Yahoo! page as well. So, when you're ready to get rid of the dedicated window, just close it as you would any window on your screen. No need to add the content again to My Yahoo!. It's still there.

All three editing buttons aren't present on all content modules. Some features can't be detached into separate windows, and some features can't be internally edited. But all features do contain the Remove button.

Playing art director

After you have a number of content modules placed on your page, it's time to arrange them in the order you prefer. Of primary importance is moving to the top whatever features you want displayed when you *first* enter My Yahoo!. It's nice to make the important stuff visible without scrolling the page downward. I like to put the Message Center and Portfolios modules near the top of the left column, and certain news headline groups atop the right column. But you may prefer seeing a horoscope on the left and the Fitness Feature on the right. Sports scores are also a good "up-top" left-column candidate.

You can't mix and match right-side and left-side features. They are locked to their respective sides.

Follow these steps to arrange your page's layout:

1. **On your My Yahoo! page, click the Layout button.**

   The Layout button is located atop the left column. When you click it, the Personalize Page Layout page appears, as shown in Figure 2-6.

2. **In the window titled Narrow Column, click to select any content module listed.**

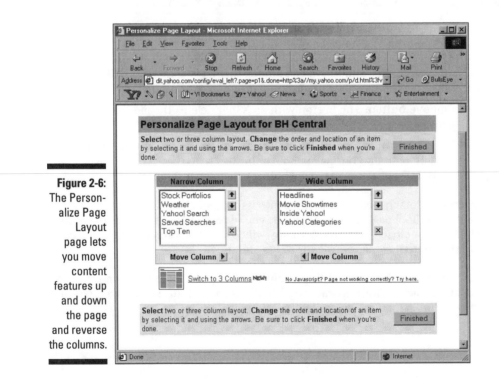

Figure 2-6:
The Person-
alize Page
Layout
page lets
you move
content
features up
and down
the page
and reverse
the columns.

3. **Use the up and down arrow buttons to move the selected module higher or lower on your page, or use the X button to eliminate it.**

   You may move any module as many steps upward or downward as you like. Just keep clicking the arrow button of your choice.

4. **Repeat Steps 2 and 3 for the window titled Wide Column.**

5. **Use the Move Column buttons to switch the position of the wide and narrow columns.**

6. **Click the Finished button.**

You may also use a three-column layout (the contents of the narrow column are divided into two narrow columns), but I don't recommend this option if you have a small monitor or use a screen resolution of either 640 x 480 or 800 x 600. Those conditions make the three-column layout too crowded to use easily. If you have a large monitor or run the screen at a high resolution, however, the three-column layout can shorten a long page, making it easier to navigate. Click the <u>Switch to 3 columns</u> link. As with the two-column layout, you can adjust the position of the columns on the page.

Playing news editor

My Yahoo! is many things, but its default format devotes most of the screen space to news headlines. You can choose from a lot of news covering current events, sports, and finances. Many of the smaller features are newsy, too. This section talks you through some of the editing choices you have for your page.

Selecting the main news portions of your page is probably the biggest editing job you have, simply because so many news sources are available. The following steps familiarize you with adding and removing specific news features:

1. **On your My Yahoo! page, click the Edit button on the My Front Page Headlines banner.**

   The My Front Page Headlines banner is at the top of your right-side content when you begin creating a My Yahoo! page. If for some reason it's not there (perhaps because you deleted it), scroll to the bottom of the page, use the right-side drop-down menu to select News Headlines and then click the Add button. Look at the previous "Plugging in some content" section for complete instructions.

2. **On the Edit your Headlines Module page, click any topic link from the list.**

   I chose the Current Events & Politics link.

3. **From the Available Sections list (see Figure 2-7), select any topic by clicking it.**

   Use the scroll bar to see items lower on the list.

4. **On the Edit your Headlines page, check the boxes next to the news sources you want to include on your page and then click the Finished button.**

5. **Back on the Edit your Headlines Module page, select another topic and repeat Step 4.**

6. **When you've finished adding topics and news sources, click the Finished button on the Edit your Headlines Module page.**

TIP

You can adjust your Headlines settings at any time. To remove a previously selected news source within any news topic, simply uncheck it.

Yahoo! starts you off with a single page but doesn't limit you to just one. You may add up to six other pages, which appear as links in the title banner of your main page. Whenever you surf to the basic My Yahoo! address (my.yahoo.com), your main page is displayed first.

To create a second (or third) page, click the Add Page link from My Yahoo! and then select the type of page you want. Follow the same process to delete a page.

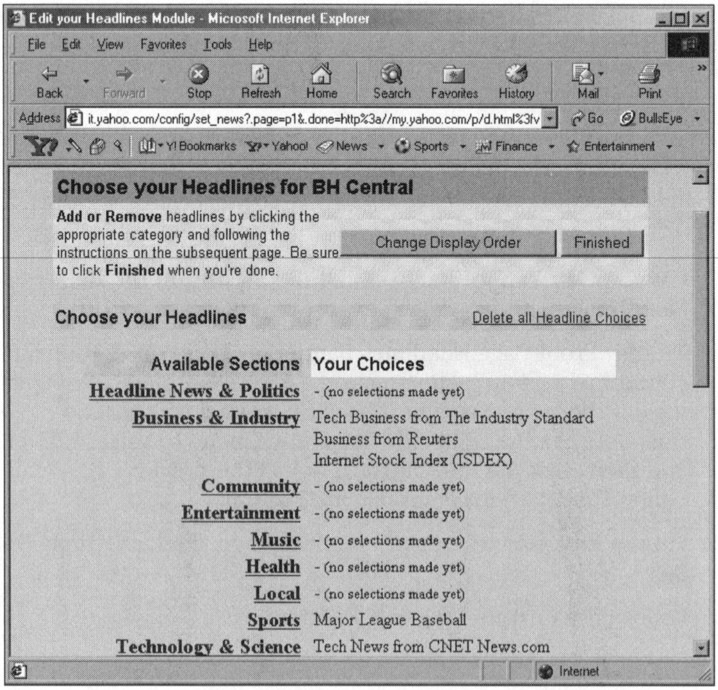

Figure 2-7:
Use this page to specify which news topic sections appear in the Headlines portion of your page.

Searching Yahoo! from My Yahoo!

Because Yahoo! is well known as a Web index and directory, you'd think there would be some way of browsing and searching Yahoo! from My Yahoo! There is. The keyword-entry form for searching the Yahoo! directory (see Chapter 7) appears by default in the left column of your main My Yahoo! page.

If you delete the search form from your narrow column (I explain how to delete things in this chapter), the form reappears at the top of the page. (Use the move to bottom link to shift the search form to the bottom of the page.)

You may also add categories from the Yahoo! directory to My Yahoo!, but the process is more complicated. Here's what to do:

1. **At the bottom of your My Yahoo! page, under the Personalize This Page heading, use the right-hand drop-down content menu to select Yahoo! Categories.**

2. **Click the Add button.**

3. **On your My Yahoo! page, scroll down to the Yahoo! Categories banner and click the Edit button.**

4. **On the Choose your favorite categories page, click the Start Here link.**

   The main Yahoo! home page is displayed, showing the top-level directory categories (see Chapter 7).

5. **Browse through the Yahoo! directory, clicking the Personalize link at the top of any category you want to add to My Yahoo!.**

You don't need to follow the first four steps every time you want to add new categories. Any time you're in the Yahoo! directory (when logged into your Yahoo! ID), you may select the Personalize link to add a category. You'll see that category added to the Yahoo! Categories content module next time you visit your My Yahoo! page.

Chapter 3

Neither Rain, nor Sleet, nor . . .

Guess what the most-used feature of the Internet is. Go on, guess. Okay, I'll tell you — it's e-mail. E-mail is used more than the Web.

E-mail has traditionally existed in its own realm. It's not the Web, it's not Usenet newsgroups, and it's not instant messaging. It has been a separate product of the online experience. When you get an online account (through an Internet service provider or an online service such as America Online), you automatically receive an e-mail box and the capability to exchange letters with anyone else with an account.

Built-in e-mail accounts are convenient and are usually accessed with dedicated e-mail programs such as Outlook Express, Netscape Messenger, or Eudora. In the last few years, though, *Web-based e-mail* has become popular. *Web-based e-mail* really is part of the Web and is accessed through regular Web pages, viewed in a Web browser. Although slower and more cumbersome than regular e-mail, the Web-based version has some compelling advantages:

  ✔ Web-based e-mail is free, though you still need an online access account to get on the Web.

  ✔ Web mail is accessible from any computer logged on to the Internet, so it's great when traveling.

  ✔ Such mail accounts can be more permanent than online access accounts. If you switch from America Online to Mindspring to some other Internet provider, you get a new e-mail address each time, but your Yahoo! Mail address remains constant.

Each of your Yahoo! IDs has its own e-mail box. This chapter explains how Yahoo! Mail works and unravels its most important features.

Getting Ready for Yahoo! Mail

Setting up your Yahoo! Mail account is an easy matter, especially if you've already created a Yahoo! ID. If not, now is a good time to make one — you can't have Yahoo! Mail without an ID. You get one Yahoo! mailbox per password. Different IDs accessed by one password all share a single e-mail box. You may give out those different IDs as distinct e-mail addresses, each with the @yahoo.com suffix. But all incoming mail lands in the single mailbox assigned to the first ID you created. You can access that mailbox while logged on to any of the IDs.

Follow these steps to set up your Yahoo! mailbox:

1. **At the top of the Yahoo! home page, click the Check Email button.**

   The Welcome to Yahoo! Mail page appears.

2. **Fill in your ID and password and then click the Sign in button.**

   If you don't have a Yahoo! ID yet, click the <u>Sign me up!</u> link and continue from there or get some help from Chapter 1.

3. **On the setup page, read the Yahoo! Mail Terms of Service Agreement and then click the I Accept button at the bottom of the page.**

   The mail summary page you see next should bear a strong resemblance to Figure 3-1.

Yahoo! Mail has its own log on and log off procedure, distinct from the ID sign in and off process. When you exit Yahoo! Mail, it's not necessary to sign out from your Yahoo! ID account. By the same token, you sometimes need to take an extra log on step to get your mail, depending on the length of time since you last got it. Yahoo! Mail has a *timeout* feature that closes your mailbox after a certain time, requiring you to type your password to get back in, even if you're already signed in with that mailbox's ID. The extra security is for your protection; if you leave your computer unattended for an extended period, others won't be able to peek at your letters.

E-Mail Coming and Going

I'm a much more active correspondent in the realm of e-mail than I ever was with paper letters. This discrepancy could be due to my latent fear of post offices, but more likely it's because e-mail is so easy. No envelope. No stamp. And best of all, no delivery delays. E-mail is fast, and I have fun chatting with friends and acquaintances throughout the day. E-mail is informal and conversational.

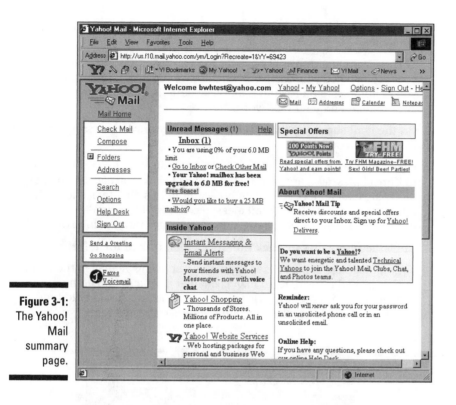

Figure 3-1:
The Yahoo!
Mail
summary
page.

Checking your Yahoo! Mail

It's a good idea to bookmark your Yahoo! Mail page or the main service page
at the following URL:

```
mail.yahoo.com
```

That URL (or bookmark) will deliver your personal mail page or sign-in page
(if you haven't checked your mail for a while) when you're signed in to your
Yahoo! ID. Perhaps the best way to stay in touch with your mailbox is to keep
Messenger or Companion (or both) running. (Messenger is explained in
Chapter 15, and I wax euphoric over the Yahoo! Companion in Chapter 20.)
Both (free) programs alert you to incoming e-mails and give you one-click
access to your mailbox. (Neither one can be held responsible for inserting
too many parentheses in a single paragraph.)

Here's how to check your mail. Note that in the following steps, I assume that
you haven't yet set up Messenger or Companion:

1. **On the Yahoo! home page, click the Check Email button at the top of the page.**

   The mail summary page (Figure 3-1) appears. If it has been a while since you last checked your mail, you might have to enter your password. If you're not logged on to your Yahoo! account ID, you definitely need to enter both it and your password.

2. **On the mail summary page, see whether any unread messages are waiting for you.**

   Figure 3-1 shows a single unread message, indicated in parentheses next to Unread Messages and also by the Inbox (1) link. You can set up multiple incoming-mail folders (I explain how later in this chapter), and each folder shows up in the Unread Messages list with the number of unread messages. But at the beginning, new mail comes into the Inbox.

3. **Click the Inbox link or click the Check Mail link in the left sidebar.**

   Your Inbox page appears (see Figure 3-2), showing all mail in the Inbox, both read and unread. Read mail is shaded gray, and unread mail isn't shaded. Furthermore, the titles of unread messages are in bold type, which thins out to regular type after you read the message.

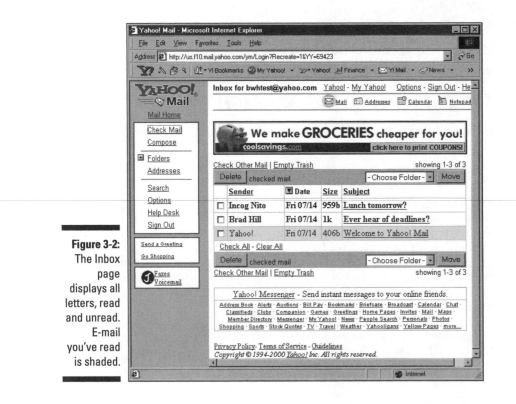

Figure 3-2:
The Inbox page displays all letters, read and unread. E-mail you've read is shaded.

The fine print

Most Web-based e-mail services require that you read (or at least say that you read) a Terms of Service (TOS) agreement, which spells out the basic rules of the service. Yahoo! is no different. Because the e-mail service is free, following the commonsense rules isn't too much to ask.

What is it that you're agreeing to? Basically, you agree to do three things with Yahoo! Mail:

✔ You agree to provide accurate information about yourself in the registration process.

✔ You agree to avoid all illegal, harmful, libelous, abusive, and generally obnoxious uses of the e-mail service.

✔ You agree to not send *spam* (bulk e-mail advertisements) through Yahoo! Mail.

The coup de grace is a clause that says Yahoo! can nuke your account whenever it wants. But don't worry, no one gets their plug pulled for normal e-mail usage.

4. Click the subject of any letter to read it.

Figure 3-3 illustrates what a letter (albeit an extremely brief and impatient one) looks like in Yahoo! Mail.

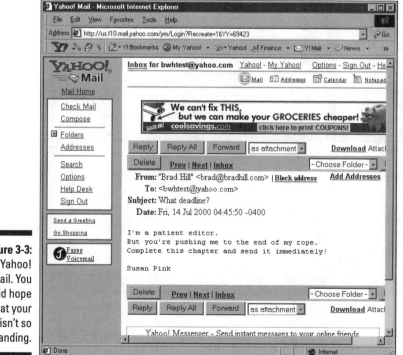

Figure 3-3:
A Yahoo!
e-mail. You
should hope
that your
mail isn't so
demanding.

Responding to e-mail

It's only polite to write back. And it's easy — Yahoo! keeps the whole process in the same browser window, unlike dedicated e-mail programs that open new windows for writing mail. The following steps show how to respond to an e-mail:

1. **On any Read Message page, click the Reply button.**

   The Compose Mail page appears (see Figure 3-4).

2. **Use the large text-entry form to type your letter.**

   Notice that the text of the letter you're replying to is placed in the text-entry box. In all e-mail formats, it's typical to *quote back* the letter you're responding to, so the recipient doesn't have to remember what the conversation is about. Typically, you type your response above the quote. Quoting back is not a requirement, though, so feel free to highlight and delete the quoted letter before sending your reply.

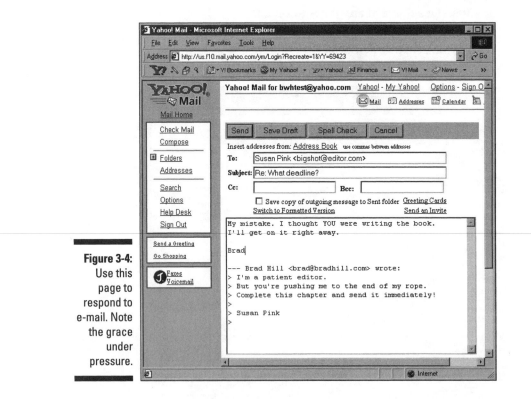

Figure 3-4:
Use this page to respond to e-mail. Note the grace under pressure.

3. **Click the Send button.**

   If you're not ready to send the letter yet, but are tired of working on it (or can't think of how to finish your missive), click the Save Draft button. The letter-in-progress is placed in your Draft folder. (Every mailbox has a Draft folder — you don't have to create it.)

4. **To keep a copy of your reply after sending it, click the box next to Save copy of outgoing message to Sent folder.**

   As with the Draft folder, the Sent folder already exists.

While writing long e-mails, use the Save Draft button to occasionally save the letter-in-progress to the Draft folder. Then, if your computer crashes and you lose your screen, you don't have to start from scratch upon your return to Yahoo! Mail. Each time you click that Save Draft button, Yahoo! places another copy of the letter in the Draft folder. On a long letter, saved frequently, you might end up with ten versions of the letter in various stages of incompletion. They all stay there (until deleted) after you finally send the letter.

You can use the Spell Check feature on outgoing messages. On the Compose Mail page, click the Spell Check button before sending the mail. Perhaps unfortunately, Yahoo! Mail checks the spelling of e-mail addresses as well as the message itself, resulting in almost inevitable spelling "errors" because the system doesn't recognize e-mail aliases as real words.

To fix a legitimate spelling error, do this:

1. **Click the question-mark button next to any suggested error.**

2. **In the pop-up window, select a correct spelling from the drop-down menu (see Figure 3-5).**

Figure 3-5:
The Spell
Check
correction
window.

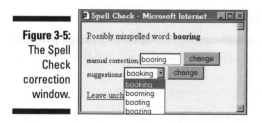

If you don't see a correct spelling in the drop-down menu and you know what the correct spelling is, just type the replacement manually.

3. **Click the change button.**

   If you prefer the misspelling for some reason or you realize it's not a misspelling after all, click the <u>Leave unchanged</u> link.

4. **On the Spell Check Message page, click the Done button.**

   Clicking the Done button returns you to the Compose Mail page, where you can edit the letter, add to it, or send it.

To start an e-mail from scratch (as opposed to replying to an e-mail you've received), click the <u>Compose</u> link in the left sidebar. The Compose Mail page appears, as when you're replying to a message, but without an address in the To: field. You must enter the recipient's e-mail address yourself and type a subject for the letter also. Use the Send, Save Draft, and Spell Check buttons as described previously.

You may enter a recipient's address of a letter you're composing directly from your Yahoo! Address Book, which I describe a bit later in this chapter.

Organizing your mail

If you're an active e-mailer, you know how letters can pile up and how the ol' Inbox can become a cluttered mess. Dedicated e-mail programs let you create multiple folders for organizing mail, and Yahoo! Mail emulates that system in its Web mail.

If you're relatively new to e-mail, or if you already have e-mail and just aren't sure how you're going to use your Yahoo! mailbox, it might not be immediately apparent what folders you need to create. Not a problem — you can make them at any time, as you need them. I'm always creating folders, moving mail around, deleting old folders, and generally wasting more time organizing my mail than if I left it in one big stack. But I'll proceed on the assumption that you're better at this than I am. Here's how to create a new folder in Yahoo! Mail:

1. **In Yahoo! Mail, click the <u>Folders</u> link in the left sidebar.**

   Click the link itself, not the + box beside it. That little box opens a drop-down menu showing your current folders. When you click the link, your folders page appears.

2. **In the Create a personal folder field, type a folder name.**

   A *personal folder* is any folder added to the collection of default folders Yahoo! provides to every mailbox. The default folders are Inbox, Draft, Sent, and Trash.

3. **Click the Create folder button.**

   Your folders page reloads, this time listing your new folder and a new Edit a personal folder section. Whenever you return to this page, you may use the drop-down menu to select one of your personal folders and then rename or delete it.

Your mailbox starts of with four default folders: Inbox (where incoming personal mail automatically gets placed), Draft (where your letters-in-progress get stored), Sent (where outgoing mail gets stored if you select that feature), and Trash (where deleted mail gets stored until you click the [Empty] link). Another folder, called Bulk, automatically receives junk mail, and springs into existence when you first receive such an e-mail.

The Bulk folder works with an effective filter that is surprisingly good at distinguishing between personal mail you want to read and junk mail you want to ignore. Every so often you should delete the contents of the Bulk folder, but not before checking to make sure it contains nothing worth saving.

Immediately after you create your first personal folder, incoming mail still goes directly to your Inbox. From there, you may move it to any folder, default or personal. Here's how:

1. **On your Inbox page, click the check box next to any message you want to move.**

2. **In the Choose Folder drop-down menu, select the folder you'd like to use to hold the selected letter.**

3. **Click the Move button.**

   The Inbox page reloads, with your selected message no longer present in your Inbox list. To view the contents of any of your folders, click the Folders link in the left sidebar.

Your Virtual Black Book

It's so easy to make friends in Yahoo! through chatting, the message boards, and Yahoo! Messenger that you might quickly develop a large and varied correspondence. It's impractical to keep your e-mail addresses on paper. The best system is to have an online address book. Yahoo! Mail provides such a thing. Here's how to get it started:

1. **In Yahoo! Mail, click the Addresses link in the left sidebar.**

   A window titled *Address Book for* appears, as shown in Figure 3-6.

2. **Click the New Contact button.**

   The New Address Book Entry page appears.

3. **Fill in the fields.**

   All that's really necessary is a name and an e-mail address. You don't need to use the Yahoo! Address Book to keep track of phone numbers and company names if you don't feel so inspired. If you really do get inspired, click the Add More Detail button — the Add/Edit Contact Details page gives you enough information fields to spend the night entering everything you know about someone. Use the Category drop-down list to select where in your book to place this address.

4. Click the Save button.

Figure 3-6 illustrates an address book with a few entries. This option-packed page has a number of features:

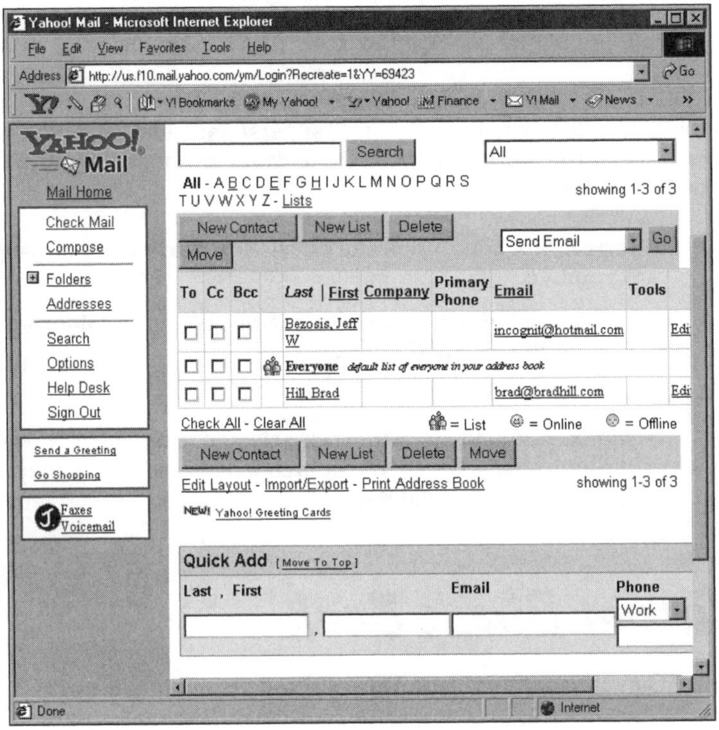

Figure 3-6:
A working address book with a few entries.

➤ Use the Search field to enter a name or part of a name if your address book is large and you've lost someone. The search engine is pretty smart — you can enter a name, a nickname as entered in the address book, a fraction of a name, an e-mail address, or a portion of an e-mail address, such as the domain name.

➤ Click the check boxes next to names, turning them into recipients of your outgoing mail when you select Send Email from the drop-down menu and click the Go button. You may check as many as you like. The Cc column is for copies sent to addresses besides the main recipient(s). The Bcc column is for recipients whose names *will not* appear to all other recipients. (Bcc stands for Blind carbon copy.)

✔ Click any letter to see address book entries for that letter only.

✔ Click the <u>First</u>, <u>Last</u>, <u>Company</u> or <u>Email</u> links to sort the list by that criterion, alphabetically. (If <u>First</u> is clicked, <u>Last</u> becomes a link.)

✔ Use the <u>Check All</u> link to select every name on the current page as a recipient.

✔ Use <u>Clear All</u> when you realize using the <u>Check All</u> link was a terrible mistake and you want to start over.

✔ Click any name to see all the information you've entered for that person.

✔ Use the <u>Edit</u> link to change the information entered for any name.

✔ Use the <u>Delete</u> link to kick someone out of your address book. (You may also use the Delete button to mass-annihilate any number of checked names.)

✔ Use the Move button to shift any entry to a new category.

You might want to organize your names into group lists, if you mail repeatedly to certain groups of names in your address book. Here's how to create your first group:

1. **In your address book, click the New List button.**

   The Edit Distribution List page appears.

2. **Click any name from the address book list on the left side.**

   You may use the Shift key to include all names between two clicks or the Ctrl key to select noncontiguous names.

3. **Click the Add>> button.**

   Your selected names move, as if by psychic powers, to the Members of List window.

4. **To eliminate names from your list, select the names and click the <<Remove button.**

5. **In the Members of List field above the right-hand list, type the name of your new list.**

   You might need to scroll your browser window to the right to see this field.

6. **Click the Done button.**

   Your distribution list is now added to the Distribution Lists page. When you want to send an e-mail to the entire list, simply click the To check box, and all list addresses are automatically inserted as recipients. You may also click the Cc or Bcc check box for an entire list of names.

It's come to this: You have so much e-mail stashed in your Yahoo! mailbox folders that you can't find that crucial invitation to the office party. Fortunately, a search engine lurks inside Yahoo! Mail to bail you out of just such a gaffe. Click the <u>Search</u> link in the left sidebar. Figure 3-7 illustrates the search form. If normal searching doesn't do it for you, try the <u>Advanced Search</u> link. It displays the Power Search page, which uses a series of drop-down menus to fine-tune what Yahoo! is looking for and where it looks.

Getting Your Mail from All Over

If you have Yahoo! Mail, chances are you have another mailbox. You might use other Web-based mail services and almost certainly you have an Internet mailbox associated with your online service or Internet service provider. You can receive your mail from other mailboxes through the Yahoo! Mail interface if you like.

Under normal circumstances, you might have little reason for reading non-Yahoo! mail in your Yahoo! mailbox. But I can tell you from experience, the feature comes in handy when you're traveling. Using Yahoo!, you can check your mail from a library computer, an Internet café, or any computer connected to the Net.

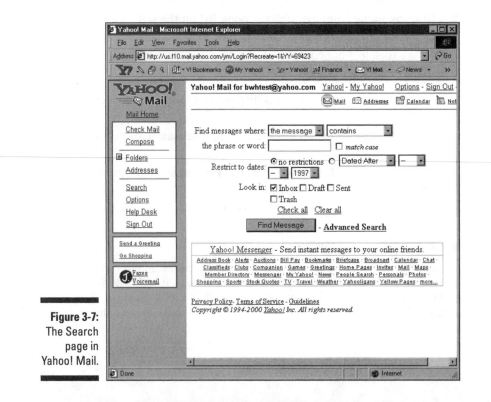

Figure 3-7:
The Search page in Yahoo! Mail.

Here's how to set it up:

1. **In Yahoo! Mail, click the <u>Options</u> link from the left sidebar.**

   The Options page appears.

2. **Click the <u>Check Other (POP) Mail</u> link.**

3. **Click the Add Mail Server button.**

   The Mail Account Information page appears.

4. **Fill in the fields that define your external mailbox.**

   The Mail Server is probably the trickiest. You might need to ask your Internet service provider for the mail server domain name. Usually, the format is `mail.server.com` (or `mail.server.net`). The `server` in this example is normally the name of the Internet service provider.

   In most cases, your Username is the first part of your e-mail address, before the @ symbol. Only you know the Password. Leave the Port Number set at the default, 110.

5. **Using the check box, decide whether you want your mail left on the server.**

   I always click Yes because I know I'm going to want the mail in my normal e-mail program eventually. But if that isn't important to you, click No so that your mail doesn't pile up on the server, forcing you to download it all again at some point.

6. **Using the check box, decide whether to get all messages or new messages only.**

   Yahoo! Mail keeps track of which messages you've collected from your server. This selection is relevant only if you selected to leave mail on the server (Step 5).

7. **Using the drop-down menu, select which folder to use for your external mail.**

   I find that it's a good idea to create a new folder exclusively for external mail.

8. **Use the check box to indicate whether you want to apply your filters (described next) to your external mail.**

9. **Using the color-coded radio buttons, decide how you would like your external mail distinguished.**

   The color-coding is a good feature but necessary only if you don't create a dedicated folder for external mail.

10. **Click the OK button.**

11. **To get your external mail, click the <u>Check Other Mail</u> link on your Inbox page.**

The Options page is stuffed with other useful tools and perks. The following brief descriptions explain what's so great about some of them:

- ✔ **Mail Preferences.** The most-changed feature of this option set is the name that gets attached to outgoing mail. This is the name that appears in the heading of any e-mail you send, as it shows up in another person's mailbox. You can put any name here, your full name, or just your first name. You can also place any e-mail address as a reply-to address. Adjust certain colors here, and turn your Bulk folder on and off. A number of other settings affect how your mail is displayed and ordered.

- ✔ **Signature.** This is where you determine what automatically appears at the end of your outgoing messages, if anything. You can include HTML tags, if you know them.

- ✔ **Vacation Response.** This handy feature sends preset responses during periods when you can't check your mail. You can even specify a special response for up to two individual incoming e-mail domains.

- ✔ **Block Addresses.** Somebody really getting on your virtual nerves? You can assign up to one hundred e-mail addresses. Incoming mail from those addresses is deleted before it hits your mailbox.

- ✔ **Filters.** Force incoming mail to certain folders depending on its header, subject, or words in the message body.

Getting Attached

One of the greatest inventions in the e-mail space has been attachments. *Attachments* are binary (usually non-text) files that can't be placed in the body of an e-mail. Pictures are the most common attachments. Other types of computer files that can be attached to an e-mail include word-processing files and digital music files.

Yahoo! Mail remains fairly fluent with attachments, though the service hasn't upgraded its attachment flexibility in a while. You still can attach only three files at a time — which is perfectly sufficient for most people. Here's how you do it:

1. **In Yahoo! Mail, click the Compose link or the Reply button of a displayed e-mail.**

   You attach files to outgoing mail, either initiating an exchange or responding to a letter.

2. **On the Compose page, scroll down and click the Edit Attachments link.**

   This link may seem oddly named, because you haven't yet made any attachments to edit. Nonetheless, click it. The Attachments window pops open, as shown in Figure 3-8.

3. Click the Browse button to select a file from your hard drive.

In Windows, the Choose file dialog box lets you browse your hard drive's directories. Double-click a file to attach, and it appears in the topmost field of the Attachments window.

4. Click the Attach File button.

Now your file appears in the "Attached files" space.

5. When you've attached all the files you want (no more than three), click the Done button.

Your files now appear beneath the main text-entry field of the Compose page.

When e-mails arrive with files attached, a paper-clip icon appears next to the message header in your Inbox. Click the icon to download the attachment. Most picture attachments appear in the body of the e-mail when you open it; after viewing the picture in that fashion, you can decide whether to download it to your hard drive.

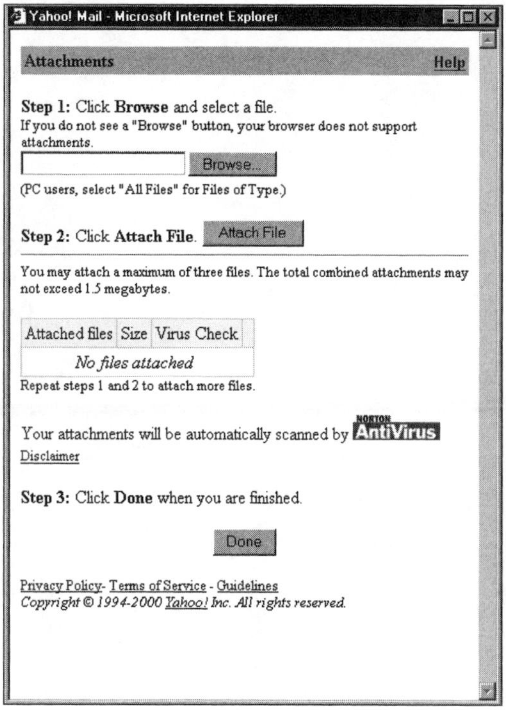

Figure 3-8:
The window in which you specify files to be attached to outgoing e-mail.

Part II
Building Your Yahoo! Nest

The 5th Wave   By Rich Tennant

"It's a letter from the company that installed our in-ground sprinkler system. They're offering Internet access now."

In this part . . .

This part concentrates on building an online home that others can visit. GeoCities is a full-featured Web-page community, and Chapter 4 describes exactly how to settle in and develop your own site. Chapter 5 takes virtual homesteading to the next level with Yahoo! Website Services, where you can purchase your own URL domain and build a more elaborate home. Finally, the Briefcase and Photo Album features fill up Chapter 6, where you discover how to store pictures and other files in your personal Yahoo! computer space.

Chapter 4

Settling into GeoCities

● ●

In This Chapter

▶ Starting your free GeoCities account

▶ Designing a Web page quickly with PageWizards

▶ Constructing a Web page easily with PageBuilder

▶ Becoming a power-Webmaster

● ●

*W*hat defines your online home? Your e-mail address? Your Yahoo! ID, which identifies you in Messenger and Chat? Your My Yahoo! page? In the physical world, your home defines your permanent presence. What's the comparable home in the virtual world?

Nothing quite says cyber-home like a Web site. A site may be a single page or a complex labyrinth of linked pages. Yahoo!, complete online provider that it is, offers a free service for establishing your Web-based home. This service is called Yahoo! GeoCities, and this chapter takes you through getting started in GeoCities and building a Web page.

Moving into GeoCities

GeoCities began as an independent community whose members enjoyed free page-hosting service. Yahoo! left the basic idea intact when it acquired GeoCities and then repackaged the service into a clearer, more coherent interface. Yahoo! GeoCities is still free (for the basic service) and provides all the help you need to build a simple or complex online home.

All you need is a Yahoo! ID (also free, as described in Chapter 1) to establish your space in GeoCities. What exactly do you get? Primarily, some server space. *Server space* is computer memory on the GeoCities computers, in which you store your pages and the files (such as pictures) used by your pages. Everybody gets 15 megabytes of server space, free of charge.

The first thing to do is establish your free GeoCities account. Then, whenever you're ready, use the later sections of this chapter to help you build a page. Or three. First, follow these steps to begin your account:

1. **On the Yahoo! home page, click the <u>Home Pages</u> link.**

   The <u>Home Pages</u> link is located near the bottom of the Yahoo! home page, in the More Yahoo! area, to the right of Publishing. You can also go to GeoCities directly at the following:

   ```
   geocities.yahoo.com
   ```

   You must be logged into your Yahoo! ID to use GeoCities.

2. **On the About Your Home Page page, write a short description, choose a topic from the list, and click the Submit button.**

   Filling out this page identifies the purpose of your page and helps place it in the GeoCities community directory of sites.

3. **Review the GeoCities Terms of Service and click the I Accept button at the bottom of the page.**

   See the "Rules of the game" sidebar for a bit of explanation about the Terms of Service.

4. **On the Yahoo! GeoCities for *YourID* page, select one of the page-building tools to get started.**

You might think you need to know about HTML, the underlying language of all Web pages, to have a Web page of your own. But it ain't so. (By the same token, you don't need good grammar to write books, apparently.) Yahoo! GeoCities provides three methods of creating pages, two of which hide the cryptic details of HTML code entirely:

- ✓ **Yahoo! PageWizards.** This method of page building is the easiest. The Wizards let you choose a basic design from a preset selection and then slap together a simple page on the basis of a few pieces of information supplied by you.

- ✓ **Yahoo! PageBuilder.** PageBuilder is a Java program that lets you drag text and graphic boxes around the page and then publishes the result with all the correct HTML code in the background. The program is reasonably powerful and very easy to operate if you have some experience with using computer software.

- ✓ **Advanced HTML Editor.** This is a tool for Web veterans who are comfortable digging their hands into the HTML code itself. This editor opens in your Web browser and allows you to manipulate the code itself, tag by tag. You never need to use the Advanced HTML Editor if you don't want to.

If you already have Web pages of your own and already use an HTML editor or page builder, that's no problem. You can upload your finished pages to GeoCities and either continue using your regular software or give Yahoo! PageBuilder a whirl. Be careful, though, about migrating to PageBuilder, because you might not be able to load a file back into your regular editor after PageBuilder has applied its touch to it. Always back up your coded pages before loading them into PageBuilder.

If you use Microsoft FrontPage 2000 and the FrontPage ServerExtensions, everything should work just fine in GeoCities. The server there supports FrontPage's extensions. Publish your pages to GeoCities in the normal fashion through FrontPage 2000 — click the Publish button and then enter your Yahoo! ID and password.

The following two sections walk you through the basic features of PageWizards and PageBuilder.

A Quick and Easy Page

When you want to get started fast, when you want to get a basic page up on the Web without fuss, who you gonna call? PageWizards! Remember, this service is absolutely free — free of charge and free of hassle. Within fifteen minutes from the time you first surf into Yahoo! GeoCities (signed in with your ID), you can have a Web site published and ready to show your friends — even if you have absolutely no Web-page experience.

PageWizards is probably the best way for novices to start. If it seems too limiting, you can always move your work to PageBuilder, which offers many more tools and options. Following is the simplest path to your first Web page. After Step 4, the details of the process may vary depending on which PageWizard you choose.

1. **Go to the main Yahoo! GeoCities page at the following address:**

   `geocities.yahoo.com`

2. **Click the <u>Yahoo! PageWizards</u> link.**

   The PageWizards page displays several templates from which to choose the basic design of your page. Each design is a separate PageWizard. The Quick Start templates are slightly easier than the Popular Themes choices.

3. **Click any PageWizard.**

   A new Wizard window opens with simple instructions for proceeding.

4. **Click the Begin button.**

5. **Choose a style for your page and then click the Next button.**

   I know what you're thinking — you already chose a style on the main PageWizards page. That's true, and now you have a chance to change your mind. Click any radio button to see that style.

6. **Enter a page title and any text you'd like on the page and then click the Next button.**

   This is your only opportunity to write some text. So make it Pulitzer-worthy. Actually, immortal prose isn't as important as basic information.

7. **Select a picture for your page, type a caption, and click the Next button.**

   This is the picture page. In these Wizards, you may place only one picture on the page. You can use the default picture that comes with the style or upload a photo from your computer's hard drive. If you have a scanned picture of yourself, that's a possibility. The Wizards accept pictures in .jpg and .gif formats. Click the Browse button to select a file from your computer — the Wizard uploads it automatically.

8. **Put some links on your page and then click the Next button.**

   You don't need to put links on your page, but doing so is a long-standing Web tradition. The Wizard comes with default links, and guess what? They all lead to Yahoo! destinations. (See Figure 4-1.) That's a surprise! Feel free to take those links out and replace them with your own favorites. You must know the URL of your links for this feature to work correctly for visitors.

9. **Enter your personal information and then click the Next button.**

   This page is where you put your name and e-mail address if you want that information to appear. You also have the option of placing the I'm Online indicator on the page — this icon, which appears throughout the community portions of Yahoo!, lets your page visitors know when you're logged into Yahoo! through Messenger or Yahoo! Chat.

10. **Name your page and then click the Next button.**

    The name you select here becomes the last part of your URL, or Web address.

11. **Click the Done button.**

    This final page spells out your new site's URL as a link, which you can click to see your page.

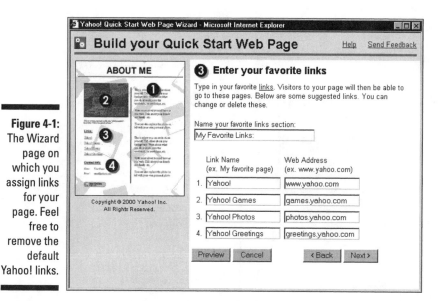

Figure 4-1:
The Wizard
page on
which you
assign links
for your
page. Feel
free to
remove the
default
Yahoo! links.

As you move through the Wizard's instruction pages, you can back up at any time using the Back button. Clicking the Preview button on any page opens a Web browser window and displays your site-in-progress. The Cancel button gets you out of the Wizard entirely and does not save your page.

The information fields that you fill in during the Wizard process are optional. You can always leave them blank and move onto the next page. Of course, if you do that too often, you'll end up with one mighty boring Web page. But the point is that nothing is mandatory — you're not required to upload a picture, assign links, or enter your contact information.

The result of your Wizard work is a simple, informative personal page. (See Figure 4-2 for an example.) Note the little Y!GeoCities box in the upper-right corner of the page. That's an ad. You (and any other visitor to your page) can remove it by clicking the small X in the corner, but it will always reappear when someone surfs to your page, even if that person removed it last time. There's no way to remove this small promotion at the code level, but you can get it off your page by using the GeoGuide, described later in this chapter.

There isn't anything extra you can add to your page within PageWizards, though you can change your text, links, picture, and personal information at any time. You can't add a second picture, place a new text box, or put new headings on the page. If you get ready to bring your site to the next level, move to Yahoo! PageBuilder. See the next section for a profoundly meaningful discussion of that program.

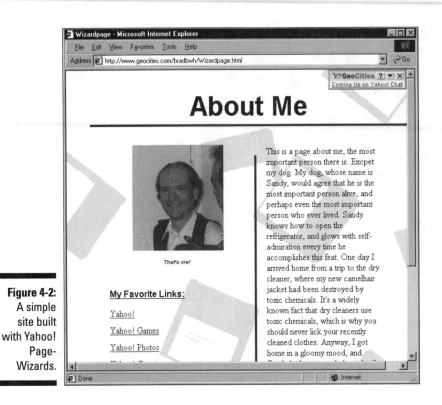

This is a page about me, the most important person there is. Excpet my dog. My dog, whose name is Sandy, would agree that he is the most important person alive, and perhaps even the most important person who ever lived. Sandy knows how to open the refrigerator, and glows with self-admiration every time he accomplishes this feat. One day I arrived home from a trip to the dry cleaner, where my new camelhair jacket had been destroyed by toxic chemicals. It's a widely known fact that dry cleaners use toxic chemicals, which is why you should never lick your recently cleaned clothes. Anyway, I got home in a gloomy mood, and

Figure 4-2:
A simple
site built
with Yahoo!
Page-
Wizards.

Page Construction Made Easy

Yahoo! PageBuilder is an intermediate tool, much more sophisticated than PageWizards but still sparing the rigors of HTML code. Moving from PageWizards to PageBuilder is a natural progression, and the slight learning curve rewards users with much greater power and flexibility. Pages designed in PageBuilder can be far more interesting and varied than Wizard pages.

You can use PageBuilder to start a page from scratch or to upgrade any page originally built in PageWizards. You can start a new PageBuilder page even if you have created Wizard pages and want to leave them as they are.

The following steps get you started with Yahoo! PageBuilder:

1. **On the Yahoo! GeoCities home page, click the <u>Yahoo! PageBuilder</u> link.**

2. **On the next page, select a theme or click the <u>Launch PageBuilder</u> link.**

   PageBuilder provides pre-built templates within which you can enter your content, just as PageWizards does. The PageBuilder templates (sometimes called *themes*) are more complex than PageWizards templates, and they can be much more flexibly adjusted. If you click a theme link, that template is displayed — if you open PageBuilder from that page, it automatically starts with that template ready to be filled in. If you launch PageBuilder without clicking a template link, the program starts off with a blank page.

One way or the other, launch PageBuilder at this point. A small window with the heading Yahoo! PageBuilder Running pops open. Do not close that small window while working in PageBuilder.

Yahoo! PageBuilder is a Java program that downloads into your computer. The process might take as long as five minutes if you use a 28.8k modem. After it opens (see Figure 4-3), PageBuilder operates just like a Windows application. The first thing you see is a blank page (if you didn't select a template and this is the first time you've used PageBuilder), a template page (if you selected a template), or one of your previously edited pages (if you've used PageBuilder before).

To start a new page in PageBuilder, click the New icon in the toolbar. To work on a page you've already created, either in PageBuilder or PageWizards, follow these steps:

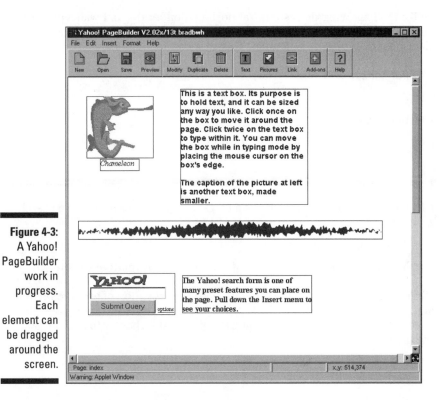

Figure 4-3:
A Yahoo!
PageBuilder
work in
progress.
Each
element can
be dragged
around the
screen.

1. **In PageBuilder, click the Open icon in the toolbar.**

   The Open Page panel displays a list of all the pages you've created in the GeoCities account of your current Yahoo! ID.

2. **In the Files Available window, double-click any page.**

   That page opens in PageBuilder. Everything on the page is translated to PageBuilder's underlying language, so you can manipulate page elements in PageBuilder fashion (see the following section) even if you didn't create the page in PageBuilder.

Two things in PageBuilder you should know about right away and remember as you work. First — the Preview button. Use this button at any time to see what your page looks like in a Web browser. Using the Preview button is the only way to find out how some of the interactive elements actually work. Second, save your work frequently. If you undergo a computer crash or lose your Internet connection, your page-in-progress is not automatically saved. Click the Save button to name your page and save it.

Dragging stuff around in PageBuilder

Unlike the PageWizards system, Yahoo! PageBuilder doesn't walk you through the creation of a page. The tools are easy to use, but you must initiate the placement of every page element. Those elements include:

✔ Portions of text

✔ Pictures

✔ Buttons and bullets

✔ Horizontal and vertical lines for borders

✔ Games

✔ Animated images

✔ Information elements such as a clock, a page-hit counter, and a search form

✔ A message board

✔ Interactive forms that allow visitors to send information to you

All the elements offered in the program, with the exception of text, are pre-built. No expertise is required to add a game or a message board to your page. Just select it from the menu (keep reading this part of the chapter to find out how) and plug it in.

All page elements appear in PageBuilder enclosed in a box. This box is PageBuilder's unique feature and enables you to design your page without worrying about HTML code. Every box on the page can be dragged around and dropped somewhere on the page. Furthermore, every box can be resized. Before you drag or resize boxes, though, you need to place at least one element on the page. Here's how to add a text box and put text into it:

1. **In PageBuilder, choose Insert ⇨ Basics ⇨ Text.**

   An empty rectangular box appears on the page. (See Figure 4-4.) At the same time, the PageBuilder toolbar changes to a text-formatting toolbar, with buttons and drop-down menus for changing the font, size, boldness, color, and other qualities of the displayed text.

2. **Click your mouse cursor inside the text box.**

   A place-marking cursor appears in the text box, showing that it is ready to receive text.

3. **Type your text into the text box.**

   Be as brief or verbose as you like. Text boxes can be used for major expositions, simple picture captions, or anything in between.

4. **Click anywhere outside the text box.**

   The box changes to a single, thin blue line, ready to be moved or resized.

Inserting text, as just described, requires more work from you than inserting any other element. That's because you must type the text. You can't copy and paste text from another program.

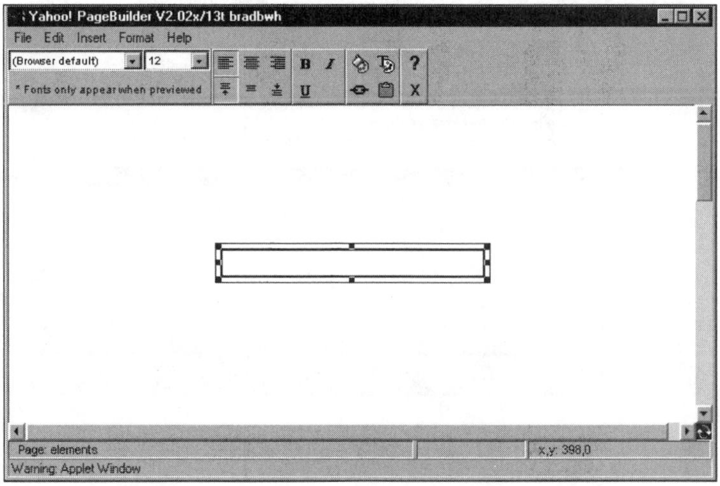

Figure 4-4:
An empty text box in PageBuilder.

After you have a text box with text in it (or any other type of element), you're ready to move it around and resize it. The following illustrated steps walk you through both procedures, illustrating how to move a text box from above a horizontal divider to below it and then how to resize the text box to the width of the divider. The divider is in a box, too, just like any other element, but it will remain in place during this exercise.

1. **Click any text box, keeping the mouse button held down.**

   The box changes to thicker lines with eight small squares spaced around it, as shown in Figure 4-5. You use those little squares to resize the box.

2. **Still holding down the mouse button, drag the box below the horizontal divider by moving the mouse.**

   When passing across the horizontal divider, a bright red grid appears in the area of overlap. Never let two boxes remain in an overlapped position — no red grids should be showing in the final version of your page. Figure 4-6 shows the text box in its new position below the horizontal divider.

3. **Position the mouse cursor over one of the small squares on the right edge of the text box.**

   When the mouse is positioned correctly, the cursor displays a short line with an arrow at each end. That cursor is your sign that you can grab the box's edge by clicking and holding the mouse button.

4. **Click the small square and hold down the mouse button.**

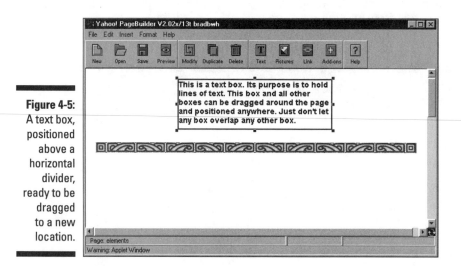

Figure 4-5:
A text box, positioned above a horizontal divider, ready to be dragged to a new location.

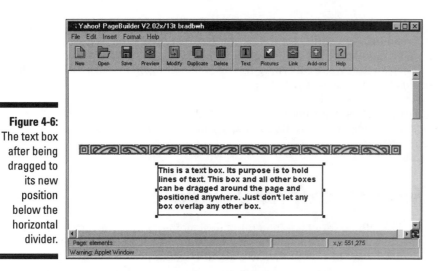

Figure 4-6:
The text box
after being
dragged to
its new
position
below the
horizontal
divider.

5. **Drag the right edge of the text box to the right, until the edge is aligned with the edge of the horizontal divider.**

   Of course, you can stop dragging at any point — I'm aligning with the edge of the divider for illustrative purposes. Note that the text in the box adjusts to fit the new box size. Text always fills out the width of a larger box, leaving room at the bottom.

6. **Drag the left edge of the text box to the left, until the edge is aligned with the edge of the horizontal divider.**

   At this point, the lower half of the text box has a lot of room, because the text has adjusted upward into the larger width. See Figure 4-7. You can drag the bottom edge upward to close that space or leave it alone. Leaving the space there creates a buffer into which no other page element can be placed without overlapping boxes. (You can also type more text by clicking your mouse cursor inside the box and typing.)

7. **Click anywhere outside the text box to remove the resizing squares.**

When you resize a graphic element box, the picture inside stretches or squashes to fit the new box size. Clipart is distorted by this adjustment, so it's generally a good idea to leave those boxes at their original size. Of course, you can move them around just like text boxes without distorting them.

You can't perform a cut-and-paste or copy-and-paste operation using the Windows or Mac Clipboard with PageBuilder. In other words, you can't copy text from another Windows or Mac program into a PageBuilder text box. This limitation is because PageBuilder is a Java program, not a Windows or Mac program. PageBuilder has its own Clipboard, however, and you can cut text from one text box and paste it into another text box. You lose the formatting (font, size, color) of the text when you paste it, but you can always reformat it. Doing so is easier than typing the text all over again in a new box, which would also require formatting.

You can delete any element on your page. Just click that element and then click the Delete button in the toolbar. (You can also use the keyboard's Delete key.)

Choosing stuff for your page

Yahoo! PageBuilder puts quite a bit of designer content up for grabs. Diving deep into the Insert menu reveals a large library of graphics and interactive elements. I can't be comprehensive about PageBuilder's content without devoting the entire book to this one program. Instead, this section explores the high points of the six categories of content in the Insert menu.

Basics

Basics cover the basics. (Duh.) You can easily create an entire Web site using only the choices in the Basics portion of the Insert menu .This is where you find text boxes, picture boxes, border lines, backgrounds, buttons and bullets, and a page-hit counter. I describe the operation of text boxes in the preceding section.

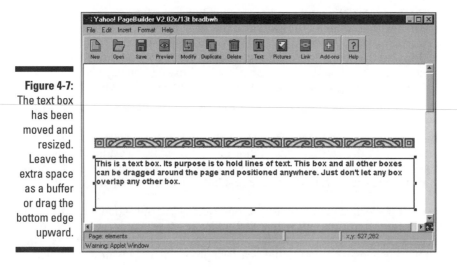

Figure 4-7:
The text box has been moved and resized. Leave the extra space as a buffer or drag the bottom edge upward.

PageBuilder dishes up plenty of pictures, both of the clipart and photographic variety. You can also upload your own picture files and place them on your page. If you have no pictures of your own but want to spice up your page with graphics, PageBuilder storms to the rescue with an extensive library of free choices. Here's how to browse in that graphics library:

1. **In PageBuilder, choose Insert ➪ Basics ➪ Pictures.**

   The Select Picture panel appears, as shown in Figure 4-8.

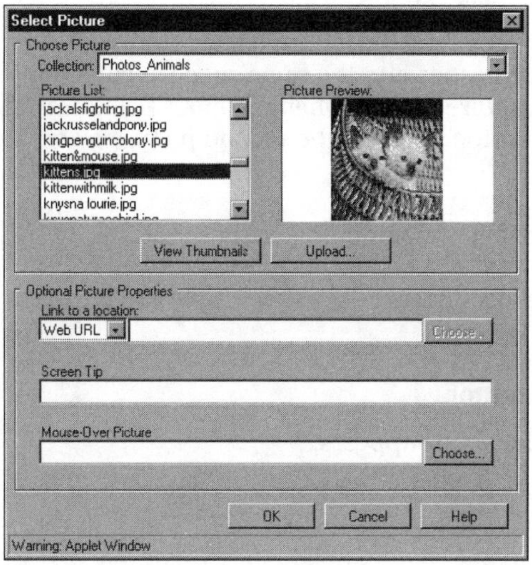

Figure 4-8:
You can select from several libraries of graphic photos and clipart. It's all free.

2. **In the Collection drop-down menu, select a picture group.**

3. **In the Picture List selection, click any picture file.**

   A small version of the picture appears in the Picture Preview pane. You can view thumbnail versions of all the pictures in the currently selected Collection by clicking the View Thumbnails button. Clicking any thumbnail displays a slightly larger view in the Picture Preview pane.

4. **Click the OK button.**

   The Select Picture panel disappears, and your selected picture appears on the page you're currently building. You can move it around the page; resizing is usually a bad idea because it distorts the picture.

Three other features appear under Optional Picture Properties in the Select Picture panel, as shown in Figure 4-8. They are

✔ **Link to a location.** Activating this feature turns the picture into a hyperlink on your page. That means if a visitor clicks the link, something happens. Use this property to determine what happens. Use the drop-down menu to link the picture to any URL on the Web, your e-mail address, or another of your Yahoo! GeoCities pages. The Choose button is active when you link to another one of your pages.

✔ **Screen Tip.** This feature displays a small pop-up tool tip when a visitor runs the mouse cursor over your picture. Use this field to determine what that pop-up flag says.

✔ **Mouse-Over Picture.** This feature lets you choose a second picture that appears when a visitor runs the mouse cursor over your first picture. The second picture flashes into the same space occupied by the first picture. The first picture returns when the mouse cursor is moved away. Click the Choose button to select the second picture from the Select a Picture panel.

Uploading a picture from your computer is fairly simple:

1. **In PageBuilder, choose Insert ➪ Basics ➪ Upload Picture.**

   The Upload Image panel appears.

2. **Click the Browse button.**

   The Choose file dialog box appears.

3. **Select a picture file in .gif or .jpg format to upload and then click the Open button.**

   Or just double-click the picture file to upload.

4. **Click the Upload button.**

   PageBuilder copies the picture file from your computer to your GeoCities server space and adds the picture as an element on your page-in-progress.

When uploading pictures to your page, copies of the pictures are stored in your Yahoo! GeoCities server space. You have 15 megabytes of space, which can hold a lot of pictures in most cases. If you do a lot of uploading or if your picture files are large (hundreds of kilobytes), you can fill up your available memory. Use File Manager (described later in this chapter) to manage your server space.

Other portions of the Basics menu include the following:

✔ **Background.** A background can be a simple color selection of a design. Some backgrounds contain a left-hand border. PageBuilder provides a large selection of backgrounds, which you may preview and select just like you do pictures.

✔ **Background music.** You can set music to play when a visitor arrives at your page. As of this writing, PageBuilder is providing the menu selection but no music selections. Possibly by the time you read this, PageBuilder will be equipped with MIDI and small WAV files to choose from.

✔ **Buttons and bullets.** You may use these small graphic elements to offset and emphasize text.

✔ **Horizontal and vertical lines.** These are custom-designed graphic dividers with which you can organize your page.

✔ **Counter.** This is an automatic gadget that counts the number of visitors to your page and displays the result. Most people put their counters near the bottom of the page.

Fun and Games

PageBuilder has some interactive programming modules that you can plug into your site. There's nothing to it; simply choose Insert ➪ Fun and Games and then click a game. PageBuilder does the rest, and you can move the game display around your page like any other element (some can't be resized).

You can't play the game from within PageBuilder. So if you want to find out how the game works and whether you want to keep it on your page, click the Preview button and try the game in your Web browser.

In addition to games, the Fun and Games menu contains . . . well, fun. You can select content that drops into your page on a regular basis, such as the Recipe of the Day. The Baseball module lets visitors look up statistics about teams. In all these cases, the content is taken from parts of the Yahoo! service, and some of it is similar to what you can put on your My Yahoo! page (see Chapter 2).

Animation

The Animation section of the Insert menu offers graphics that just won't stay still. Animated graphics are a great way to enliven a Web page. Creating them from scratch is no day at the beach, so these files are a welcome addition to the PageBuilder toolbox.

Most of the animations are picture-displaying tricks that slide or fade one picture into an element box while the previous picture slides or fades out. They provide a terrific way to showcase personal photos. In PageBuilder, animated graphics appear as generic element boxes — that is, the animations don't animate. You can't see any of the pictures you selected. To see what any file looks like when it's doing its thing, you need to Preview your page after inserting the animated element.

Instant Info

The Instant Info selection in the Insert menu contains information modules that deliver a bit of time-sensitive data to your visitors. There's a clock, a stock charter, a Yahoo! search form, a birthday count-down, a mortgage calculator, and a few other gadgets. These info-perks are easy to place on your page. Simply select one from the menu, and it appears. The modules don't actually work within PageBuilder — you can't, for example, call up a stock chart — but they appear just as they do on the Web page. When your site "goes live," these things work just fine.

Interactive

Perhaps the most important of the three Interactive selections in the Insert menu is the GeoGuide. GeoGuide appears within PageBuilder as a generic element box and appears on your Web page as a banner ad for GeoCities. Why would you choose to place an ad on your page? Because it's the only way to eliminate the GeoCities Ad Square that otherwise appears in the upper-right corner of your page. It also eliminates annoying pop-up advertising windows that otherwise plague your visitors.

Choosing GeoGuide is a trade-off of advertising methods. You can't get away from some kind of promotion on your page. At least with GeoGuide, you can position it wherever you want, even at the very bottom of the page.

The Yahoo! Presence is another Interactive selection. This icon is the familiar I'm Online! graphic that appears throughout Yahoo! communities. Use it if you want your visitors to know when you're available through Messenger or Yahoo! Chat.

The final Interactive selection is Message Board, which places a fully functioning message center right on your Web site.

Forms and Scripts

The final category of the Insert menu invites you to place interactive text-entry forms, check boxes, and radio buttons on your site. When visitors use these features, an e-mail containing their entries is automatically sent to the e-mail address listed in your Yahoo! profile for the ID currently in use as your GeoCities identifier. (That's a bit complex. Whatever ID you used to sign into GeoCities gets the e-mail containing text entries and check-box results.)

These forms, which use invisible segments of code called *scripts* (that you don't need to know anything about), are great for compiling a mailing list or running a survey. If you know HTML or want to copy a script from another page, choose HTML code.

Two more points to remember about Yahoo! PageBuilder. First, you can't use the program to construct pages that reside anywhere outside GeoCities. You simply can't save a page to any location except your GeoCities server space. Second, remember that the PageBuilder templates provide a good starting point, and they can be edited and altered with all the power and flexibility you have when starting from scratch.

Becoming a Power Host

Hosting your own site might be so much fun that you want to get serious about it. Yahoo! GeoCities keeps pace with your rising ambitions with a suite of services that can turn your hobby into . . . well, a serious hobby.

The two most common needs of experienced Webmasters are more space and better management tools. Yahoo! GeoCities covers both bases.

Please sir, can I have some more?

Your free GeoCities account starts with 15 megabytes of space, which is a fairly generous allotment. But if you start building a complex, multipage site, filled with space-hogging graphics, you may bump your head against that space memory ceiling at some point.

You can order more memory, in increments of 5 megabytes, at any time. Each chunk of 5 megs costs $2.50 per month (as of this writing). Here's how to order more server space:

1. **On the Yahoo! GeoCities home page, click the <u>Extra Space</u> link.**

   The Account Status page appears.

2. **Under <u>Additional Disk Space</u>, click the <u>Add</u> link.**

   The Change Disk Space page appears.

3. **Use the drop-down menu to select an amount to add.**

4. **Make sure the Add radio button is selected, or select the Subtract radio button to remove previously added space.**

5. **Click the Confirm button.**

   As with any other purchase of features in GeoCities, you must have a valid Yahoo! Wallet. (For more on Yahoo! Wallet, see Chapter 24.)

Master of your domain

File management is always an issue with sites that exceed about five pages or even fewer pages if many graphics and other elements are uploaded to the GeoCities server space. You need an on-screen tool that displays all your pages and uploaded files. That's just what you get with File Manager, a GeoCities program that operates right in your Web browser.

File Manager allows you to view, edit, copy, rename, delete, and move files in your server space. The program may look a little intimidating at first, but it's intuitively designed and easy to use. Some of its features are quite slick.

Follow these steps to get started with GeoCities File Manager:

1. **On the GeoCities home page, click the <u>File Manager</u> link.**

2. **On the next page, select what types of files you want to appear in File Manager.**

   The default settings are preferable in most cases. Leave them alone and File Manager displays all your files. If you want to see only your page files, leaving all graphic files and other elements off the list, check the html box. Leave that box unchecked to see only supporting files, not the pages themselves.

3. **Click the <u>Open File Manager</u> link.**

   The File Manager appears, as shown in Figure 4-9, displaying your files with check boxes next to them. You can use the boxes to decide which files will be affected by the commands you give File Manager.

File Manager provides a quick overview of what you have in your server space and how the HTML files (your pages) were created. The icons with little gears indicate a PageWizards creation; icons with a little house indicate a PageBuilder creation.

Beyond the overview, File Manager provides three important links and six buttons that help you assess and manipulate your files:

- ✔ **The <u>View</u> link.** Click this link to view any graphic or page file in your browser.

- ✔ **The <u>Stats</u> link.** This link displays statistics about any page (.html file) in your account. The stats (see Figure 4-10) show the number of visits to that page and let you select other statistical reports.

- ✔ **The <u>Setup</u> link.** Use this link to set up a hit counter for your page. A detailed array of variations lets you customize the counter to your specifications.

✔ **The New button.** Clicking this button displays an HTML editing page for creating a new page or excerpt of code. If you normally work in PageWizards or PageBuilder and don't want to get your hands dirty with raw HTML code, don't ever click this button.

✔ **The Copy button.** This button enables you to make a copy of any file in your server space (check the box next to the file you want to copy). You must give the copied file a new name.

✔ **The Rename button.** Renaming is different than copying, even though both operations create a new name. Rename a file that you don't want a second copy of.

✔ **The Edit button.** Like the New button, the Edit button links to an HTML editor. You can view and alter the code of any .html file, which is to say, any of your pages. The Edit button doesn't work with picture files. If you prefer adjusting your pages in PageWizards or PageBuilder, avoid the Edit button.

✔ **The Delete button.** Careful with this one. The Delete button does what it says, erasing any selected files (those with checked boxes).

✔ **The Move button.** If you've created at least one subdirectory, you can move files among your directories with the Move button.

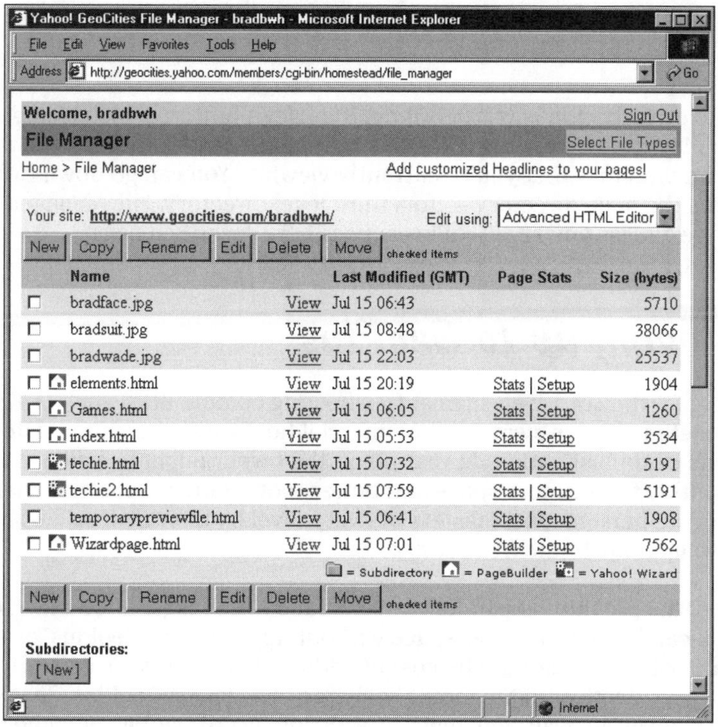

Figure 4-9:
GeoCities
File
Manager.

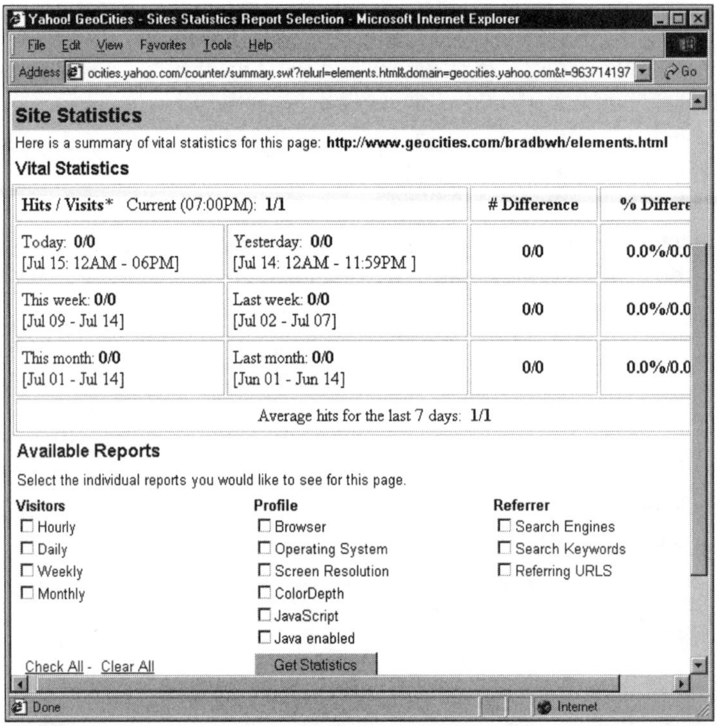

Figure 4-10:
The Site
Statistics
page. Use
the check
boxes to
view more
stats.

One other button is worth noting: the [New] button, which is under the
Subdirectories heading. Click this button to create a directory within the
main directory that you're currently viewing. You can go down two levels
from the main directory — to a third-level directory. File Manager stops you
there, unless you're a GeoPlus subscriber (described next).

Moving up to GeoPlus

People who start Web sites at free hosting communities such as GeoCities
sometimes move away to a commercial host when their site attains a certain
level of sophistication. At that point, the owner might be willing to pay a
monthly fee for more space and better tools. Yahoo! GeoCities tries to accommodate personal Webmasters of every level by offering GeoPlus, an inexpensive upgrade to the free service.

GeoPlus provides expanded server space — 25 megs, to be exact. Of course,
you can buy extra server space without upgrading to GeoPlus, as described
earlier in this chapter. The cost of adding 10 megabtyes to the original 15
megs is identical to the monthly charge of $4.95 for GeoPlus. So if you're up
to 25 megs anyway, you might as well convert to GeoPlus membership for the
other benefits, which include

✔ A large library of CGI scripts for building sophisticated interactive additions to your page

✔ A Java applet library for adding small programs to the page

✔ More sophisticated site statistics, with graphic displays

✔ Deeper subdirectory structure, down to five levels

✔ Online support from staff Web developers

To find out the details of the GeoPlus subscription plan, go to the Yahoo! GeoCities home page and click the <u>GeoPlus Members</u> link.

Chapter 5

Master of Your Domain

- -

- -

*Y*ahoo! is nothing if not hospitable. The service provides several ways to build a virtual home, a stable Internet identity and address. My Yahoo! is your information center; Yahoo! Companion is your bookmarking center; Yahoo! GeoCities is a Web-site community center; Messenger and Yahoo! Mail are communications centers; and Yahoo! Clubs is a recreation center. For those ready to stretch a bit beyond the Yahoo! umbrella, Yahoo! Website Services provides a home away from home.

Yahoo! Website Services is the Web hosting branch of Yahoo!. Hosting companies furnish leased server (remote computer) space for placing Web pages. Yahoo! GeoCities (Chapter 4) is a Web host and a free one. So why go anywhere else to build a Web page? Yahoo! GeoCities trades no-charge service for an ad-infested page design. Website Services, on the other hand, charges for the hosting but keeps its hands off your pages.

All Web hosting operates pretty much the same way. You pay a monthly leasing charge for the server space plus related services, and you are responsible for designing and uploading your pages. Typically, Web hosts are transparent partners — they don't assist with your pages or in managing your server space. As such, these services are for the more experienced Web resident or for anyone who wants to become more experienced.

Another reason many people are willing to pay for Web hosting is to acquire and use their own domain name. Domain names are the portions of URL addresses after the .www and before the .com (or .net or .org). My domain name, for example, is bradhill. Fabulous, isn't it? I haven't yet won prizes for originality, but I'm still hoping.

Yahoo! Website Services covers the usual bases — lots of server space, related services, and domain registration. All for an attractive price. This chapter spells out how to understand and sign up for Yahoo! Web hosting.

The Hosting Deal

I've shopped extensively for Web hosts and used several of them over the years. So I can say confidently that the Yahoo! arrangement is a good deal. Here's what you get in the basic plan, called the Starter Web Package:

- **100 megabytes of server space.** This is a lot of space — more than most people use for personal Web sites. If you become ambitious with multi-media (memory-gobbling) content, Yahoo! has a Plus Web Package that includes 250 megs.

- **Ten e-mail boxes.** Whether you use your own registered domain or not, you can use ten different addresses. You could, for example, set up mailboxes for yourname@yourname.com, yname@yourname.com, yn@yourname.com, and yourn@yourname.com. You could send e-mail subscriptions to one address, an e-mail discussion group to another, use one for your personal box, devote another to your girlfriend or boyfriend — you get the picture.

- **Web Console.** Web Console is a browser interface that helps you manage your account, divide your server space, assign folders, create e-mail boxes, and accomplish all the chores of administering a domain.

- **Free domain registration.** Yahoo! is not an official domain registrar, but it works with Network Solutions (one of several companies that registers domain names) and doesn't charge you for the connection to Network Solutions. Furthermore, Yahoo! pays for the initial registration and ongoing renewal fees for the domain. As of this writing, domain names are purchased for an initial period of two years, and the cost is $75 for the entire two-year period. You can renew domains for single-year increments after the first two-year period. The deal as it stands at this writing is that Yahoo! pays all the registration fees for as long as you host the domain at Yahoo! Website Services.

As of this writing, the Starter Web Package costs $14.95 per month, after a one-time setup charge of $14.95. The Plus Web Package costs $19.95 to set up and then carries an ongoing $39.95 charge per month. In addition to more server space and more mailboxes, the Plus arrangement includes two major features for advanced Web residents:

✔ **Merchant Auctions Manager.** This is an auction managements system for use with Yahoo! Auctions. Serious auctioneers can set up their Web-based business with the Plus Web Package and use Merchant Auctions Manager to run the auction side of the operation.

✔ **Media Boost.** This feature fortifies your server space, enabling it to accommodate more listeners to streaming media.

These two aspects make the Plus Web Package appealing to auction businesses and multimedia programmers. Most other people who want an ad-free hobby site would be happy with the Starter Web Package.

Setting Up Your Account

One peculiar feature of Yahoo! Website Services is that you must start by acquiring a domain. Many hosting companies allow you to buy a domain name *or* create a user account under the host company's domain name. Not so here. Because Yahoo! is paying for the domain name, there's really no disadvantage to acquiring the domain, as long as you stick with Yahoo! as your host. That's exactly why Yahoo! is doing it this way.

As a result of this policy, setting up a Yahoo! Website Services account is a triple process in which you must:

✔ Search for an unregistered domain

✔ Acquire a domain

✔ Set up your account

In the following, I step you through the process.

1. **On the Yahoo! Website Services home page, shown in Figure 5-1, click the <u>Place Your Order</u> link for the Starter Web Package.**

   The quickest way to get to the Website Services home page is to enter the following URL in your browser:

   ```
   website.yahoo.com
   ```

2. **On the next page, search for an unregistered domain name.**

   This step takes time and creativity. You can start with your own name, which might be available if it's an unusual one. Or you may prefer to invent a new name for your site. Take your time with this step. Some people spend weeks finding the perfect domain name.

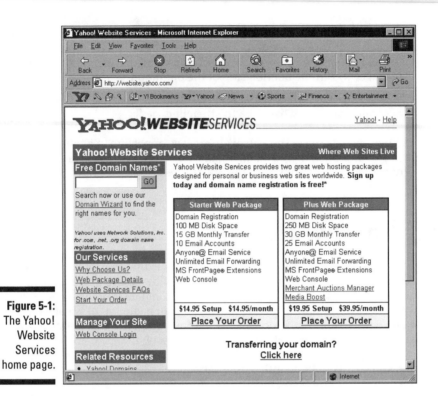

Figure 5-1:
The Yahoo!
Website
Services
home page.

Generally, short names that are easy to remember are best. People refer to site domains as "domainname dot com," so think of something that can be pronounced easily in that format.

The Domain Search on this page (see Figure 5-2) works with .com, .net, and .org domains because they are the most common suffixes. (By late 2000, new suffixes might be introduced to the domain system.) The Domain Wizard accepts up to three keywords and attempts to find relevant, unregistered domain names.

3. **On the Search Results page, click the Buy Now! button to register a domain name.**

   The Domain Search and Domain Wizard forms are below the Search Results, so you can continue searching without backtracking.

4. **Enter your Yahoo! Security Key for your Yahoo! Wallet and then click the Enter Secure Area button.**

   I explain how to get a Yahoo! Wallet in Chapter 24 — you need one to host a site at Yahoo!. The Yahoo! ID you're currently using must be the same as your Wallet ID.

5. **Review your Yahoo! Wallet information and then click the Finished button.**

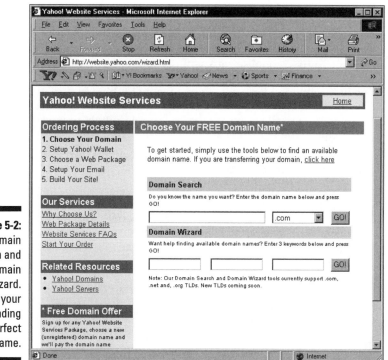

Figure 5-2:
The Domain
Search and
Domain
Wizard.
Take your
time finding
the perfect
name.

6. **Create a password for your domain and then click the Register Your Domain button.**

This is the first page of a six-page registration process. You need to type your password twice — both times it appears on your screen as a row of asterisks. That's so the snoop looking over your shoulder doesn't decipher it. In most cases, the Promotion Code and Reseller fields are left blank.

7. **On the Step 2 of 6 page, fill in all required fields and then click the Select Your Web Package button.**

Required fields are marked with asterisks. Your Yahoo! Profile information has probably filled in most of the fields for you. The Domain Name Registrant is almost always the person filling out this form — that would be you. The Administrative Contact is the person handling renewals and general upkeep of the hosting situation — that most likely would be you again.

The Administrative Contact has complete control over the domain name, where it's hosted, and whether it's renewed. Do not capriciously put someone else's contact information in this form unless you're willing to lose control of the domain name and its site content. If you're giving a domain name and hosting service as a gift, however, you might want to make the recipient the Administrative Contact.

Every domain registration has an Administrative Contact and a Technical Contact. You see no mention of a Technical Contact during this process because Yahoo! makes itself the technical contact. This default is necessary so that Yahoo! Website Services can apply your domain to the Yahoo! servers without hassling you with technical details. Believe me, if you're not technically minded and don't enjoy filling in bewildering forms, you don't want anything to do with the technical chores. However, if you — as the Administrative Contact — close the account, you need to change the Technical Contact to yourself and do the technical dirty work of moving the domain to another service.

8. **Select a service plan, check the User Agreement box, and then click the Review Your Order button.**

   Use the drop-down menu (see Figure 5-3) to select either the Starter Web Package (sufficient for most people) or the Plus Web Package. You can add extra e-mail boxes in increments of five mailboxes with the lower drop-down menu. Remember to check the User Agreement box and click the Yahoo! Website Services Agreement link to see the agreement document.

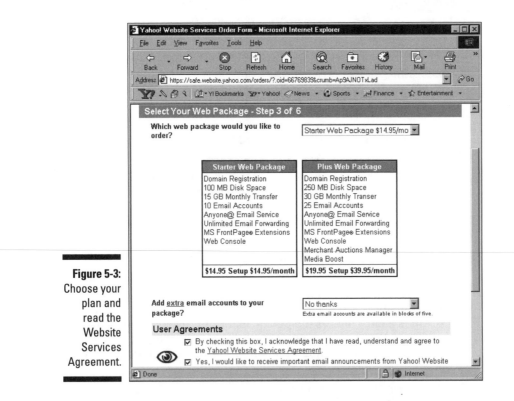

Figure 5-3:
Choose your plan and read the Website Services Agreement.

9. **Review your order and the charges and then click the Complete Your Order button.**

   The Order Confirmation page appears, which you can print as a receipt. At the same time, Yahoo! is e-mailing important information to the mailbox listed in your Yahoo! Profile (not to a mailbox in your newly created domain). Save all e-mails that arrive! They give you valuable information about accessing your Web Console (for managing your server space) and uploading files to an FTP (File Transfer Protocol) address. One of the e-mails serves as another receipt of payment.

Discovering Web Console

After your account is set up, you may interface with it, change it, and manage it with something called Web Console. The only task that you don't accomplish through Web Console is uploading pages to your server space — use standard FTP transfers for that. (Yahoo! sends you e-mails regarding that process the moment your account is set up.)

Get to Web Console at the following URL:

```
console.website.yahoo.com
```

You can also click the <u>Web Console Login</u> link on the Website Services home page (see Figure 5-1).

Enter your new domain name (complete with the .com, .net, or .org suffix) and password. The Console is called My Yahoo! Website Services on the page but *Web Console* in the browser title bar. Throughout this chapter, I refer to it as Web Console.

Changing passwords

At first, the Web Console password is identical to your general account password. To change that password (though you don't need to) and to change the FTP Access Password (you don't need to change that either), follow these steps:

1. **On the Web Console page, click Password Manager.**

   The Password Manager page appears, as shown in Figure 5-4.

2. **Choose a Web Console Password and then click the Change Web Console Password button.**

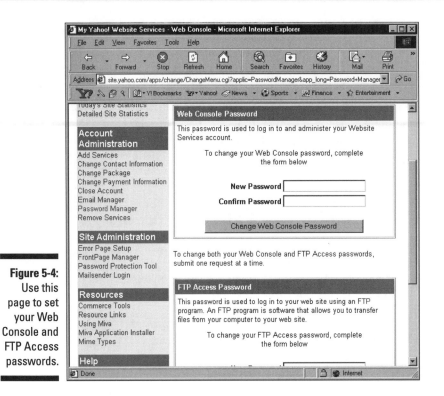

Figure 5-4:
Use this
page to set
your Web
Console and
FTP Access
passwords.

3. **Use the Back button of your browser to return to the Password Manager page.**

4. **On the Password Manager page again, choose an FTP Access Password and then click the Change Web Console Password button.**

   You have now created three passwords: an account password, the Web Console Password, and the FTP Access Password. They can be identical if you choose.

Putting up a mailbox or two

Your next step should be to set up some mailboxes or at least one mailbox. Follow these steps to begin setting up the mailboxes at your new domain:

1. **On the Web Console page, click Email Manager.**

   The Email Manager page of Web Console appears, as shown in Figure 5-5.

2. **Click the New Email Box button.**

   This should be the first button of the three you select, because the first thing you need to do is establish at least one mailbox.

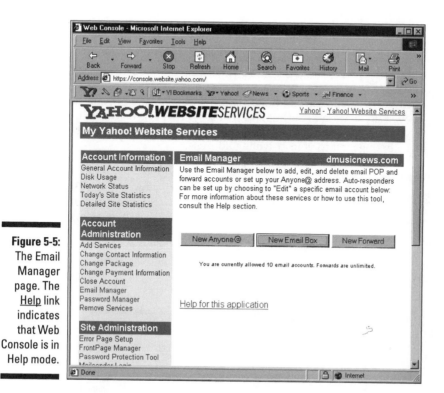

Figure 5-5:
The Email
Manager
page. The
Help link
indicates
that Web
Console is in
Help mode.

3. **On the next Email Manager page, shown in Figure 5-6, create your new mailbox by filling in the fields and selecting radio buttons.**

   As you can see, each mailbox can have its own password. In fact, you *must* enter a password, even if it duplicates your account password, Web Console password, or FTP Access password. The Forward To field is optional but watch out — if you place an address in that field, the mailbox doesn't hold any mail it receives. In other words, it doesn't copy incoming mail and forward it. It just forwards it right out of the mailbox. The Auto Reply function is for mailboxes that act like robots — they send a form response to everything that comes in, which is convenient if you're going to be on vacation.

4. **Click the Submit button.**

   All mailboxes that you create appear on the Email Manager page, with Edit and Delete buttons.

Two other buttons enliven the Email Manager page. They are

✔ **New Anyone@.** This cryptic button lets you create a mailbox that accepts mail addressed to any name (or random string of characters) placed before the @ sign that precedes your domain. This feature helps catch misspellings and typos. If your real e-mail address is `namehere@ yourname.com`, for example, and someone addresses you at `namehear@ yourname.com`, that letter can be collected by an Anyone@ box. You can assign one of your `yourname.com` mailboxes or any mailbox at all as the Anyone@ catchall.

✔ **New Forward.** You can put Forward status on any of your mailboxes, even if you didn't set them up that way. This is great when traveling — you can arrange for your main mailbox (or more than one) to pass incoming mail to your traveling address.

You can access your mail with the same program you currently use to get your ISP mail. (The preceding sentence is not true for America Online users.) Microsoft Outlook Express and Netscape Mail are the two most popular e-mail programs. (America Online customers may use them also.)

Yahoo! also provides a Web-based service for reading mail in your browser (see Figure 5-7). Click the <u>Mailsender Login</u> link under the Site Administration heading in Web Console to access that page.

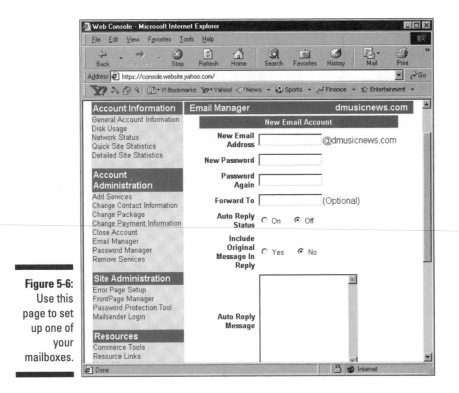

Figure 5-6:
Use this page to set up one of your mailboxes.

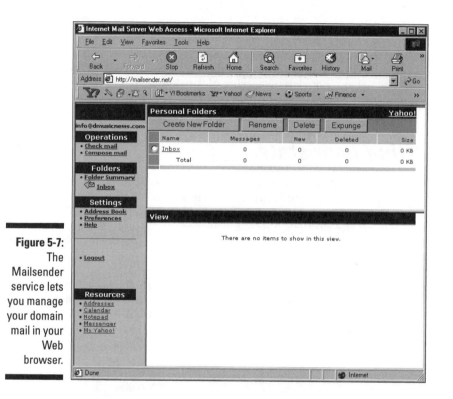

Figure 5-7:
The
Mailsender
service lets
you manage
your domain
mail in your
Web
browser.

Managing your account

Under the Account Administration heading in Web Console, several links connect you to pages in which you can change aspects of your account. The previous sections of this chapter describe the Email Manager and Password Manager, two of the most important links under Account Administration. Briefly, here's a rundown of what the other links do:

✔ **Account Services.** On this page, add additional e-mail accounts and media boosts. This is *not* where you create one of your mailboxes within your included allowance of mailboxes. If you need more than your included allowance, order them here in increments of five mailboxes. The media boosts are helpful when serving many simultaneous multimedia streams — for example, if you've set up an MP3 radio station and you're getting more traffic.

✔ **Change Contact Information.** Your contact information for the Website Services account is stored in Yahoo! Wallet, so this link sends you to the Wallet to make changes.

✔ **Change Package.** Use the radio buttons on this page to upgrade to the Plus Web Package or downgrade to the Starter Web Package.

✔ **Change Payment Information.** As with your contact information, payment information is changed in Yahoo! Wallet. That's where this link sends you.

✔ **Close Account.** On this page, you need to fill in several required fields. Remember that closing the account puts you in charge of paying ongoing domain renewal fees. You also must remove Yahoo! as the Technical Administrator and take charge of finding a new host for your domain. You can also relinquish ownership of the domain name by simply not renewing it when your two-year registration expires.

Getting your stats

The Account Information heading of Web Console links you to pages that display details of your account's activity. This is where Yahoo! communicates with you about server issues and maintenance and where you see statistics related to your site's traffic (how many people are visiting). You can also check how much of your allotted server space you're using. The following rundown briefly describes the functions under the Account Information heading:

✔ **General Account Information.** This simple page, shown in Figure 5-8, tells you whether your account is active, what the current contact e-mail address is, whether FrontPage ServerExtensions (software on the server for people who use the FrontPage program to design Web pages) are installed, and what operating system is running the account's server.

Figure 5-8:
The General Account Information page of Web Console.

✔ **Disk Usage.** This simple table indicates how much of your server space is occupied by pages, graphics, and other files associated with your site.

✔ **Network Status.** This page, which is shown in Figure 5-9, is Yahoo!'s message board to its customers. Check the page often to find out about scheduled maintenance downtimes and other issues.

✔ **Today's Site Statistics.** This link displays a simple report indicating the number of *hits,* or visits, that have been made to your site's pages.

✔ **Detailed Site Statistics.** This page is an elaborate form with which you can order a complex report of your site's traffic statistics. As you can see in Figure 5-10 (which illustrates only part of the form), you can get quite specific in what you want to see. The form is delivered by e-mail.

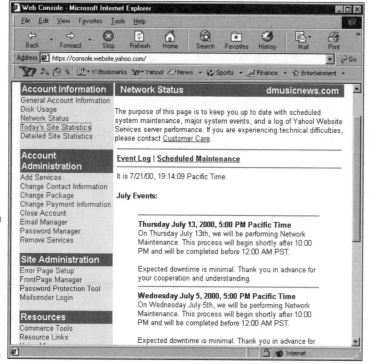

Figure 5-9:
The Network Status page is Yahoo!'s message board to its customers.

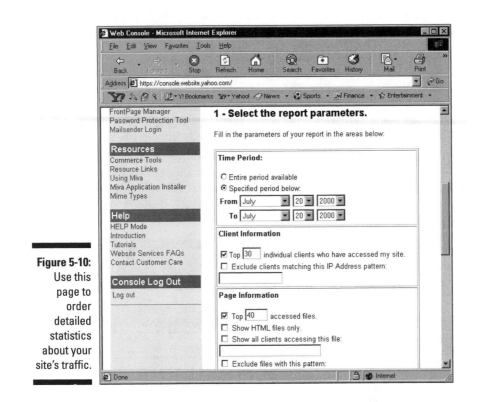

Figure 5-10:
Use this page to order detailed statistics about your site's traffic.

Chapter 6

Your Virtual Photo Album

Two parts of the Yahoo! service are so inextricably bound together, it's as if they are married. And like some married folks, they've begun to look like each other. I'm referring to Yahoo! Photos and Yahoo! Briefcase.

Although this chapter is purportedly about online photo albums, its broader purpose is to show how you can store all kinds of computer files online, courtesy of Yahoo!. To that end, I've bonded Yahoo! Photos and Yahoo! Briefcase into a single chapter. Likewise, Yahoo! itself bonds them into a single service, wherein the Photos part is a subset of the Briefcase part. Photos also exists alone, like a married woman taking a solo vacation. However, the Briefcase can't live without her. Perhaps it's best to end this marriage analogy now. But I can't promise I won't come back to it.

Opening Your Yahoo! Briefcase

Yahoo! Briefcase is a personal storage area set aside for anyone with a Yahoo! ID. Three crucial facts hold true for your briefcase:

✔ Each briefcase contains 25 megabytes of storage space.

✔ Within that space, you can store up to 36 files.

✔ No file can be larger than 5 megabytes.

These limitations cover the Briefcase and the Photo Album, taken as a single storage entity. In other words, the Photo Album is part of the Briefcase.

Yahoo! Photos is specifically intended for uploading and storing photos, and it operates identically to Yahoo! Briefcase. The Photo Album is displayed as part of Yahoo! Briefcase. Figure 6-1 makes the arrangement clear:

- ✔ Under the File Folders heading, your main Briefcase folder is listed. That's where you keep non-photo files.
- ✔ Under the Photo Albums heading, your folders for photos are displayed.

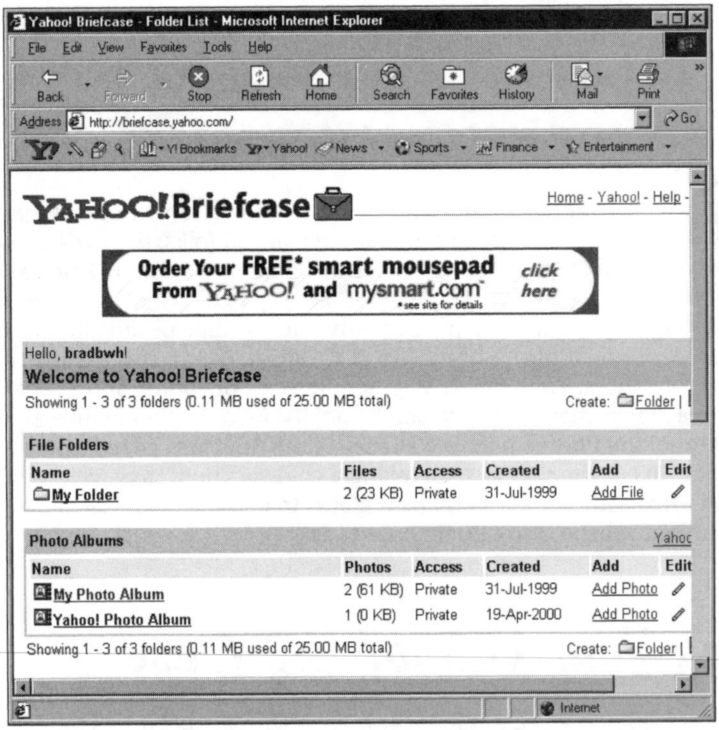

Figure 6-1: The Yahoo! Briefcase home page.

If you ever upload photos to the Briefcase instead of to the Photo Album, your computer explodes! Just kidding. What actually happens is that your uploaded pictures are automatically repositioned in the Photo Album.

The Briefcase is a convenient aid to business travelers because it can be accessed from any connected computer. You can put any kind of file in your briefcase. The service is a great way to back up crucial files, even though 25 megabytes isn't nearly enough storage space for any kind of comprehensive backup.

A Yahoo! Briefcase can be public or private. In public mode, it offers an efficient way to share files. You can even make a briefcase partially public, available to a predetermined group of people. If you make your briefcase fully public, you might want to consider listing it on your Yahoo! Profile page (see Chapter 1).

Uploading to your briefcase

There's nothing complex about Yahoo! Briefcase. You upload; you store; possibly you share. You create new folders. You move files around. You revel in coolness. Follow these steps to start using your briefcase.

1. **When signed in to your Yahoo! ID, go to the Yahoo! Briefcase home page at the following URL:**

   ```
   briefcase.yahoo.com
   ```

2. **Click the <u>My Folder</u> folder.**

   A Briefcase folder is shown in Figure 6-2.

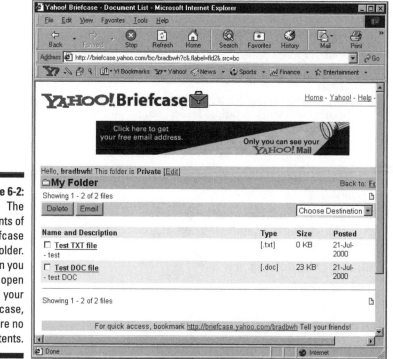

Figure 6-2:
The contents of a Briefcase folder. When you first open your briefcase, there are no contents.

3. **Click the <u>Add File</u> link.**

   The link is hidden to the right in Figure 6-2. You may need to scroll your window to the right to find it.

4. **Under the Locate your file heading, click the Browse button.**

5. **In the Choose file window, select a file to upload from your computer.**

   If you're testing the Briefcase, choose a small file to minimize upload time. Use the <u>link to a file on the Web</u> link to copy a file that's already uploaded somewhere.

6. **Under the Name your file heading, enter a name and a description of the file.**

7. **Click the Upload button.**

   Your Briefcase folder reappears with the new file listed.

Sharing your briefcase

As mentioned earlier, you can make your briefcase public, private, or semi-private. Here's how:

1. **On the Yahoo! Briefcase home page, click the Edit icon (it looks like a pencil) next to any folder or Photo Album.**

   The Share Folders page appears, as shown in Figure 6-3.

2. **Choose a radio button to determine the privacy of your folder.**

   A private folder can never be viewed by anyone logged into a different Yahoo! ID (even you). A public folder can be viewed by anyone who surfs to the following URL:

   ```
   briefcase.yahoo.com/yourID
   ```

   A friends folder can be viewed only by the Yahoo! IDs you list in the Friends field.

3. **If you want to make the folder accessible only to Yahoo! IDs regis-tered to users over eighteen years old, click to add a checkmark to the Age restriction box.**

4. **Click the Continue button.**

   The Yahoo! Briefcase home page appears.

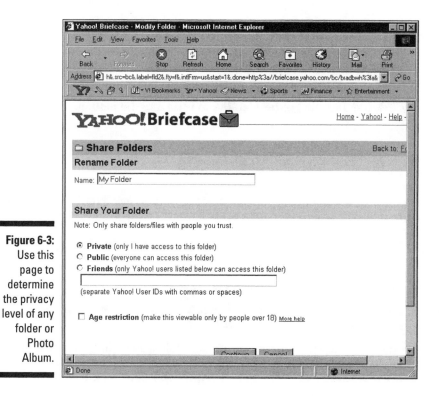

Creating Folders

You can set up several new folders and Photo Albums. The folders and albums are not in a box-within-a-box hierarchy as on a computer hard drive. Every folder is on the same level. Still, the feature is convenient and helps keep things organized. You can assign one folder to a certain type of file or a certain project. Furthermore, each folder can have its own privacy level, so you can separate private files from public ones. (Same with pictures in the Photo Albums section.)

Follow these steps to create a new folder:

1. **On the Yahoo! Briefcase home page, click the Create: <u>Folder</u> link.**

   The Create a New Folder page appears.

2. **Type a name for the new folder.**

3. **Select the privacy level of the new folder, as described in the previous section.**

   4. **If you want to exclude minors, click to add a checkmark to the Age restriction box.**

   5. **Click the Create Folder button.**

      The new folder page appears, with no file listed.

   6. **Click the Back to: Folder List link to return to the main page.**

Organizing Your Files

After creating a few folders, you may feel the need to move files around from time to time. File shuffling is not a problem. Just do the following:

   1. **On the Yahoo! Briefcase home page, click any folder link.**

      The folder page appears.

   2. **Click to add a checkmark to a box next to any file or files.**

   3. **From the Choose Destination pull-down menu, select one of your other folders.**

      You cannot move a file from a Briefcase folder to a Photo Album folder or vice versa. Although the two services are presented together on the Briefcase page and operate similarly, Yahoo! keeps their files separate.

   4. **Click the Move button.**

      The destination folder's page appears, showing the moved file.

You can e-mail a file from the folder page, too. Just select any file or files and click the Email button. The page shown in Figure 6-4 appears, asking for at least one e-mail address (you may enter up to five) and a personal message, which will appear in the body of the received e-mail. In truth, you are e-mailing only a link to the file, not the file itself. The link doesn't work with private folders, although the system doesn't stop you from sending the e-mail.

Fun facts about Yahoo! Briefcase

Maybe they're not fun, but they are facts.

✔ You can open files stored in your briefcase, right from the folder page. But you must have the appropriate program installed — such as Microsoft Word for .doc files — to see the file.

✔ Your briefcase is easily accessible from Yahoo! Companion (see Chapter 20). Click the Yahoo! button, select Tools, and then click Briefcase.

✔ Your Briefcase URL is briefcase. yahoo.com/*YourYahooID*. If your folders are public, you can send that link to friends.

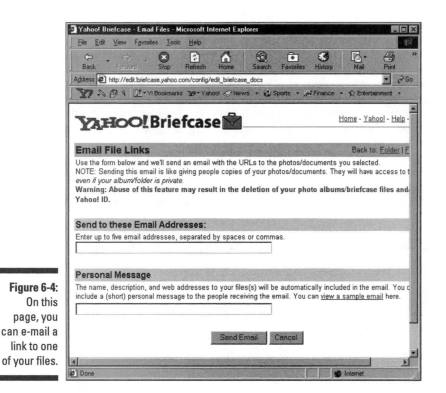

Figure 6-4:
On this
page, you
can e-mail a
link to one
of your files.

Keeping a Photo Album

If you use Yahoo! Briefcase primarily for storing photos, you might want to relate to the Yahoo! Photos section as a separate site, detached from Yahoo! Briefcase. You can see the service on its own at this URL:

```
photos.yahoo.com
```

Yahoo! Photos works in essentially the same way as Yahoo! Briefcase but with two extra features:

✔ Photos can be resized as they are uploaded, to conserve storage space.

✔ You can order inexpensive prints of any photo(s) stored in your albums.

Figure 6-5 shows the upload page for Yahoo! Photos, which is identical to the Briefcase upload page described previously. The Resize Photo feature is near the bottom. Clicking the Don't resize option maintains the proportions of the photo and is the best choice with moderately sized pictures. Use the Large selection with tiny photos, the Medium selection with very large photos, and the Small selection with large photos when conserving space. Check the results with the Preview button before clicking the Upload button.

Each Photo Album page contains an Order Prints button. Click it to see an order form you use to select the photos you want printed and to determine quantities and print sizes. Figure 6-6 shows the order form. Use the Express Checkout button to purchase prints quickly using Yahoo! Wallet (described in Chapter 24).

Any visitor to a public photo album can order prints of your photos. You can disable the print-ordering feature while keeping the album public. To do so, click the Edit link on any album page and then check the Order restriction box.

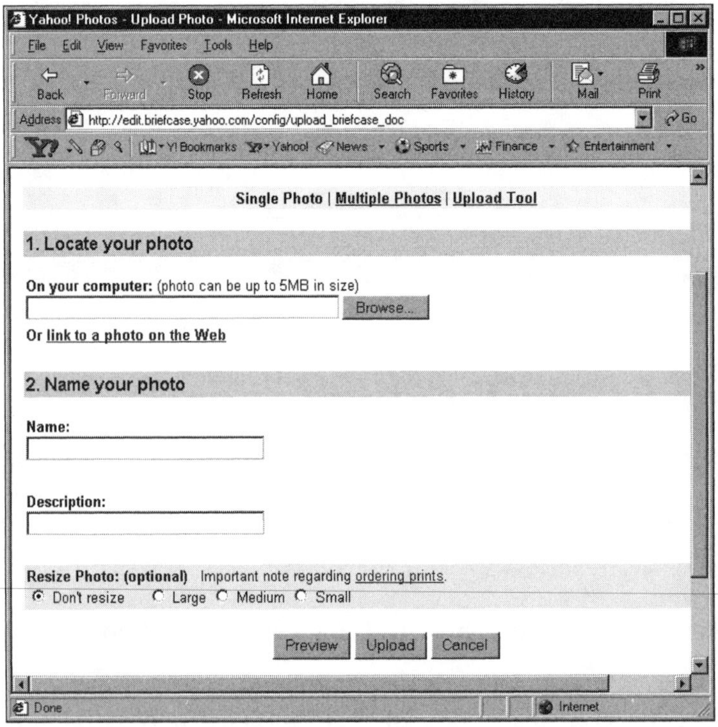

Figure 6-5:
Use this page to upload photos — it works just like uploading to Briefcase.

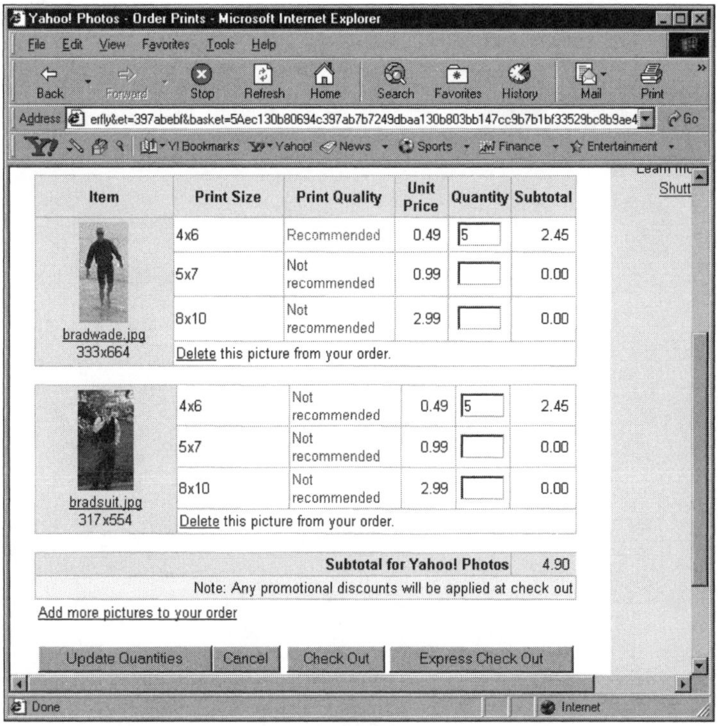

Figure 6-6:
This is where you order prints of your Photo Album photographs.

Part III
Knowledge and Fun

The 5th Wave — By Rich Tennant

@RICHTENNANT

"Children- it is not necessary to whisper while we're visiting the Vatican Library Web site."

In this part . . .

Yahoo! has long been known for its excellent directory and search engine, and the first chapter in this part explains how to get the most from those core features. News, sports, finances, and music each get their own chapter in this part. The last chapter introduces you to Yahoo! Games, where you can meet others for interactive board and card games.

Chapter 7

Navigating the Web

• •

• •

Think of it. The Internet can be considered the planet's largest library. And Yahoo!, which started as a directory of the Web, is arguably the most detailed card catalogue to the Internet. *Arguably* is a key word, though, because several other directories would lay claim to the honor of being the most thorough menu of Web pages. The argument has been raging for years, but it's pointless. The Web is so huge and so kaleidoscopic in its tendency to shift and evolve that no online service in the world can take the ultimate snapshot of all Web pages at any given moment.

Yahoo! built the reputation of its directory on the twin values of size and organization. Although some other directories apply severe editorial guidance by pointing visitors to selected sites, Yahoo! became famous for its lengthy directory pages that *seem* to link every Web site ever created on a certain topic. But that's not exactly true — in fact, Yahoo! employs its own selection process when adding to the directory, which I cover later in this chapter. And, indeed, some Yahoo! directory pages point the visitor to content destinations within the Yahoo! service. But these subjective factors notwithstanding, the Yahoo! directory is renowned for its detail and elaborately useful organizational structure.

Yahoo!'s directory, and the related search engine, remain core features of the entire online service. The directory is an astounding menu of Web sites, and the search engine is a great way to navigate it. When you want an overview of Web destinations on a certain topic — general and detailed, good and bad, corporate and personal, famous and obscure — Yahoo!'s directory is the place to turn.

Although the directory and search engine aren't difficult features to use, they represent a massive catalogue of content that can be intimidating. Luckily, navigating this catalogue succumbs nicely to a few tricks and shortcuts. That's the purpose of this chapter. Here, I tackle Yahoo!'s sprawling, magnificent information menu, which played a huge part in popularizing the Internet and still provides a daily virtual map to millions of online citizens.

Understanding the Yahoo! Directory

I might have titled this section "Understanding the Toaster" because the Yahoo! directory is somewhat easier to comprehend than piloting an airliner. This isn't brain surgery or even a relatively simple appendectomy. (For information on those topics, please see *Scalpel Techniques For Dummies*.) But this *is* where the aforementioned tricks and shortcuts come in. I'll guide your mouse through the points and clicks of Yahoo!'s directory, adding my tips along the way.

Start with the main directory page, as pictured in the lovely Figure 7-1. Get there by using the primary Yahoo! URL:

```
www.yahoo.com
```

The main Yahoo! directory page doesn't waste any space on decoration or unnecessary prettiness. Perhaps that's a kind way of saying it's ugly but useful. Its plain look brings an advantage to the user, though — without graphics and lots of advertisements, the directory is quick loading, easy to navigate, and down to earth.

The home page displays a Search button above the directory topics, but ignore them for the time being. (I explain how to use keywords and the search form, later in this chapter.) Likewise, disregard the auction links and all those other tempting links immediately below the Search button. I get into each one of those features later in the book.

Scroll down to those big, fat directory topics — Arts & Humanities, News & Media, and the twelve others. These are the *top-level,* or *first-level,* directory topics. Each one is a link leading to a *second-level* directory page. Each second-level page contains subtopic links leading to *third-level* pages, and so it goes for several levels. How many levels, exactly? It depends on the topic. Some subjects reach down eight levels.

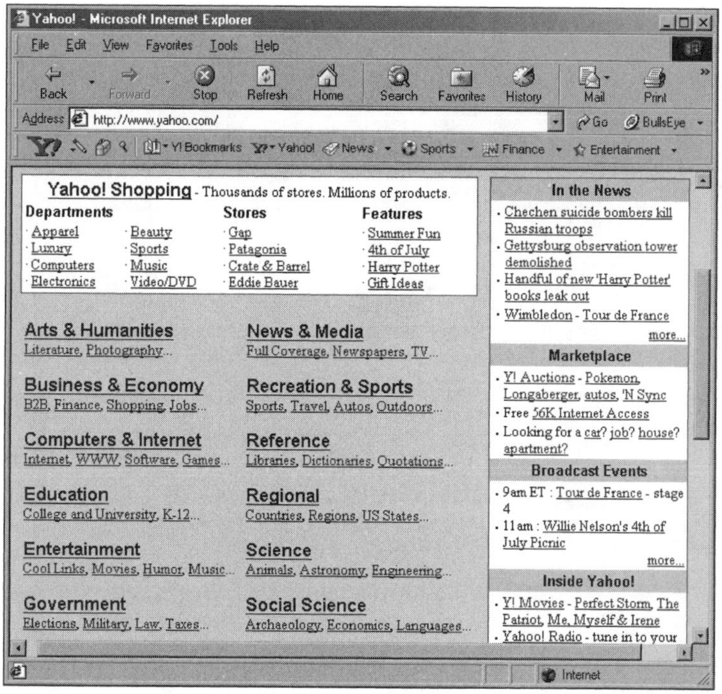

Figure 7-1:
The main
Yahoo!
directory
page.

Site links versus directory links

It's a fight! Not really. Site links and directory links work together to bring
sparkle and joy to many directory pages. Well, they work together, anyway. I
mention site links versus directory links to draw a distinction between when
you're linking to a Web site (leaving Yahoo! to visit another site) and when
you're linking to a lower-level page in the Yahoo! directory.

Some directory pages have only directory links. (They tend to be upper-level
pages representing broad topics.) Some directory pages have only site links.
(They're lower-level pages representing highly specific topics and containing
links to other sites on those topics.) The middle ground is populated with
pages that have both directory and site links, and in those cases the directory links are always above the site links and are displayed in **bold** type.

Figure 7-2 shows a hybrid directory page. The figure illustrates the Trivia portion of the Entertainment topic. Trivia subcategories are placed above the
site links. Clicking a subcategory leads to another directory page (third level
in this case), and clicking a site link takes you to that site, outside Yahoo!.

Directory links

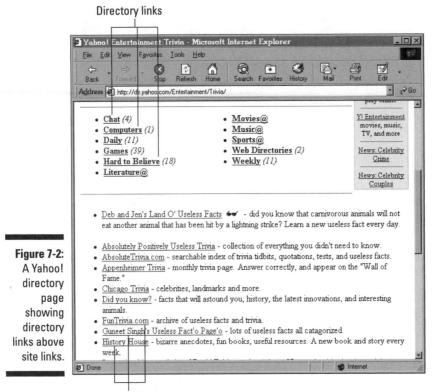

Figure 7-2:
A Yahoo!
directory
page
showing
directory
links above
site links.

Site links

The numbers next to directory links throughout the Yahoo! directory give you an indication of how many site links are within that topic and its subtopics. As you begin working with the directory, it might seem that those numbers are inaccurate. Next to Chat in Figure 7-2, for example, four site links are indicated. Yet clicking that directory link reveals only one site link on the next page. That's because *another* directory link (with a 3 in parentheses) is featured on that page, and clicking it reveals the missing site links on the next page. In other words, the site links indicated in parentheses might be distributed among several layers further down in the directory.

Fun with shortcuts

When I was a kid, I cut through a neighbor's yard on the way to school, trampling flowerbeds in my haste to educate myself. Who knew that a life of juvenile crime would prepare me to be a famous author? Or even an obscure one? Anyway, Yahoo! lets you take shortcuts for the sake of education, too.

Getting your bearings

The Yahoo! directory is as complex as a labyrinth. It's a marvel of organization, actually, but even highly organized structures can leave your head spinning if they're complicated enough. The Yahoo! directory is definitely complex. Fortunately, it delivers a helpful feature that marks your place in the overall structure at any given moment. And you can use this feature to quickly get out of any tangled trail.

Near the top of every Yahoo! directory page is a succession of links, the leftmost of which is a <u>Home</u> link to the top page of the directory (Yahoo!'s home page). The links get more topic specific as you track them to the right. Moving up to a higher-level directory page is as simple as clicking any of the links.

It's tempting to think that the string of links represents a trail of your journey into the directory, but in fact it doesn't always work that way. As you navigate through the directory, you might notice that the entire string changes from one page to another, when you'd expect only the last link to be added to the previous string. This discrepancy is due to the cross-referencing of the directory, wherein some very specific topics might be listed in more than one main topic's directory pages.

If you look back at Figure 7-1, you see a few links in small type beneath the main topic categories. Each link takes you directly to a third-level directory page, skipping over the second level with the same blithe spirit I felt when thrashing through tulips as an eager young lad. Yahoo! attempts to place the most popular, in-demand subcategories as these shortcut links. But if you don't see what you're looking for, you might need to click the main category, get to the second-level page, and find your subtopic there. On the other hand, if your goal falls within one of the shortcut links (such as a film title within the Movies shortcut), you'll save some time by cruising directly to the third level.

I told you that would be fun. I'm great at parties, too.

Little tiny icons

Diminutive icons are sprinkled through the Yahoo! directory like sprouts on a health salad. Two types of icon are likely to catch your attention:

- ✔ **NEW!**. The yellow NEW! icon, displayed next to directory links, can mean only one thing — something is NEW!. It's not the subcategory link that's new, though. The NEW! icon indicates that new site links have been added to the category.

- ✔ **Glasses.** The glasses icon is a miniature graphic of a pair of glasses (sunglasses, it appears). It indicates that a site link is worth investigating — worth a closer look, you might say.

Steroid-Infused Tips

As the preceding section makes clear, the Yahoo! directory is a marvel of organization and complexity. It contains an astounding number of topics, subtopics, and directory pages. Navigating within the directory isn't hard, after you grasp the multilayered architecture of the thing. (All Web directories are structured in essentially the same way.)

This section highlights two tricks for any would-be power Yahoo!'er. The following points are habits I've incorporated in my constant quest for more, faster, and better content.

Use multiple windows

One important detail that can escape the attention of Internet newcomers, and even folks of greater experience, is that browsers can replicate themselves in multiple windows. Whether you're using Internet Explorer or Navigator, you may at any time generate a new browser window.

In both programs, using the Ctrl+N keyboard command opens up a new window, displaying the same page as the original window. Navigator keeps added windows the same size as the original, but Explorer is more capricious in that regard. (Explorer users can always resize the new window to their taste.)

When using the Yahoo! directory, I usually open new browser windows in the process of clicking a link. Both popular browsers give you the option of opening a link in a new window by using the right-click menu. Here's how it works:

1. **When you find a site link you'd like to visit, place your mouse cursor over it and click the right mouse button.**

   (Or click the left button if you have reversed the default function of the buttons. At any rate, use the mouse button you don't normally use to click a link.) A menu drops down beneath the mouse cursor.

2. **Move the cursor to the Open in New Window selection and then left-click it. (Use the normal mouse button.)**

   The site you're visiting appears in a new browser window.

3. **Resize the window if necessary.**

   You may switch back and forth between the site and the directory page.

If creating multiple browser windows gives you concern about using up your computer's resources and slowing down its performance, stop worrying. Opening another window doesn't boot up a cloned version of your browser. It's just one program running, with the capability to reach several tentacles into the Net simultaneously. Sort of like one room with many windows. Each extra window does chew up a small portion of your desktop resources, but in most cases you won't notice the difference. If your machine has no more than 32 megs of RAM, however, and you notice slower-than-normal page loads when using more than one browser window, go back to a single window.

Opening multiple browser windows helps you avoid getting lost. Keep in mind that finding good stuff through the Yahoo! directory is a hit-or-miss business. The directory exposes you to a gigantic range of sites on almost any topic, and — even using the URL pointers I describe in the preceding section — bouncing back and forth between Yahoo! and outside sites is commonplace. That bouncing is a lot easier if you keep one browser window dedicated to the directory page you're linking from.

It's easy to get involved in a site, exploring its pages and layers. In so doing, you can lose track of where you were in the Yahoo! directory. Keep clicking for long enough, and even the Back button and History list of your browser won't help you. Anchoring one browser window on the directory page and linking sites into new browser windows is the answer.

Using a fresh browser window isn't a bad idea even while you're staying within the Yahoo! directory. I sometimes link from one subcategory to a lower-level topic in a new window so as not to lose track of the subcategory. Whether you rely on your Back button or keep things organized in different windows depends on how you like to view things and how big your monitor is. Multiple browser windows on 15-inch monitors (or smaller) can get cluttered and confusing.

Bookmark your Favorites

If you're the adventurous sort, the Yahoo! directory is made for you. During your explorations, you will no doubt investigate many a terrific Web site. One common downfall of surf-loving folks is forgetting to bookmark sites and then never finding them again.

The Navigator browser has its Bookmark feature, and Internet Explorer uses lists called Favorites. Although the two browsers implement these features somewhat differently, they both serve the same essential function, which is to put reminder links to sites in the browser itself, so you don't have to track them down the hard way a second time. Both Bookmarks and Favorites allow you to accumulate many such links and organize them into named folders.

The rule is bookmark first, sort later. If you go into a site that looks halfway decent and might possibly be worth a second visit sometime, just add it to your Bookmarks or Favorites list immediately. It's a lot easier to remove a bookmark than to find an obscure site a second time.

Adding a Site

Yahoo! is a highly interactive online service. You might be surprised to discover that the directory relies on its visitors for additions to its extensive menu of sites. The Yahoo! editors perform a small portion of the selecting and reviewing of new directory sites, but most additions result from the suggestions of users.

If you have a Web page of your own, submitting it to the Yahoo! directory is free and doesn't take much time. You must follow a certain procedure, however, or you'll get bogged down in error messages. When sending in the name and URL of a site, you must also select a subcategory page where you think the link should be. You must submit a subcategory, not one of the 14 main topic areas that appear on the Yahoo! home page. Note, though, that the Yahoo! Surfers (the Yahoo! team) might change the location before adding your site.

Although you have no assurance that a site will be added to the Yahoo! directory, Yahoo! isn't in the business of turning sites away from the directory. So as long as you have a legitimate URL and follow the procedure, it should get added within a reasonable time. (It sometimes takes a few weeks.)

When looking for your site's listing in the Yahoo! directory, search the directory by keyword. Don't just look in the subcategory you selected because the editors at Yahoo! might have decided your page fit better elsewhere. If, after two months, you're convinced your site has not been added to the directory, resubmit it following the directions in the following sections.

Finding the category

Choosing a good subcategory page for your site submission enhances your chances of getting the site added — and added quickly. Because of that fact, choosing the subcategory is probably the most important part of the entire process. Don't slight it by taking a hasty or ill-informed guess at where your site belongs. Digging around the directory until you find the best spot is worth the time.

Following are a few pointers for finding the best subcategory:

✔ When choosing a subcategory, the first thing you should look for is the presence of site links on the subcategory directory page. (I explain the difference between site links and directory links earlier in this chapter.) If the page has only directory links leading to more specific subtopics, you're still too high in the directory and need to dig deeper to find your category.

✔ When examining a possible subcategory directory page, look for sites that are similar to the one you're submitting. You might even want to visit a few or you might be able to see immediately, from the site title, whether it's the page for you.

✔ When assessing where your site belongs, distinguish between a personal site and a topical site. By this I mean, is your site about anything besides yourself? Is it an online personal scrapbook, or is it about a hobby? Are the pages about your family, vacations, pets, and home? If so, it's a personal site. Are the pages about your hobby, favorite TV show, or research into a medical condition? If it's along some specific subject line, it's a topic page. All personal sites get listed in the "Society and Culture: People: Personal Home Pages" category. Topic sites fit into other directory subcategories.

You might be tempted to try pushing your site as high in the directory as possible. Resist this temptation. Suggesting an inappropriately high placement just makes the Yahoo! editors' job harder and slows the process of getting the site listed at all. Remember that Yahoo! enjoys a gigantic audience, and any listing in the directory is good exposure for your site.

After you decide on a subcategory directory page for your site submission, follow these two simple steps:

1. **Click the <u>Suggest a Site</u> link at the bottom of that directory page.**

   The link appears on every level-three and lower directory page. Keep in mind that second-level directory pages rarely contain site links. If you try to suggest one of those directory pages for your site, you'll probably encounter the dreaded "Please be more specific!" rejection. The rule of thumb is this: If the directory page doesn't contain any site links, the system will probably reject your suggestion to be placed on that page. Find a more specific subcategory that already has site links.

2. **On the next page, click the Proceed to Step One button.**

Submitting the site

After following the preceding steps, Yahoo! tosses you into a four-part Suggest a Site process. Don't be put off by all the steps — Yahoo! could have just as easily put the whole shebang on one page. The four-page design spreads out the forms you need to fill in but doesn't make them difficult. Here's what you need to do:

1. **In Step 1, fill in the Title, URL, and Description forms and then click the Proceed to Step 2 button.**

   Follow the instructions below each form. The title doesn't need to be the page title as it appears in the title bar of a browser visiting that page, but it's probably less confusing to visitors if you keep them the same. In the Description form, take the time to write a concise, positive description of the site. Remarkably, most submissions don't contain descriptions; a short blurb encourages users to link to your site.

2. **In Step 2, fill in the Category Suggestions fields and then click the Proceed to Step 3 button.**

   Remember that Yahoo! already knows your first choice for a category in which to list your site. On this page, you have the chance to specify a second (or new) category where your site should *also* be listed. Some sites are cross-referenced in two categories — such as an investment company specializing in local accounts that might be listed in a regional category and a financial category.

   You can't be vague about the alternate category suggestion. Make a suggestion for an alternate listing only if you have the exact category on hand. If you want to do further research in the directory, open a new browser window so that you don't lose your place in the submission process.

3. **In Step 3, fill in the Contact and Geographical information and then click the Proceed to Step 4 button.**

   This page is where Yahoo! learns who you are (in a perfunctory way; you don't have to discuss your troubled childhood), how you can be contacted, and where your site is geographically located.

4. **In Step 4, fill in the applicable fields and then click the Submit button.**

   The Time-Sensitive Information fields on this page apply only to pages that describe, promote, or host an event. If your page isn't associated with any deadlines or ending times, ignore these forms. The Final Comments form is the place to type anything that will help the Yahoo! team understand or place your site.

You're finished! Have patience as Yahoo! checks out your site.

Starting the Yahoo! Search Engine

You've probably heard the slightly intimidating phrase, *search engine.* Sounds like something you don't want to get your hands dirty on. Actually, search engines are extremely sanitary and useful. They help you find things on the Internet without spending all night browsing through directories.

If browsing directories is like window shopping, using a search engine is like striding into a store, plastic in hand, with intent to purchase. Browsing goes for the haystack; searching goes for the needle. (My Bachelor of Metaphor degree is really coming in handy.)

The remaining portion of this chapter describes how Yahoo! differs from other search engines and explains how to use keywords in Yahoo! to find stuff on the Net.

Yahoo! searching secrets revealed

Yahoo! became famous several years ago as an Internet directory with a search engine attached. This chapter describes how searching in Yahoo! works, but it's important to distinguish between two types of search engines you can find on the Web. Many search engines use automated software to continually troll the Net, learning about new sites. Those sites then become part of a massive, searchable index of Internet destinations.

Yahoo! operates differently, without any such automated indexing software (sometimes called *spiders, robots,* or just *bots*). The Yahoo! search engine performs only within the Yahoo! directory. (See the first portion of this chapter to find out more about the directory.) The difference between Yahoo!'s search engine and others might seem subtle — after all, a directory is nothing more than a big index. Although that's true, a fairly big difference exists in how different indices are compiled. For example, automated Web-trolling software picks up individual pages of multipage sites, whereas Yahoo! — which relies on site owners to submit their URLs to the directory — might contain only the main page of a site.

Other differences distinguish bot-based search engines from Yahoo!'s directory searching feature. When you perform a search in one of the major, non-Yahoo! search engines, the results you get are slanted according to a number of factors that may exist in the pages' underlying code. The search engine in Yahoo!, by contrast, looks only at the page title and description as submitted by the page owner and listed in the directory.

Going beyond the directory

Recognizing that its users sometimes want to search beyond its directory, Yahoo! provides an automated link to another, Internet-wide search engine. (That engine is called Google. You should probably never say the word "google" out loud.)

Every Search Results page that you see has a <u>Web Pages</u> link near the top. When you click that link, Yahoo! automatically feeds your keyword(s) into the Google search engine and displays the results. Now you're seeing the results of Google's *spider,* which scours the Web all the time finding new sites and multiple pages within sites. Unlike Yahoo!'s own search engine, the Google engine looks at all the words on every page it finds, so your search runs much deeper into the Web's content.

Generally, a <u>Web Pages</u> search returns more results (sometimes a *lot* more) than the standard directory search. Some of the search results can seem bafflingly irrelevant, if your keywords are matching some bit of text buried deep within the page. Deeper searching is not always better searching, but it's good to have the option.

This is all very interesting (or not), but what do these differences mean to us, the users? They add up to one central fact: Each search engine is different and produces distinctive search results for any given query. Yahoo! is unique in that its directory is so gigantic and targeted to main pages of sites. On the other hand, if a site owner hasn't submitted his or her site to Yahoo! for inclusion in the directory (a somewhat time-consuming process described earlier in this chapter), it doesn't exist on Yahoo!'s radar. Search engines that run automatically might well turn up that same site, thanks to the work of their tireless software robots.

Sleuthing with keywords

Keywords are clues. Computers, being the dense creatures they are, need all the clues they can get. Keywords are cryptic hints that lead you to specific topics on the Internet.

Using keywords to search in Yahoo! is the reverse of using the directory, which gives *you* keywords. Consider the categories and subcategories of the Yahoo! directory, as pictured in Figure 7-1. Each topical link provides a keyword that leads you to more detailed subjects. Typing your own keywords in the search form (also pictured in Figure 7-3) lets you cut to the chase by zooming directly to directory pages and site links on highly specific topics.

A keyword can be anything related to what you're looking for. You may also enter more than one keyword, called a *keyword string.* A certain craft is involved in determining what keyword(s) will give you the best results. This part of the chapter gets you started on the right foot for the Yahoo! search engine and provides some helpful tips. In fact, I see a helpful tip coming up next.

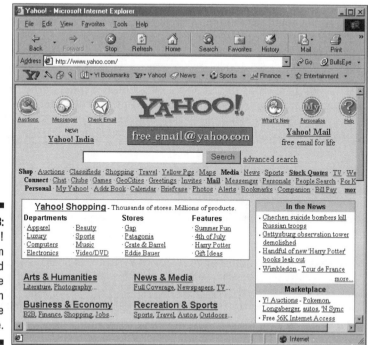

To search effectively in Yahoo!, you must attain a literal state of mind. It doesn't do any good to speak colloquially to Yahoo! or to ask it questions. For example, if you're interested in finding a Web page with a stock market summary, you might be tempted to type what's really on your mind, like this search string: *Did the stock market close up or down today?* Yahoo!, struggling in its literal-minded way to please you, would search for matches to every one of those keywords and (I just tried it now) would deliver a history page about the role of Australia in the evolution of Homo Sapiens. (Don't ask.) Entering the search string *stock market summary,* however, brings up links you can use, unrelated to prehistoric matters.

You need to remember a few basic points if you're just starting to use keywords in Yahoo!. The following might seem obvious, but I'll get to the more sophisticated stuff later in this chapter:

✔ **No caps.** Capital (uppercase) letters are not important when searching in Yahoo!. It doesn't hurt your search to use them, but there's no point knocking yourself out unnecessarily. The search engine is not *case sensitive.* Even when using proper names as your keywords, feel free to use lowercase letters, as in *kevin costner.*

✔ **Don't forget the spaces.** Yahoo! may be literal, but it can't understand multiple keywords if you don't have a space between each word. You can enhance your search by inserting things in those spaces. I'll get to them later in this chapter.

✔ **Watch your spelling.** Spelling counts when searching. You can get away with sloppy spelling in just about every other aspect of the Net — e-mail, chat rooms, message boards — but it'll kill a search. Many times, I've scratched my head over a puzzling set of search results, only to finally realize that I made slip of the typing finger.

Just a simple search

Getting started with a simple Yahoo! search is so easy it's almost embarrassing. Follow these steps and you'll be lasering into the Web in no time:

1. **Go to the Yahoo! home page (refer to Figure 7-1) at this URL:**

   `www.yahoo.com`

2. **In the keyword-entry form, type a keyword or a keyword string.**

3. **Click the Search button next to the keyword-entry form.**

In a few seconds, a search results page appears, unsurprisingly called Yahoo! Search Results. Figure 7-4 illustrates the search results for the keyword string *anthony hopkins*. Because I searched for a particular person, as opposed to a general topic, I got a manageable number of results (called *hits*). Had I searched for a more general subject, I would have been deluged with hits (ouch!), which Yahoo! would have organized in groups of twenty hits per page. Whenever you get more than twenty hits, you can move among your Search Results pages using links at the bottom of each page.

Simple searches are a little more complicated than they seem. Yahoo! is really performing three functions:

✔ First, it is searching for internal destinations within the Yahoo! service that match your query.

✔ Second, the search engine is looking through the many categories of its directory.

✔ Third, the engine is searching the site links of its directory.

The upshot of this three-pronged approach is a results page divided into what are called Inside Matches, Category Matches, and Site Matches. Figure 7-4 shows how results are organized in a typical simple search.

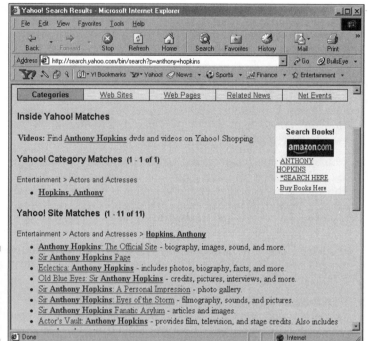

Figure 7-4:
A Yahoo!
search
results
page.

Category matches bring up directory categories and subcategories that include all your keywords. Each category link takes you to that directory page, where you may browse for sites and perhaps drill down further into the directory. Site matches show links to outside sites whose titles or descriptions match at least one of your keywords. (Sites that match *all* your keywords are listed first.) Additionally, the site links are organized by the directory subcategory under which they are listed. As you can see in Figure 7-4, site matches may be grouped on directory pages that do not appear in the category matches. That's because certain directory page titles might not contain your keywords but still house links that do contain your keywords.

Getting your bearings on the Search Results page

The Yahoo! Search Results page has a few features worth investigating. In addition, I want to get into some tricks to working with the category matches. This section helps you make the most of your search results.

If you look once again at Figure 7-4, you can see a horizontal bar with five links. The left-hand selection, Categories, is highlighted when you first see your search results. These five links are important because they give you new ways of making your keywords work for you. Whenever you use these links, Yahoo! remembers your most recent keywords and matches them to its database in certain ways. Here's how the links work:

- ✔ **Categories.** The default selection when you perform a simple search, the Categories page displays category matches to your keywords first, followed by site matches.

- ✔ **Web Sites.** If you want to skip the category matches, click this selection to display a page containing only the site matches to your keywords. This tack is especially useful when using broad, general keywords or just a single keyword. In those cases, it's possible to generate so many category matches that your site matches don't even appear on the first Search Results page. (Remember that Yahoo! places only 20 results on any page.) Try searching on the single keyword *movies* to see what I mean. Later in this section, I'll show you another way of dealing with extensive category matches.

- ✔ **Web Pages.** As I mention in the "Going beyond the directory" sidebar, Yahoo! lets you break out of its directory whenever you want to take advantage of a Web-spider search engine called Google. After performing your simple search, click the <u>Web Pages</u> link from the Search Results page to apply your keyword to Google. Google inspects every word of all the Web sites in its index, so your results draw a deeper portrait of what's available on the Internet for any topic. The numbers bear out that added depth: In my original simple search for *anthony hopkins,* the Yahoo! directory came up with eight site matches, whereas Google delivered over fourteen thousand hits. Remember — bigger is not necessarily better! Those eight Yahoo! directory hits are well targeted because the keywords appear in the site title or description. If you were to investigate all the Google hits (which would probably damage your mental health), you'd find many irrelevancies and dead ends.

- ✔ **Related News.** Yahoo! maintains an extensive database of up-to-the-minute news stories from a number of wire services and other sources (see Chapter 8). The <u>Related News</u> link sends your keywords into that database and returns hits that match any words in any stories. The searching in this department is thorough, and you're likely to see matches that don't seem, at first, to bear any relationship to your keywords. Then, if you read a seemingly irrelevant news story, you always find your keywords in there somewhere. This feature is good to use when searching on proper name keywords or places.

- ✔ **Net Events.** This link notifies you of scheduled online events that relate to your keywords. In the *anthony hopkins* search, <u>Net Events</u> hit on a weekly fan chat about the actor. Some searches don't bring up any events; my search for *dump trucks,* for example, returned more site matches than *anthony hopkins* but failed to uncover any chats about six-wheelers. (Maybe there's not much to say about them.)

When conducting a simple search, you're more likely to get a lot of category matches when you use fewer and broader keywords as opposed to more and specific keywords. Knowing that, a strategy should begin to take form in your mind. When you know exactly what you want, and you desire to get outside Yahoo! to the sites that deliver your subject, spell out your need with a string of precisely targeted keywords.

From any directory category page, you can perform a secondary search within that category. Using the keyword-entry form near the top of any category page, select the Just this category option, enter your keyword(s), and click the Search button. Figure 7-5 illustrates the search form on a category page.

You can always start over in the midst of any Yahoo! search. Near the bottom of every Search Results page is a keyword search form. Yahoo! remembers your previous keywords, but you can type over them to begin a new search. By the same token, you may begin a search from any directory page — the keyword search form is located near the top of each of them.

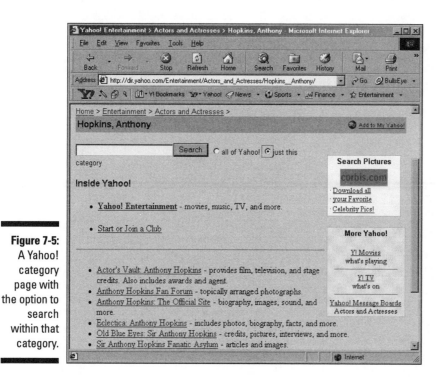

Figure 7-5:
A Yahoo!
category
page with
the option to
search
within that
category.

Show-off searching

From any Search Results page or from the Yahoo! home page, you can opt for a more sophisticated set of options for your keywords. On any of those pages, click the <u>advanced search</u> link to see the Search Options page. On this page, you can give Yahoo! more clues than the raw keywords that you use in a simple search. Here, you can

✔ Choose between Category and Site searching

✔ Apply search operators to your keywords

✔ Select to avoid the Web entirely in favor of Usenet newsgroups

✔ Alter the time period of your search

Advanced searching works in the same fundamental way as simple searching, in that you type a keyword or three and click the Search button to launch your inquiry. The difference lies in settings that control how Yahoo! treats your keywords, giving you a more precise searching focus. Figure 7-6 shows the Search Options page; you might want to refer to it or get the page on your computer screen as you go through the next section.

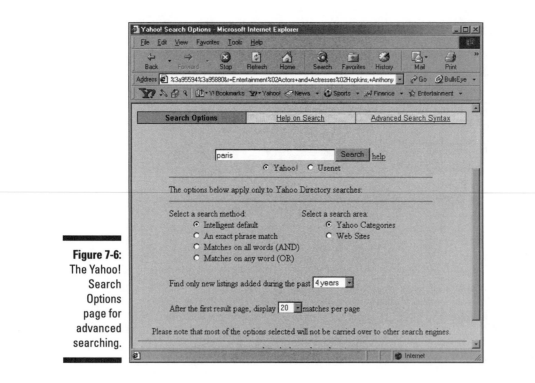

Figure 7-6:
The Yahoo!
Search
Options
page for
advanced
searching.

Getting precise with search operators

Search operators are words or symbols added to your keyword string that tell Yahoo! how to interpret your request. On the Search Options page, the AND and OR options refer to two basic search operators that instruct the search engine to find matches for *all* keywords (AND) and *any* keywords (OR). You can bypass the Search Options page by becoming acquainted with the search operators and typing them manually into your search string.

In Yahoo!, symbols and single-letter abbreviations indicate search operators. As always when dealing with simple-minded computers, you must be literal and use the correct spelling and syntax — the symbols must not be varied or positioned in the wrong place. This section summarizes the search operators recognized by Yahoo! and specifies how to type them:

- ✔ **AND.** The AND search operator is symbolized with +, the addition sign, and is placed immediately before any keyword that must be included in the search results. This operator tends to narrow the search, delivering fewer, better-targeted results. An example of its use is the search string *baltimore +orioles,* which eliminates sites about the city of Baltimore that don't include a reference to its baseball team, the Orioles. If you're concerned about getting sites about birds, you could extend the string to *baltimore +orioles +baseball* which would force Yahoo! to return sites that include all three words.

- ✔ **NOT.** The NOT operator is very useful and is not included on the Search Options page. NOT excludes keywords from being matched and is symbolized by -, the minus sign (the hyphen key of your keyboard). As with the AND operator, the NOT symbol is placed immediately before any word you want to exclude from matching. An example is *orioles -baseball,* which would match to sites about birds but not the baseball team.

- ✔ **Document titles only.** Yahoo! can restrict the search to Web site titles only, disregarding descriptions and URLs. To do so, put **t:** immediately before a keyword or keyword string. (If you're using multiple keywords, you need place only one t: in front of the whole string.) An example is *t:anthony hopkins,* which searches for sites with Anthony Hopkins in the title but not necessarily in the site description or URL. At the same time, it eliminates matches of Anthony Hopkins in the description if it doesn't also appear in the title.

- ✔ **Document URLs only.** As a reverse of the preceding search operator, Yahoo! can limit the search to URLs, excluding Web page titles and descriptions. This is a great option for zooming in on specific Web sites. Simply place **u:** in front of the keyword string (or single keyword). Try it when searching for a company name. A good experiment is to search on the company name without the u: operator and then with it and then compare the results.

- **Exact phrases.** The Search Options page allows you to specify exact phrase matches, and you can do the same thing using quotation marks (" and ") around the keyword string. If you're searching for a person's name, for example, and the first and last name could be mistaken for words with other meanings (such as Jack London), the phrase operator comes in handy. Try the *"jack london"* keyword string.

- **Wild card.** This search operator lets you get away with not knowing how to spell something and is also an easy way to broaden a search. The symbol is an asterisk (*), and it must be placed immediately after a word or partial word. An example is *paris**, which matches up with Paris and Parisian. :

Search operators can be combined! Stay calm; don't get too excited. I know this is good news. You can mix and match the preceding operators in any way that remains logical. Here are two examples based on keywords I already used:

- If you want to find sites about the Baltimore Orioles baseball team but specifically exclude bird information, try

  baltimore +orioles +baseball -birds

- If you want pages about Anthony Hopkins, but don't care to read about the "Silence of the Lambs" movie, try

  anthony +hopkins - "silence of the lambs"

Generally, when you combine search operators with the number of keywords, you can drastically enlarge or shrink your search results. Here are two rules:

- To get fewer hits, add keywords and use the + search operator.

- To get more hits, subtract keywords and use the - operator on the Search Options page.

Chapter 8

All the News That's Fit to Link

*1*nformation **wants to be free**. That's the motto of the **Internet. Whether** information actually has desires is a question beyond my metaphysical capacity, but it **does seem as if** Yahoo! adheres to the **sentiment**. Free news is provided in almost embarrassing wealth. Big, sloppy buckets **of news**. Up-to-the-second, **comprehensive news**. You can get a broad **overview** or drill deeply into a topic.

Best of all, Yahoo!'s plain, straightforward display style makes the experience fast and generally without hassle. Unlike other news **magazines on the Web** that force you to load graphics-intense, feature-laden pages, Yahoo! gets a lot of its news from wire services and sticks to the stark headline style that characterizes those sources. It's not that Yahoo! News pages **are unattractive, but** neither are they unnecessarily encumbered with fancy borders, pictures, and advertisements. It's a clean viewing experience. News photos **are gathered** into separate areas for those who want to take the time to view them.

This chapter walks you through the sometimes labyrinthine hallways of the Yahoo! newsroom.

Finding the Front Page

Getting started is perhaps the trickiest part of enjoying news, Yahoo! style. The Yahoo! home page doesn't make a big **deal of the rich news resources** that await you, so your mouse might circle the page a bit before knowing how to proceed. Here's the solution:

1. **On the Yahoo! home page, click the <u>News</u> link next to Media.**

   Alternatively, you can go directly to the Yahoo! News home page (Figure 8-1) with this link:

   ```
   dailynews.yahoo.com
   ```

2. **On the Yahoo! News home page, click any story headline from the center of the page or any topic from beneath the News Topics heading.**

   Clicking a news topic takes you to a Yahoo! News topical front page. The topical pages are the *real* front pages, in my view, the ones that should be bookmarked for the future. I dissect the topical pages in the next section.

You can angle into the Yahoo! News section in other ways. The Yahoo! directory features links to news on many second- and third-level directory pages (see Figure 8-2). Those directory links take you to the news page relevant to the directory topic you linked from. Such cross-referencing makes it handy to relate your Web surfing to outside-world current events.

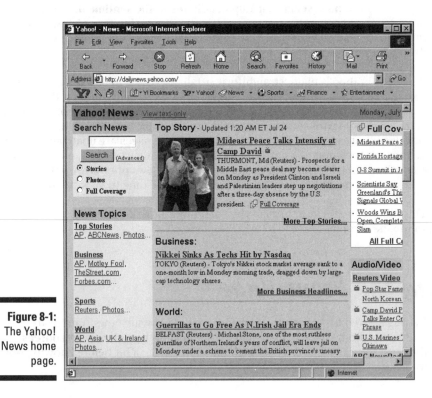

Figure 8-1: The Yahoo! News home page.

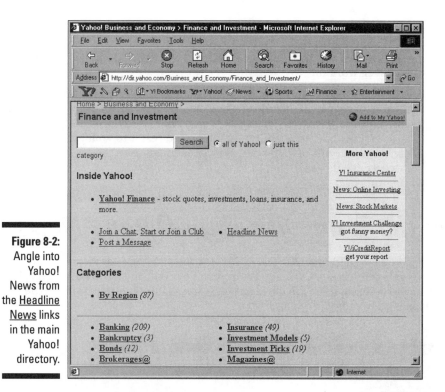

Figure 8-2:
Angle into
Yahoo!
News from
the Headline
News links
in the main
Yahoo!
directory.

Yahoo! News also borrows heavily from other sections of Yahoo!. Sports news takes information and pages from Yahoo! Sports; business news borrows from Yahoo! Finance. You shouldn't think of Yahoo! News as an isolated warehouse of current event information. It's best to familiarize yourself with many Yahoo! sections and treat the whole thing as an organic information entity. How you pursue your interests through Yahoo! and how you bookmark its pages are a matter of taste, and you'll develop your own system over time as your understanding of the whole service grows.

Notice the Search form in Figure 8-1. The form exists on every Yahoo! News page, and searching for news is useful in some situations. Here are some hints for productive news searching:

✔ Remember that Yahoo! News searching is literal and detailed. Every word of every story is compared to your keyword(s), including the writer's name. So a search for *O.J. Simpson* might deliver an unrelated story written by Ian Simpson, the writer for Reuters news service.

✔ The Yahoo! News search engine finds every matching story in its archived database, which goes back ten days. If you want to avoid scrolling through page after page of results — going further and further back in time — select keywords that deliver narrower results. (See Chapter 7 for keyword help.)

✔ Very general searches that deliver hundreds of results are not particularly useful — it's better to browse your way through the Yahoo! News pages to find current headlines and stories. General searches for photos, however, work nicely.

✔ Search results in Yahoo! News are displayed on a general Yahoo! Search Results page, which includes links to search results (for your keywords) among Yahoo! directory categories, Web Sites, Web Pages, Related News, and Net Events. The upshot is an integrated result to your search that covers categories of Web sites, Web sites themselves, and scheduled Internet events — all related to your search query.

Filling the Tank with High-Octane News

When you proceed past the Yahoo! News main directory page, the search for news gets interesting. Click any topic you like on the main directory page. For the sake of illustration, I'm clicking the <u>Business</u> link. Figure 8-3 shows the Business news directory page.

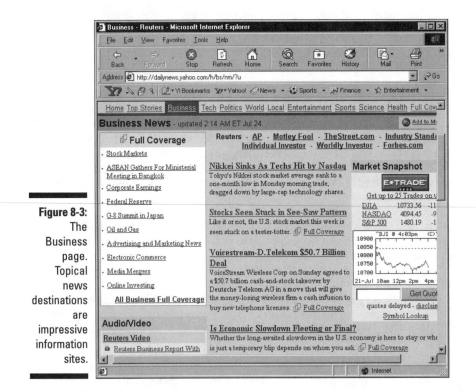

Figure 8-3:
The
Business
page.
Topical
news
destinations
are
impressive
information
sites.

Each news topic presents a slightly different front page, but some elements appear on most of them:

- ✔ **Headlines.** The meat of every Yahoo! News topical front page, the headlines stretch down the main portion of the page, including the first line from each story. Click any headline to see the full story.

- ✔ **Topic menu.** The main Yahoo! News topics are presented on each topical front page, in a concise banner across the upper part of the page. Use the banner to switch from Politics to Business, Tech, or any other main news topic.

- ✔ **Full Coverage.** Full Coverage is one of Yahoo!'s most shining news features, where information from multiple sources about major news stories and subtopics is gathered in one place. You can access Full Coverage in two ways. Each news topic front page has a Full Coverage section in the left navigation bar, containing a few Full Coverage items for that topic. Figure 8-4 shows the Full Coverage page for Media Mergers, linked from the Business News page.

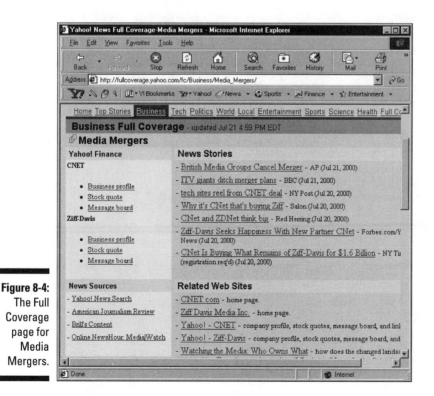

Figure 8-4:
The Full
Coverage
page for
Media
Mergers.

Click the Full Coverage link at the top of any news page to see the main Full Coverage menu, as shown in Figure 8-5. Each link on this page leads to a wealth of information and articles gathered from multiple sources. Using Full Coverage alone, you can become deeply informed in just about any current events topic.

✔ **Audio/Video News.** Some topic front pages have an Audio News section in the left sidebar, featuring links to netcasts you can listen to with RealAudio or Windows Media Player. In most cases, the links go directly to the audio file, so a minimum of clicking is necessary; you might not even have to leave the Yahoo! page to hear the netcast.

✔ **Yahoo! Resources.** This portion of the left sidebar connects you to relevant Yahoo! directory pages.

✔ **Source Links.** Above the main headlines are links to the news sources that contribute to the topic you're looking at. Wire services are almost always included. The Business section is also fed by Industry Standard, Individual Investor, Forbes.com, and Worldly Investor.

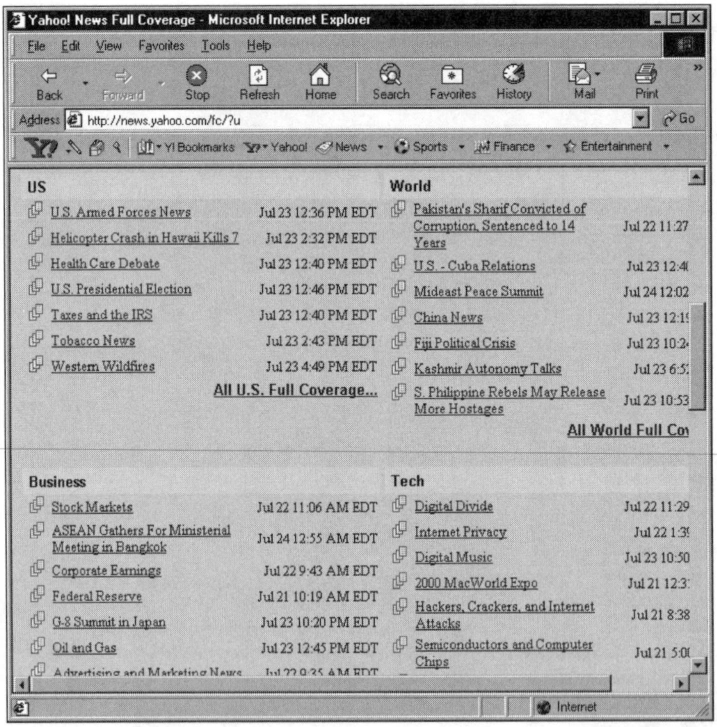

Figure 8-5:
A portion of the Full Coverage menu page.

Local news isn't given quite the same status as United States and international news in Yahoo!, but the service does take a stab at state-level information for Americans, including news on a handful of major cities. Take a look for yourself:

1. **From the Yahoo! News front page, click <u>Local</u>.**

   Or click the <u>Local</u> link from any topical front page.

2. **Under the Local News page, use the drop-down menu to select a metropolitan area of the United States.**

   See Figure 8-6, which shows the headline page for Detroit.

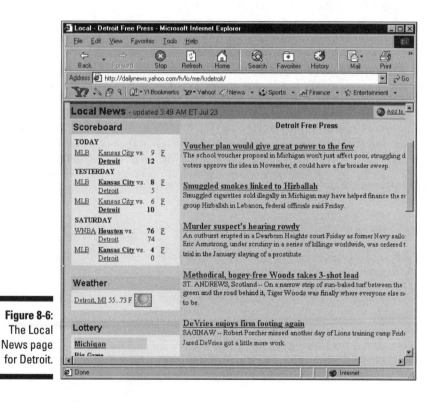

Figure 8-6:
The Local News page for Detroit.

Specialized News

A number of specialized news sources and magazines contribute to Yahoo! News. In most cases, these contributions can be accessed independently from the topical front pages. In each case listed next, the source or magazine links are placed just above the headlines. Clicking a link does not take you away from Yahoo!, which packages the content within its own pages. Here's the lineup:

- ✔ **Entertainment.** From the Entertainment front page, you can link to *E! Online, Hollywood Reporter,* and *Variety.*

- ✔ **Sports.** From the Sports front page, you can link to The Sporting News and Yahoo! Sports (which duplicates some of the sports content you find in Yahoo! News).

- ✔ **Business.** From the Business front page, you can link to *US Markets,* The Motley Fool (investment news and commentary), and TheStreet.com (more investment news and commentary).

- ✔ **Tech.** From the Tech front page, you can link to Internet Report, CNET, and ZDNet.

In the "hard news" sections, the wire services Associated Press and Reuters are used heavily by Yahoo!, and the headlines for each service are accessible separately. Just click the AP or Reuters link.

If you crave photos, Yahoo! has them, too. But the service doesn't force-feed them down your modem's throat; the Yahoo! News pages contain minimal photos, and all are small-format. (Click any photo to see a larger version.) For a more photo-rich experience, use the search form on the Yahoo! News home page. Click the Photos radio button below the Search button.

Chapter 9

Knowing the Score

In This Chapter

▶ Getting an overview of Yahoo! Sports

▶ Crunching statistics

It's not hard to find sports on the Web. ESPN, CBS SportsLine, and other media outlets share their news gathering resources with Internet citizens to some extent. But it is unusual to find an information-rich sports location that is completely free and delivers the goods with a minimum of advertisements, modem-choking graphics, registration procedures, and other hassles of Internet life. After all, when it comes to sports, don't you just want the score, and only the score, about half the time? You don't want to slog through a bunch of glitz to get it.

Now don't get me wrong. Yahoo! Sports provides more than just scores. A broad scope of information from league standings to team updates, photos, and opinion columns is presented. But Yahoo! leads with the data, not with the fat stuff such as pictures, so the pages are displayed quickly. Likewise, Yahoo! Sports doesn't push Java applets through your modem to display streaming game information. Maintaining the steely, lean interface that characterizes Yahoo! in general, Yahoo! Sports delivers the goods quickly and without headaches.

This chapter walks you through the main elements of Yahoo! Sports and helps you develop paths to certain pages you'll use over and over.

The Back Page

I don't know what it's like where you live, but some of the major New York City newspapers put their sports sections way in the back, with the back page serving as a sports front page. With that in mind, the first thing to do in Yahoo! Sports is find the front . . . er, back . . . well, the *home* page. Actually, Yahoo! has a few types of front pages, and this section explains their differences, similarities, and uses.

To get to the main Yahoo! Sports front page, click the <u>Sports</u> link next to Media on Yahoo!'s home page, or go directly to this URL:

```
sports.yahoo.com
```

Figure 9-1 shows the diversity of the Yahoo! Sports front page. This page has four basic elements:

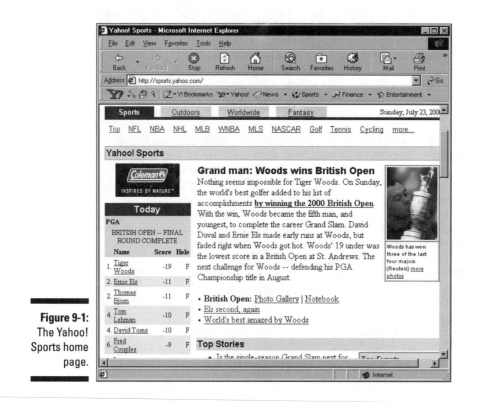

Figure 9-1:
The Yahoo!
Sports home
page.

▶ **Menu bar.** Up top, above the TOP STORIES banner, you see a series of links to subsections within Yahoo! Sports. These links are for league pages and sections on NASCAR racing, golf, tennis, cycling, and more. Click the <u>more</u> link for a detailed menu of available sports and leagues. Figure 9-2 shows that menu and provides a site overview in a glance. Some of the second-string sports coverage is impressive, such as the sections for cricket and rugby.

▶ **Top stories.** The central portion of the Yahoo! Sports front page is devoted to headlines and story summaries from all sports — whatever is making news at the time you view the page.

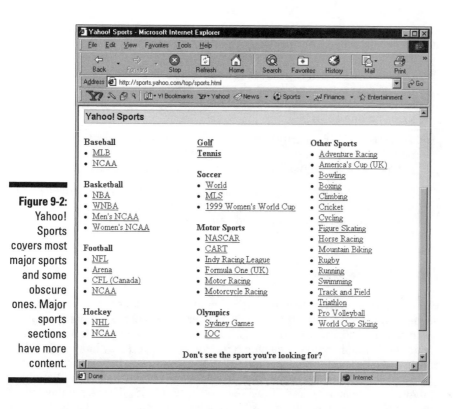

Figure 9-2:
Yahoo!
Sports
covers most
major sports
and some
obscure
ones. Major
sports
sections
have more
content.

✔ **Scores and other links.** Stretching down the left sidebar are scores for finished games and games in progress. Early in the day (for the United States), match-ups for that day's events are listed with their starting times. Links to other sports sites on the Web (The Sporting News, Fox Sports, ESPN.com, and others) are at the bottom of the sidebar.

✔ **Expert Columns.** Near the bottom of the page, several links let you read commentary from The Sporting News and CNN Sports Illustrated.

The Yahoo! Sports front page — and every page of Yahoo! Sports that contains quickly changing information such as game scores — updates automatically every few minutes. Your browser simply reloads the page, without any intervention on your part. This is convenient because you can set up a browser window in a corner of your screen, just large enough to display a game score you're following, and continue using the Internet in another browser window.

It's possible to get lost in Yahoo! Sports, wending your way deeply into endless pages of statistics and other features. At any time, you can always get a fresh start by clicking the Yahoo! Sports logo, which is at the top of every page. That link takes you back to the main front page.

You can drill into the ever-shifting fund of sports information in Yahoo! Sports at three levels, and a front page represents each one:

- ✓ **League.** At the league level, entire sports are covered. The front pages in the league sections embrace all teams in the league. These pages are similar in design to the front page of Yahoo! Sports but with a dedicated focus on one sport.

- ✓ **Team.** If you're primarily interested in one team (or a few teams), it's possible to zip directly to team-oriented front pages. These pages cover recent news, standings, game results, and player statistics.

- ✓ **Game.** A good deal of game information is presented for all games in all major sports. Coverage includes previews, highlight articles, starting players, recaps, box scores, and game logs.

In your league

When you want an overview of a sport, complete with links that take you to deeper levels of detail, try the menu links near the top of the Yahoo! Sports home page (see Figure 9-1). Official pro leagues are linked by their acronyms, including National Football League (NFL, from which you may link to the NFC and AFC), National Hockey League (NHL), National Basketball Association (NBA), Major League Baseball (MLB, from which you may link to the National and American Leagues), and Major League Soccer (MLS). The remaining links are for NASCAR racing, golf, tennis, and cycling — sports not consolidated into ownership leagues per se. (Click the <u>more</u> link to see all the sports covered.)

Figure 9-3 shows the NHL front page. If you compare this screen to Figure 9-1, you can see that it carries the same design as the main Yahoo! Sports front page (and, at the time these screen shots were taken, some of the same stories and the same picture). The page in Figure 9-3 is devoted to NHL hockey, and all the content beneath the main banner relates to the league and its games.

The league front pages keep game scores posted for a day longer than on the main Yahoo! Sports front page. The main front page wipes the scores off the board early in the morning, replacing them with preview links for the upcoming day's games. On the league front pages, though, the left sidebar extends downward to include the previous day's action.

During a sport's off-season, the league front page for that sport doesn't contain game scores, obviously. The left sidebar consists of Resources links to other Web sites. The right sidebar includes some very useful off-season stuff, including links to player draft results, free-agent signings, trades, expansion drafts, as well as next season's calendar. The Photo Gallery remains available during the off-season, and you can link to player statistics as well.

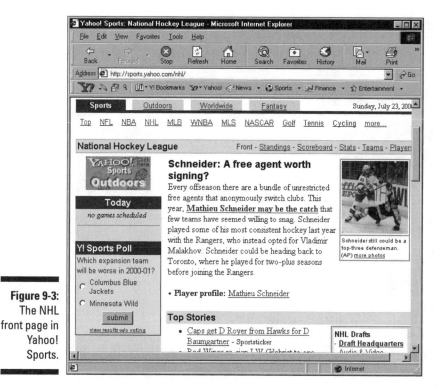

Figure 9-3:
The NHL
front page in
Yahoo!
Sports.

You can peruse links for two weeks of archived news stories. On any league front page, below the main headlines, click the <u>more news</u> link to see the day-by-day archive, such as the one shown in Figure 9-4.

Following the home team

All the major sport teams are represented with their own front pages in Yahoo! Sports. Yahoo! Sports might expand the team-by-team coverage in the future, so keep checking. For now, sports such as college baseball and soccer enjoy general reporting but lack in-depth team analysis.

You can reach your team's front page in a few ways:

✔ On game days during your team's playing season, the team is listed in the left sidebar on the main Yahoo! Sports front page. Click the team name to see the team-specific front page.

✔ On game days during your team's playing season, the team is listed in the left sidebar also on the league front page.

✔ On any league front page or any page linked from a league front page, click the <u>Teams</u> link for a complete list of teams in the league. From this list, you can display any team's front page.

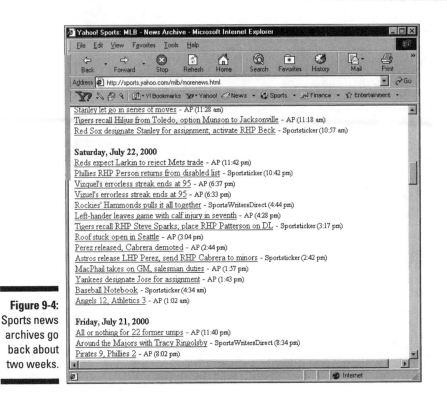

Stanley let go in series of moves - AP (11:28 am)
Tigers recall Hiljus from Toledo, option Munson to Jacksonville - AP (11:18 am)
Red Sox designate Stanley for assignment; activate RHP Beck - Sportsticker (10:57 am)

Saturday, July 22, 2000
Reds expect Larkin to reject Mets trade - AP (11:42 pm)
Phillies RHP Person returns from disabled list - Sportsticker (10:42 pm)
Vizquel's errorless streak ends at 95 - AP (6:37 pm)
Vizuel's errorless streak ends at 95 - AP (6:33 pm)
Rockies' Hammonds pulls it all together - SportsWritersDirect (4:44 pm)
Left-hander leaves game with calf injury in seventh - AP (4:28 pm)
Tigers recall RHP Steve Sparks; place RHP Patterson on DL - Sportsticker (3:17 pm)
Roof stuck open in Seattle - AP (3:04 pm)
Perez released, Cabrera demoted - AP (2:44 pm)
Astros release LHP Perez, send RHP Cabrera to minors - Sportsticker (2:42 pm)
MacPhail takes on GM, salesman duties - AP (1:57 pm)
Yankees designate Jose for assignment - AP (1:43 pm)
Baseball Notebook - Sportsticker (4:34 am)
Angels 12, Athletics 3 - AP (1:02 am)

Friday, July 21, 2000
All or nothing for 22 former umps - AP (11:40 pm)
Around the Majors with Tracy Ringolsby - SportsWritersDirect (8:34 pm)
Pirates 9, Phillies 2 - AP (8:02 pm)

Figure 9-4:
Sports news archives go back about two weeks.

Team front pages provide a current snapshot of team notes, schedules, standings, and game results during the playing season. (Off-season team front pages continue to carry update articles, team notes, and the next season's schedule if available.) Figure 9-5 shows the team page for the Cleveland Indians baseball club.

In addition to daily articles and team notes, a menu bar shows links to deeper and more statistical information about the team:

- **Calendar.** The calendar shows the team's playing schedule for the entire season. Unfortunately for fans, player birthdays are not included.

- **Log.** This page is a game-by-game recap of the team's season. The information included in this wrap-up varies from one sport to another.

- **Roster.** The roster page lists every player on the team with some basic information including — ta-da! — the players' birthdays.

- **Batting and Pitching.** Statistics pages for the team's players. The numbers provided on this page are not as extensive as the player stats at the league level, which I describe later in this chapter. But this page is offers easy answers to basic queries such as the average points per game for an NBA player. The stats pages for major league baseball teams are divided into batters and pitchers.

> ✔ **Tickets.** This link displays a page in which you may begin a process of buying tickets to your team's games over the Web. The service is provided jointly by Yahoo! and Ticketmaster.

The play-by-play

The game is where the action is. How does Yahoo! Sports measure up when it comes to delivering game results as they are happening and after the fact? Yahoo! delivers snapshot reports of games as they're being played, and those snapshots are sometimes not as up-to-the-second as might be desired. Recently, I tested the game page of an NBA playoff game during the closing minutes of the game, while following the action on TV. Yahoo! was consistently and substantially behind the real-time play, and at one point let six minutes go by without updating the score.

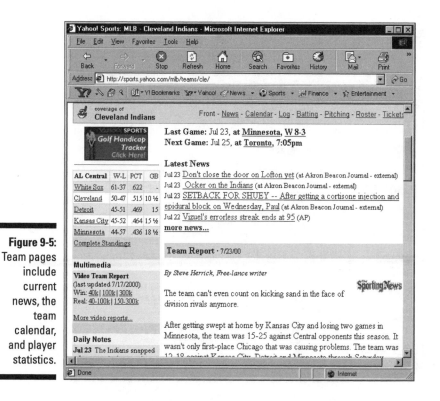

Figure 9-5:
Team pages include current news, the team calendar, and player statistics.

Yahoo! Sports does better with static content such as recaps and box scores of completed games. It gets the statistical information posted quickly, and the editorial commentary arrives whenever Yahoo!'s licensed content providers supply it (certainly sooner than if you waited for the morning paper, which might miss the end of a night game anyway).

For any games in the big four sports happening on a given day, you can click directly to game pages from the main Yahoo! Sports front page. If you refer back to Figure 9-1, you can see that all the listed games in the left sidebar are scheduled for the evening and hadn't started yet when that screen shot was taken. When a game is in progress, that starting time is replaced by an indication of where the game stands (what quarter, period, or inning it's in). When a game is over (and before the following morning, when it's removed from the sidebar), these indications are replaced by an F (for Final score).

Whether a game is yet to start, in progress, or finished, click the indicator to the right of the score to display the game page. For each game, there is (or will be, by the time the contest is over) a preview, a box score, and a recap, each on its own page. Those elements are all linkable from the main game page. Figure 9-6 shows a game page from a Cleveland Indians baseball game. Because the game is over, the link automatically displays not the game page but the recap page; the <u>preview</u> and <u>box score</u> links are also available.

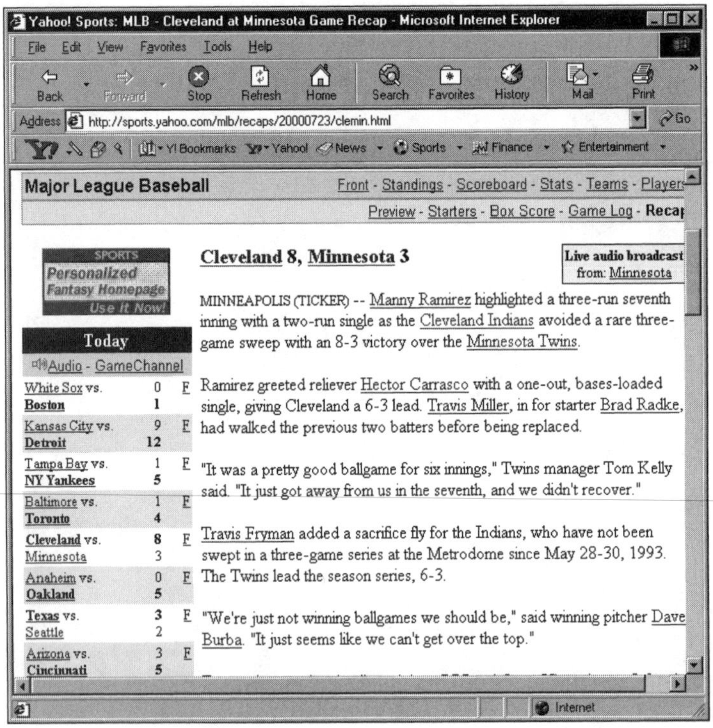

Figure 9-6:
The game page of a Cleveland Indians baseball game.

Crunching the Stats

As a stock chart is to an investor and a recipe is to a chef, so are statistics to a sports fan. Statistics explain, clarify, and reveal by comparison. A particular fascination exists for individual player statistics in team sports. Even in a team effort, each player is competing with himself or herself and with historical standards of excellence. Following a team usually means rooting for individual player's accomplishment in addition to team success.

Yahoo! Sports fares pretty well in the stat department. Throughout this section, I use baseball as an example because it is perhaps the most numbers-rich and statistically manic sport.

Yahoo! Sport has two basic types of stats:

✔ Team statistics

✔ Player statistics

It can be tricky to find exactly the type of numbers you're looking for. Allow me to mark the best paths to the best stats. To start exploring team stats, do the following:

1. **On the main Yahoo! Sports front page, click any league link.**

   In this example, I'm using the <u>MLB</u> baseball link.

2. **On the league front page, click the <u>Stats</u> link.**

   You might think it more intuitive to click the <u>Teams</u> link, but that just leads to links for team front pages, as described previously in this chapter.

3. **On the Statistics page, click any category of statistic.**

   Figure 9-7 shows the Statistics page for major league baseball. You can see that the stats are categorized by American and National League, with a column for numbers applying to both leagues. Each category is further divided into batting and pitching categories.

A slightly different path leads to the player stats. Here it is:

1. **On the main Yahoo! Sports front page, click any league link.**

   Again, let's go for the <u>MLB</u> link for this example.

2. **On the league front page, click the <u>Players</u> link.**

3. **On the Players page, click any player's name to see his or her statistical section.**

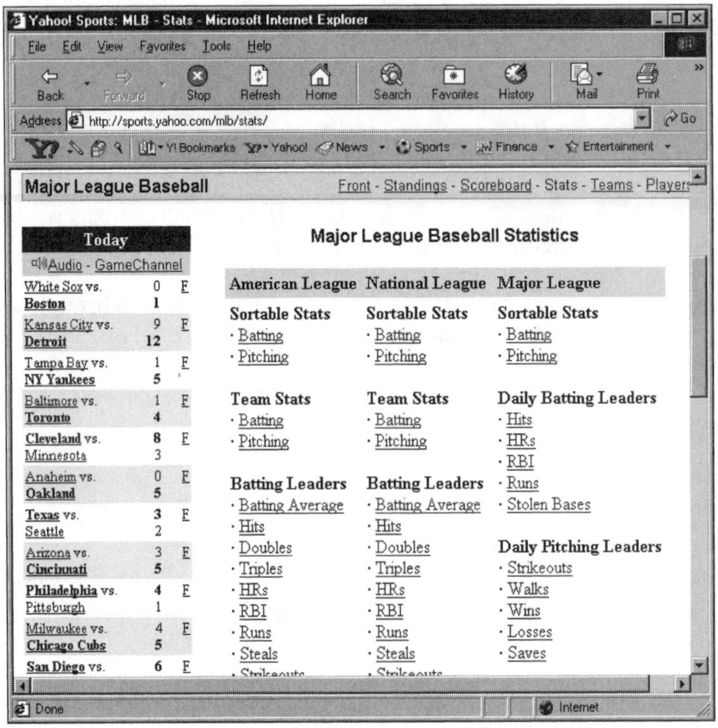

Figure 9-7:
The
Statistics
page links to
various
teams' stats.

The player statistics for major league baseball are more complex than for other sports. Figure 9-8 shows the stats page for Bobby Bonilla.

If you look at the link menu below the main banner, you can see that the Player Profile is just the first page. A few other stat pages deliver a comprehensive analysis of Bonilla's performance for the past three years, the time frame used in Yahoo! Sports statistics as of this writing. The "How Bobby Stacks Up" chart (included for each player) is a nifty at-a-glance indicator of essential performance.

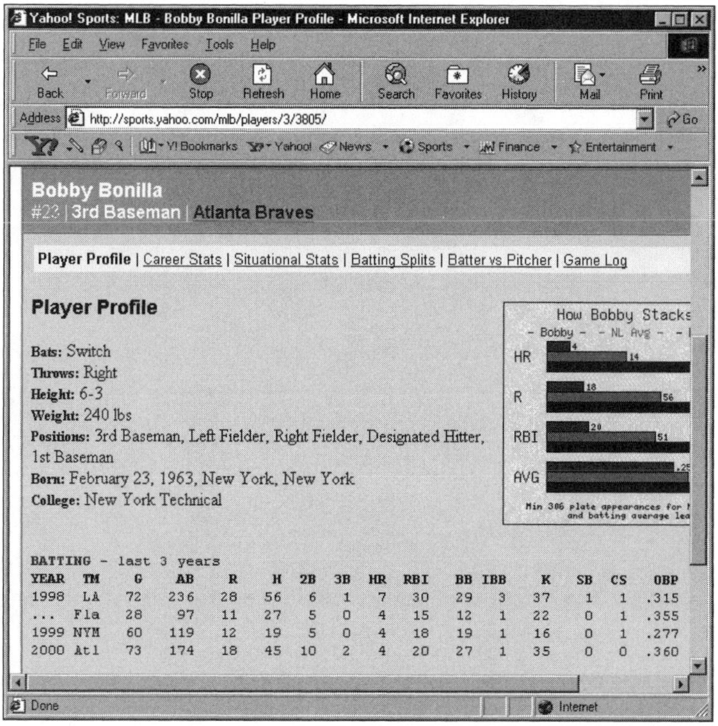

Figure 9-8:
Player
statistics go
back three
years.

Within the browser window:

Bobby Bonilla
#23 | 3rd Baseman | Atlanta Braves

Player Profile | Career Stats | Situational Stats | Batting Splits | Batter vs Pitcher | Game Log

Player Profile

Bats: Switch
Throws: Right
Height: 6-3
Weight: 240 lbs
Positions: 3rd Baseman, Left Fielder, Right Fielder, Designated Hitter, 1st Baseman
Born: February 23, 1963, New York, New York
College: New York Technical

How Bobby Stacks
- Bobby - - NL Avg - -

HR	4 / 14
R	18 / 56
RBI	20 / 51
AVG	.25

Min 386 plate appearances for
and batting average lea

BATTING - last 3 years

YEAR	TM	G	AB	R	H	2B	3B	HR	RBI	BB	IBB	K	SB	CS	OBP
1998	LA	72	236	28	56	6	1	7	30	29	3	37	1	1	.315
...	Fla	28	97	11	27	5	0	4	15	12	1	22	0	1	.355
1999	NYM	60	119	12	19	5	0	4	18	19	1	16	0	1	.277
2000	Atl	73	174	18	45	10	2	4	20	27	1	35	0	0	.360

Chapter 10

Taking Stock of Investments

● ●

In This Chapter

▶ Touring the Finance section of Yahoo!

▶ Getting up-to-the-15-minute stock quotes

▶ Tracking your holdings with an online portfolio

▶ Making the most of Yahoo! Finance

● ●

*T*he Yahoo! Finance home page is an anchor site for millions of online investors. What was once primarily a stock quote server has blossomed into a data hub and information resource. Yahoo!'s no-nonsense, fast-moving pages really come in handy for online traders who value quick, reliable information. The page design remains stark, but that just ensures fast and reliable navigation. And the range of editorial services has rounded out what was once a fairly dry set of features.

Yahoo! Finance isn't perfect. Whereas some other finance sites provide real-time stock quotes, up to the second during the market trading session, Yahoo! Finance is (as of the publication of this book) still mired in the "delayed-quote" world. Stock and option prices are delayed by fifteen or twenty minutes, depending on the exchange. Yahoo! probably realizes that the aggressive traders who most need real-time quotes get them from specialized services. Many of the big exchanges are considering reductions in the cost of obtaining prices, and Yahoo! Finance might deliver real-time quotes in the future.

Yahoo! does not maintain an in-house staff of writers like some other investment sites. Instead, Yahoo! licenses the articles and columns of other Web-based publications and presents them in the Yahoo! format.

One other feature treated lightly by Yahoo! is the stock chart. Yahoo! Finance does display stock charts along with price quotes, but the charts don't hold a candlestick to the elaborate interactive price graphs found at some other sites.

These supposed imperfections notwithstanding, Yahoo! Finance is superb in what it does best, and there is good reason why uncountable online investors consider it their home base on the Web. For gathering fundamental information about a company, no site does the job faster or more thoroughly than Yahoo! Finance.

This chapter runs down the most important features of Yahoo! Finance, including getting stock quotes, creating an online portfolio, and playing a stock-trading game.

A Basic Map of Yahoo! Finance

Following is a quick tour of the main content features of the Yahoo! Finance home page. As you can see in Figure 10-1, the home page has one heck of a lot of links — even more when you scroll down that page. Many links lead to deeply informative sites that would be worth a chapter by themselves. Because I can't do justice to the whole thing, this section provides a map of the page's basic topography so you don't miss anything important. Stock quotes and portfolios are described in separate sections later in this chapter.

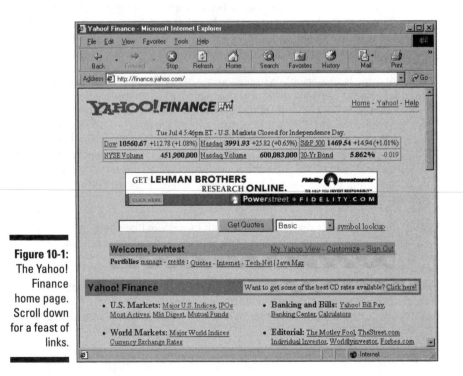

Figure 10-1:
The Yahoo!
Finance
home page.
Scroll down
for a feast of
links.

To get to Yahoo! Finance, click the <u>Stock Quotes</u> link on the Yahoo! home page or go directly to this URL:

```
quote.yahoo.com
```

Market overview

Most people who follow the financial markets check in periodically throughout the business day to get a snapshot of stock and bond activity. For most people, that snapshot is provided by the major index prices. You've probably heard them quoted on radio and TV stock market reports: "The Dow is up (or down) for the day, and the Nasdaq Composite has rallied (or slumped) throughout the afternoon. The yield on the 30-year Treasury bond is at an all-time high (or low)." Those statistics are presented at the very top of Yahoo! Finance, in real time (unlike individual stock quotes, which are delayed). If you continually click your browser's Reload or Refresh button, you can see the prices changing.

As you can see in Figure 10-1, the three index benchmarks for measuring stock market performance in the United States are on the page:

- ✔ **Dow.** The Dow Jones Industrial Average is a measure of large-company performance consisting of 30 big companies from the New York Stock Exchange.
- ✔ **Nasdaq.** The Nasdaq stock exchange composite average is generally considered a measure of technology companies because of the many such companies traded on the Nasdaq exchange.
- ✔ **S&P 500.** The Standard and Poor's index of 500 large and mid-sized companies is widely considered the most accurate barometer of broad stock market performance.

Trading volume numbers for the New York Stock Exchange (NYSE) and Nasdaq are displayed, plus the yield (but not the price) for the 30-year Treasury bond, the benchmark bond product used to evaluate the entire bond marketplace.

Click the index name for a detailed quote of that index's price, including the day's range and the 52-week range. The <u>30-Yr Bond</u> link divulges the bond yield in basis points — so 5.911 percent, for example, is represented by 59.11.

Global financial data

Yahoo! Finance is a data-rich resource, and it knows no boundaries. From Asian stock markets to currency exchange rates, Yahoo! has it. Several major sections contain links to data about the United States markets and those abroad.

Under the Yahoo! Finance banner (mid page), the U.S. Markets section offers these features:

- ✔ **Major U.S. Indices.** The Dow, Nasdaq, and S&P 500 paint the picture in broad strokes, but dozens of other United States financial market indices assign value to different sectors. Go here to see what's up with the Dow Transportation Average, the Russell 2000 index of small-cap companies, regional stock exchanges, Treasury securities, commodities, and much more. This is index-lover's heaven.

- ✔ **IPOs.** The IPO section is a detailed review and forecast of initial public offerings, including performance rankings over different time periods.

- ✔ **Most Actives.** Click this link to see the high-volume leaders at any given time for each of the three main United States exchanges: New York, American, and Nasdaq.

- ✔ **Market Digest.** Market Digest describes the *market breadth* at any given time and is a subject of great interest to most serious investors. Here, you can see at a glance the ratio of declining stocks to advancing stocks for each of the major exchanges, plus the number of new highs and new lows. The total volume for each exchange is included.

- ✔ **Mutual Funds.** Dedicated mutual fund sites can't be beat, but Yahoo! Finance doesn't try to compete with editorial content. Instead, it provides a basic fund screener, performance statistics, and news headlines.

The World Markets section goes beyond United States stock and bond exchanges to cover overseas (from the American perspective) stock exchanges, foreign currency trading, and Canadian stocks:

- ✔ **Major World Indices.** This page covers North and South America, Asia, Europe, Africa, and the Middle East (see Figure 10-2). I bet you never knew there were so many financial exchanges. And at times, even the most seemingly obscure ones may affect the stocks of your exchange — this is a good page to keep handy during those nervous midnights when you have to know what's happening on the Shanghai Composite.

- ✔ **Currency Exchange Rates.** This handy page features both a static table of major currencies and an interactive currency converter that handles just about any form of money on the planet. A drop-down menu selection lends the currency converter its flexibility. Using both menus, you can convert any national monetary unit into any other. Even if you don't trade currencies, this gadget is useful if you're interested in traveling to another country.

✔ **Canadian Markets.** The <u>Market Digest</u> and <u>Most Actives</u> links in this section deliver stock overviews for the many busy regional Canadian stock exchanges.

News and commentary

Current news headlines are located about halfway down the Yahoo! Finance home page, under the Latest Market News banner. This vortex of financial news is one of the most dynamic headline feeds on the Net. Constantly changing, it is best appreciated by clicking your browser's Reload or Refresh button every few minutes. That's not practical, of course, but the point is that Latest Market News is up to the minute no matter when you check in.

In addition to timeliness, Latest Market News doesn't pull any punches in the content department. This is a news service for the serious observer of global financial markets. Stuffed with foreign market responses to United States stocks, thorny reports about corporate boardrooms, and political news with a business slant, this editorial selection doesn't hold anyone's hand.

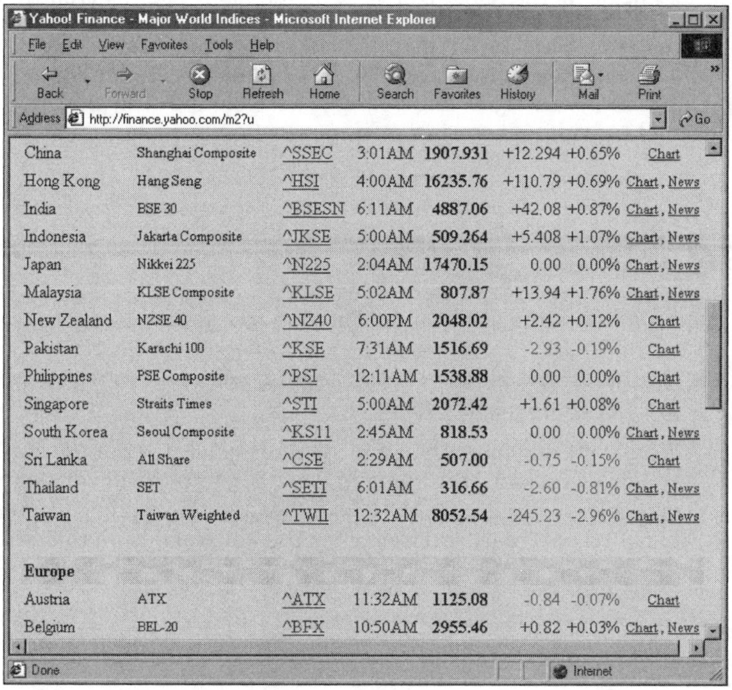

Figure 10-2:
The Major
World
Indices
page covers
basic
information
about every
national
stock
market.

Country	Index	Symbol	Time	Value	Change	%	Links
China	Shanghai Composite	^SSEC	3:01AM	1907.931	+12.294	+0.65%	Chart
Hong Kong	Hang Seng	^HSI	4:00AM	16235.76	+110.79	+0.69%	Chart, News
India	BSE 30	^BSESN	6:11AM	4887.06	+42.08	+0.87%	Chart, News
Indonesia	Jakarta Composite	^JKSE	5:00AM	509.264	+5.408	+1.07%	Chart, News
Japan	Nikkei 225	^N225	2:04AM	17470.15	0.00	0.00%	Chart, News
Malaysia	KLSE Composite	^KLSE	5:02AM	807.87	+13.94	+1.76%	Chart, News
New Zealand	NZSE 40	^NZ40	6:00PM	2048.02	+2.42	+0.12%	Chart
Pakistan	Karachi 100	^KSE	7:31AM	1516.69	-2.93	-0.19%	Chart
Philippines	PSE Composite	^PSI	12:11AM	1538.88	0.00	0.00%	Chart
Singapore	Straits Times	^STI	5:00AM	2072.42	+1.61	+0.08%	Chart
South Korea	Seoul Composite	^KS11	2:45AM	818.53	0.00	0.00%	Chart, News
Sri Lanka	All Share	^CSE	2:29AM	507.00	-0.75	-0.15%	Chart
Thailand	SET	^SETI	6:01AM	316.66	-2.60	-0.81%	Chart, News
Taiwan	Taiwan Weighted	^TWII	12:32AM	8052.54	-245.23	-2.96%	Chart, News
Europe							
Austria	ATX	^ATX	11:32AM	1125.08	-0.84	-0.07%	Chart
Belgium	BEL-20	^BFX	10:50AM	2955.46	+0.82	+0.03%	Chart, News

Further up on the page, under the Yahoo! Finance banner, the Financial News section (on the right side of the page) lets you angle into news reports by individual wire service tickers, featuring the Associated Press (AP), Canadian Corporate News (CCN), Standard & Poor's News Service (S & P), PRNewswire, the ON24 audio network, and BusinessWire. The Full Coverage link takes you to the Business Full Coverage page of Yahoo! News.

Yahoo! licenses financial commentary from a few highly regarded sources and packages it into the familiar Yahoo! page design. Here's what you can find under the Editorial section:

- **The Motley Fool.** The two brothers who achieved fame and a loyal following among investors began their online career at America Online and then migrated to the Internet. The Motley Fool blends irreverent humor with a sound investment philosophy. Yahoo! runs the Motley Fool Lunchtime News and Evening News, as well as other columns.

- **TheStreet.com.** James J. Cramer, who has attained celebrity status through his many opinionated appearances on CNBC (the financial cable channel), runs this site. TheStreet.com contributes Cramer's widely read Wrong! column and other regularly scheduled articles.

- **Individual Investor Online.** This mix of commentary and news dishes up a stock pick of the day, mutual fund analysis, and ongoing market coverage.

- **Forbes.com.** Online content from the renowned business magazine, focusing on the personalities of high finance and the companies they run.

- **Industry Standard.** A magazine of hi-tech business and new economies, The Industry Standard is a must-read publication for legions of subscribers working in, and helping to develop, digital industries. This content provides a knowing, info-age slant on business news.

Getting Stock Quotes

To get a stock quote from Yahoo! Finance, follow these steps:

1. **On the Yahoo! Finance home page, type one or more stock symbols in the Get Quotes entry form.**

   When entering more than one symbol, separate your entries by a single space. If you know the company name but not its ticker symbol, click the symbol lookup link. On the Ticker Symbol Lookup page, enter the company (or part of it) and then click the Lookup button to find the symbol.

2. Use the drop-down menu to choose the type of quote.

Yahoo! Finance offers a varying amount of data along with the simple stock price. Basic quotes are the simplest (see Figure 10-3), and Detailed quotes fill out the data snapshot with various per-share valuations (see Figure 10-4). The chart selection (shown in Detailed quotes) includes a few links for altering the time period of the chart and the size of its display. I usually select Detailed quotes. No matter what selection you make, it's easy to switch to another view using the drop-down menu. Also, note that you can switch from a Basic quote to a Detailed quote of that stock by clicking the ticker symbol.

3. Click the Get Quotes button.

Both the Basic and Detailed quote pages display a list of recent company-related headline links, below the price information.

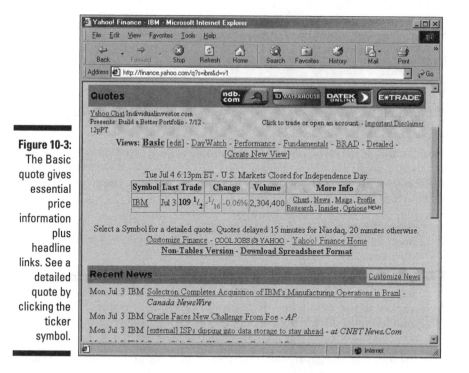

Figure 10-3: The Basic quote gives essential price information plus headline links. See a detailed quote by clicking the ticker symbol.

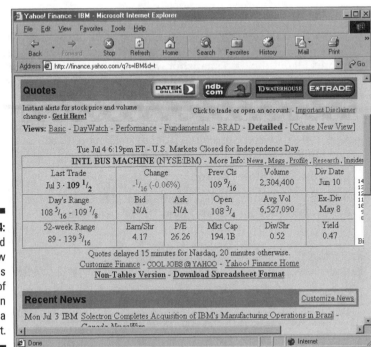

Figure 10-4:
The Detailed quote view provides lots of valuation data plus a price chart.

Price quotes are just the beginning at Yahoo! Finance. Most quotes (in Basic, Detailed, and all other views) include links to several other collections of fundamental information about the stock and its underlying company. Try any or all of these links:

- ✔ **News.** Displays a page-full of news headlines, greatly expanding the small selection visible on the quote page. Click any headline to get the full story.

- ✔ **Msgs.** This link, which stands for Messages, takes you to the Yahoo! message board related to that stock. (See Chapter 14 for an invigorating discussion of the Yahoo! boards.) The stock message boards are raucous, unmoderated destinations where investors with some time on their hands root for (and slam) companies and their stocks.

- ✔ **Profile.** This page provides a business summary of the company whose stock you're viewing, plus a range of valuation statistics too numerous to fit on the stock quote page. Here you can view data on operating margin, short ratio, size of the float, debt/equity ratios, and much more.

- ✔ **Research.** The Research page summarizes analyst recommendations, tracks past earnings on a quarterly basis, and forecasts future earnings.

✔ **Insider.** This page lists stock buying and selling activity among company executives, as filed with the Securities and Exchange Commission. Insider activity (the legal kind, not illegal trading) sometimes foretells the stock's future.

✔ **Options.** Click this link to see price quotes for the call and put options associated with the stock. This relatively new feature has been added since the first edition of this book and rounds out the scope of quote information nicely.

Creating Portfolios

If you own stocks or mutual funds, creating an online portfolio is a way to track your holdings that beats monthly brokerage reports and daily newspapers hands down. If you're accustomed to following your investments more casually, with an occasional glance at the newspaper stock listings and a monthly perusal of your brokerage statement, you might discover the fun of minute-by-minute portfolio fluctuations. Fun? Some might call it an obsession. Fanaticism isn't required, but keeping your stocks listed in Yahoo! Finance at least gives you a quick way to check your bottom line, and your individual holdings, whenever you want.

There's another reason to create an online portfolio. If you are considering becoming an online trader — the popular high-risk hobby of new-millennium investing — it's a good idea to paper trade first. *Paper trading* means buying and selling stocks in a virtual portfolio, without money. Yahoo! Finance is not a brokerage, and you can't open an account in it. So the service doesn't know or care whether your portfolio reflects actual holdings or pretend holdings. Many beginning online investors practice virtual trading through an online portfolio before putting any real money into play.

One final reason to try a Yahoo! Finance portfolio is that it's a great consolidator of stocks that interest you, even if you don't hold them. Throwing those stocks into an on-screen portfolios gathers all the information associated with each price quote (described in the preceding section) into one place. You can track news releases, price fluctuations, and constantly shifting per-share valuations whenever you want, for the whole basket of stocks.

This section describes how to create a basic Yahoo! Finance portfolio and introduces you to the free Java Portfolio Manager.

Creating your portfolio

Yahoo! Finance throws a lot of portfolio features in your face, but you don't have to use them all. You may fashion a simple list of stocks or develop a complex tool including upper and lower price alert limits, notes on each holding, commission rates to be subtracted from capital gains, and so on. A portfolio may be set up to track stocks generally (as if you didn't own them) or to track ownership of certain numbers of shares purchased at a certain price (whether you own the stock or are just pretending).

You need to display the Edit your portfolio page to begin creating your port-folio. On the Yahoo! Finance home page, click the <u>create</u> link near Portfolios (look back at Figure 10-1), and you're ready to start. Figure 10-5 shows the Edit page for stock portfolios.

You must have a Yahoo! ID to create a portfolio. See Chapter 1 for information about registering as a Yahoo! member.

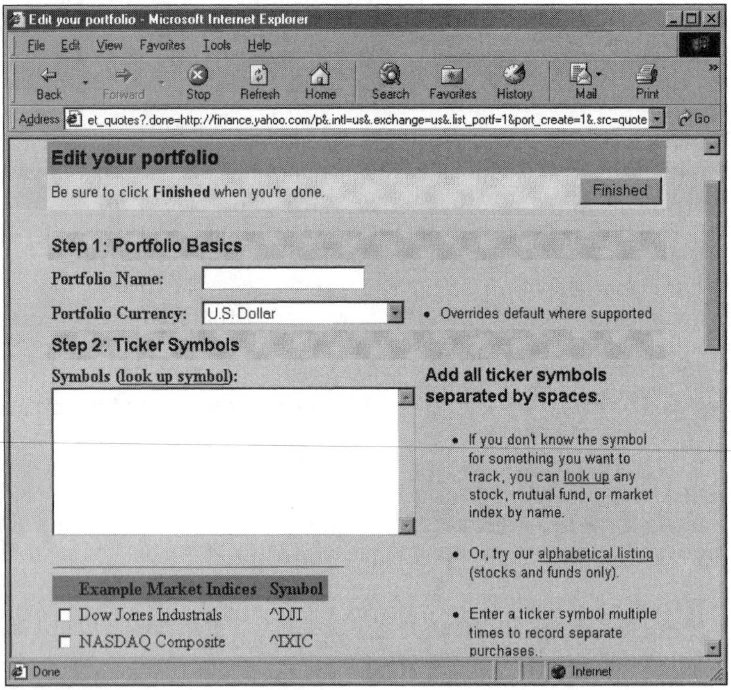

Figure 10-5:
This is
where you
begin
creating a
virtual
portfolio.

The wannabe portfolio

Most people who use Yahoo! portfolios create imaginary stock-holding sce-
narios either to test investing strategies or to follow certain companies out of
interest. Investors generally track their actual holdings using portfolio tools
provided by their online brokerage. Offline investors usually rely on their
broker statements and newspaper information. This is changing, though, as
more people experiment with managing information online.

Here, I describe how to set up a relatively simple Yahoo! portfolio — not to
track actual holdings, but to follow a group of stocks out of experimentation
or interest. The next part of this section gets into more complex features.

Follow these steps to create a basic portfolio tracker:

1. **On the Edit your portfolio page, type a name for the portfolio in the
   Portfolio Name field.**

   Because you might establish a number of portfolios, name this one
   something that indicates what is in it or give it a number. (Why am I
   being so pushy? Name it whatever you want.)

2. **In the Portfolio Currency field, use the drop-down menu to select the
   currency you want to use.**

   Yahoo! converts the native currency of the exchange where your stocks
   are located to whatever currency you *would* use if you were to buy the
   stock. This feature is only for tracking; it has nothing to do with whether
   you plan to actually buy your selected stocks.

3. **Under the Ticker Symbols banner, enter the stock symbols you want
   listed in your portfolio.**

   Put a space between all your symbols. If you don't know a stock symbol,
   use the <u>look up symbol</u> link. Enter ticker symbols in either uppercase or
   lowercase letters.

4. **Under Example Market Indices, click the check boxes next to any
   indices you want in your portfolio.**

   You may choose as many indices as you like. If the one(s) you want
   aren't on the short list, click the <u>More U.S. Indices</u> and <u>More
   International Indices</u> links.

5. **Under the Basic Features header, check the boxes if you'd like your
   stocks listed alphabetically and if you want a small-type display.**

   If you deliberately entered your stock symbols in the order you'd like
   them to appear, ignore the alphabetical option. The small font is useful if
   you choose any display option other than Basic. All the other options
   contain more information than can fit into most browser windows.
   (Although that depends on your screen size, screen resolution, and how
   wide you keep your windows.) I routinely use small fonts.

6. Using the drop-down menu, choose a profile view.

The views determine how much information is stuffed into your portfolio. The views correspond to the quote views you get when ordering a stock quote from the Yahoo! Finance home page. Basic view contains the least information and is good for quickly getting the gist of your portfolio's activity. The views get more detailed as you move down the list. Don't agonize over this decision; you can change views on the Portfolio page and also return to this page to edit your configuration at any time.

7. Click the Finished button.

Your portfolio is displayed (see Figure 10-6). To edit your options, look above the Portfolio banner, next to your currently displayed portfolio name, to find the <u>edit</u> link; click it to return to the Edit your portfolio page.

Note the <u>Create New View</u> link on the Portfolio page (refer to Figure 10-6). Use this link if you're not satisfied with the preset views available for your stocks. You might be particularly interested in each stock's P/E Ratio and Volume, but have interest also in the dividend information. The Edit your portfolio views page lets you customize what information your portfolio displays for each stock. Even better, you can use your personalized view when calling up individual quotes from the Yahoo! Finance home page. All in all, it's one kickin' feature. Here's how to use it:

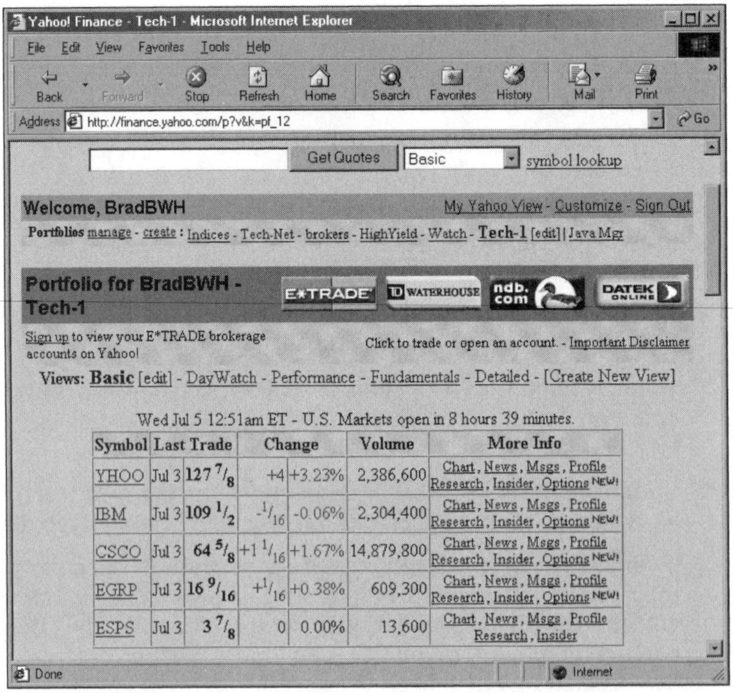

Figure 10-6:
A stock portfolio in Basic view.

Symbol	Last Trade	Change		Volume	More Info
YHOO	Jul 3 127 $^7/_8$	+4	+3.23%	2,386,600	Chart, News, Msgs, Profile Research, Insider, Options NEW!
IBM	Jul 3 109 $^1/_2$	$-^1/_{16}$	-0.06%	2,304,400	Chart, News, Msgs, Profile Research, Insider, Options NEW!
CSCO	Jul 3 64 $^5/_8$	+1 $^1/_{16}$	+1.67%	14,879,800	Chart, News, Msgs, Profile Research, Insider, Options NEW!
EGRP	Jul 3 16 $^9/_{16}$	+$^1/_{16}$	+0.38%	609,300	Chart, News, Msgs, Profile Research, Insider, Options NEW!
ESPS	Jul 3 3 $^7/_8$	0	0.00%	13,600	Chart, News, Msgs, Profile Research, Insider

1. **On the Edit your portfolio views page, name your new view in the View Name field.**

2. **If necessary, click to insert a check mark in the Show this View in the pull-down quotes menu option.**

   There is no reason to uncheck this box, which is checked by default when you first display this page.

3. **Use the drop-down menus next to each numbered field to select what information is divulged for your stocks.**

   When you drop down the menus, use the right-side scroll bars to see the entire list of options.

4. **Click the Accept Changes button.**

   Your portfolio is displayed in its new view. You may still change views easily, using the Views link directly above the portfolio. To change to another portfolio, you use the links above the Portfolio banner.

Setting up a trading portfolio

Things can get more complicated than the simple portfolio just described. Whether you own stocks or want to pretend you do for trading practice, Yahoo! Finance lets you add Buy and Sell information into your portfolio. Here's how to proceed:

1. **On the Yahoo! Finance home page, click the edit link next to any portfolio you want to alter.**

   If you're starting from scratch, use the create link next to Portfolio on the Yahoo! Finance home page.

2. **On the Edit your portfolio page, scroll down to the Step 4: Advanced Features (Optional) banner.**

   If you're starting a new portfolio, fill in the information under the first three steps on this page, as described in the preceding section. Figure 10-7 shows the advanced features.

3. **Click to add a check mark to the information features you want included in your portfolio.**

4. **Click the Enter More Info button.**

   Do not click the Finished button at this point. Checking the boxes only tells Yahoo! what fields to include in the portfolio; you still must enter basic information in those fields for the portfolio to do its work.

5. **On the Edit your portfolio details page (see Figure 10-8), type share, price, date, commission, and limit details for each stock in your portfolio, and add whatever notes you want to appear.**

6. **Click the Finished button.**

   Your new portfolio appears. To see the share, price, and gain or loss figures, you must be in Performance view. Click the <u>Performance</u> link if that is not your default view. Click the <u>edit</u> link to return to the Edit your portfolio page, where you can make Performance your default view.

Introducing the Java Portfolio Manager

The Java version of Yahoo!'s portfolios makes management much easier than in the Web-page version. After you try it, you might not want to go back to the relatively cumbersome system of surfing to the Edit your portfolio page every time you want to make a change. The Java program is far more interactive, allowing you to add and delete stocks, update prices, change portfolios, and change portfolio views without using your Web browser at all.

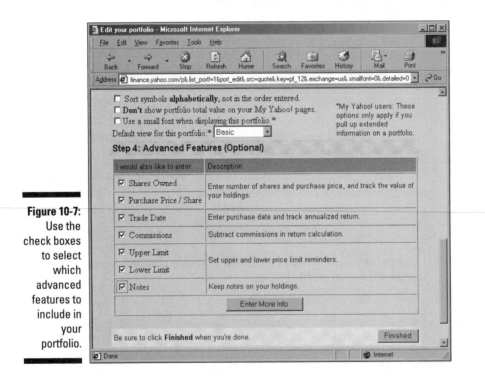

Figure 10-7: Use the check boxes to select which advanced features to include in your portfolio.

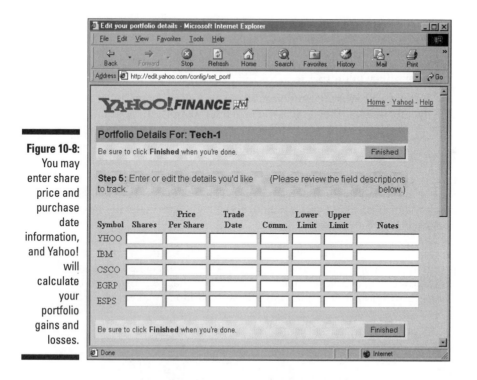

Figure 10-8:
You may
enter share
price and
purchase
date
information,
and Yahoo!
will
calculate
your
portfolio
gains and
losses.

You may use the Java Portfolio Manager on any Windows 95, Windows 98, Windows 2000, Windows NT, Macintosh, or UNIX computer that supports Java applets. Here's how to start it:

1. **On the Yahoo! Finance home page or any Portfolio page, click the** <u>**Java Mgr**</u> **link.**

   A window pops open while the Java program is automatically downloaded into your computer.

2. **When the start JPM button appears, click it.**

   The Java program appears on your screen (see Figure 10-9). It's as easy as that.

In the Java Portfolio Manager, the following features make it easy to manage your stock listing:

✔ Click the drop-down Portfolio menu to select one of your portfolios.

✔ Click the View drop-down menu to select a portfolio view.

✔ Click any stock name and drag it to a new position in the list to alter the order of stocks.

✔ Click any stock name and drag it to the trash can icon to delete it from the list.

✔ Click the Update button to get new prices. (Stock prices are delayed at least fifteen minutes.)

✔ To insert a new stock into your list, type its stock symbol in the Add Symbol field and then click the Add Symbol button.

✔ Click any column header to sort the list according to that column's data. Click it again to reverse the order.

REMEMBER

Changes made in the Java Portfolio Manager affect your portfolios as they appear in the Yahoo! Finance Web pages. The two methods of managing your stocks — Web and Java — are linked, and all changes made in one mode appear in the other mode.

WARNING!

Do not close the Java Portfolio Manager download window while the Java program is running. That's the window in which you clicked the start JPM button to launch the Java Manager. If you close that window (even though it's not the portfolio window itself), the Java Portfolio Manager closes also.

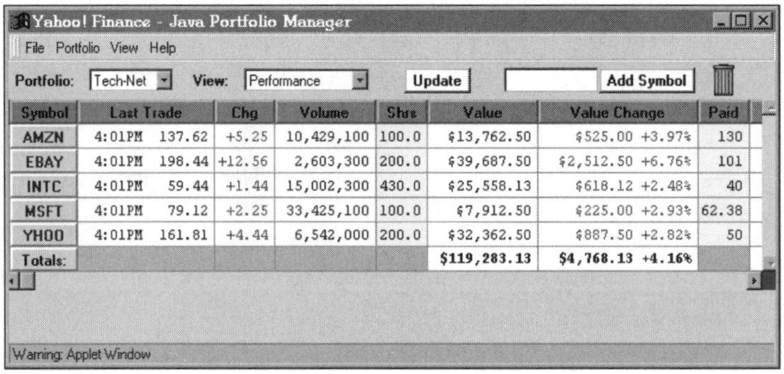

Figure 10-9:
The Java
Portfolio
Manager is
far more
interactive
than the
Web-based
portfolios.

Symbol	Last Trade	Chg	Volume	Shs	Value	Value Change	Paid
AMZN	4:01PM 137.62	+5.25	10,429,100	100.0	$13,762.50	$525.00 +3.97%	130
EBAY	4:01PM 198.44	+12.56	2,603,300	200.0	$39,687.50	$2,512.50 +6.76%	101
INTC	4:01PM 59.44	+1.44	15,002,300	430.0	$25,558.13	$618.12 +2.48%	40
MSFT	4:01PM 79.12	+2.25	33,425,100	100.0	$7,912.50	$225.00 +2.93%	62.38
YHOO	4:01PM 161.81	+4.44	6,542,000	200.0	$32,362.50	$887.50 +2.82%	50
Totals:					$119,283.13	$4,768.13 +4.16%	

Final Hints

To round out this chapter, let me offer a few final tips for making the most of Yahoo! Finance:

✔ As you wend deeply into the features of Yahoo! Finance, remember that you can return to the home page by clicking the Yahoo! Finance logo at the top of any page.

✔ Try Yahoo! FinanceVision, a real-time broadcast of market news right on your computer screen. Click the Yahoo! FinanceVision link from the Yahoo! Finance home page to get the free download. This feature works best with high-speed Internet connections.

✔ Yahoo! Companion (explained and praised to the skies in Chapter 20), offers a tremendous method of getting a grip on Yahoo! Finance and keeping its features within easy reach at all times. The Companion furnishes a dedicated (optional) Finance toolbar that makes getting stock quotes, viewing your portfolios, and researching companies a breeze, no matter where you happen to be on the Web.

✔ Stock alerts are handy for notifying you when financial events occur, such as a stock on your watch-list reaching a certain price. You can set up stock alerts through Yahoo! Messenger, which I explore with the thoroughness of a curious cat in Chapter 15.

Chapter 11

The Musical Yahoo!

*Y*ahoo! is into music in a big way. A big, scattered way. The evolution of music on the Internet has been rapid, and Yahoo! has participated in the phenomenon by adding chunks of content to its core music site. The result has become something of a patchwork.

Yahoo! currently provides five major music products — three sites and two programs:

- ✔ **Yahoo! Music.** The foundation stone of the Yahoo! music empire.

- ✔ **Yahoo! Radio.** A free on-screen gadget that tunes you in to Internet-enabled radio stations all over the world.

- ✔ **Yahoo! Digital.** The service's contribution to digital music, MP3, and related technologies.

- ✔ **Yahoo! Broadcast.** The real-time programming arm of Yahoo!.

- ✔ **Yahoo! Player.** An MP3 player and Internet-radio tuner, Yahoo! Player is a free, stand-alone program.

One day, Yahoo! might integrate this basket of content into a single coherent destination. For now, you need to find what you like in each of these services and use them to enhance your total online musical experience. This chapter covers the basics of all five Yahoo! music offerings.

Yahoo! Music

Yahoo! Music, once oriented exclusively toward rock and pop, has broadened nicely since the last edition of this book. The main Yahoo! music destination now sports five main genre divisions: Rock & Pop, Jazz & Blues, Country, Urban & Electronic, and Classical. Each of those genres spins off to a separate site. The Yahoo! Music home page also contains well-organized links to album reviews, news stories, an MP3 directory, a music shopping center, a music search engine, and various other music-related Yahoo! pages.

To see the Yahoo! Music home page (see Figure 11-1), click the <u>Music</u> link near the bottom of the main Yahoo! home page (in the *Entertainment* group of links) or go directly to the following URL:

```
music.yahoo.com
```

Finding your type of music

If you favor any of the five main music genres listed in the preceding section, Yahoo! Music makes it very easy to get information about the stars and not-stars of that style. On the Yahoo! Music home page, under the Select a Genre heading, click any of the genre links. (See the Rock & Pop page in Figure 11-2.)

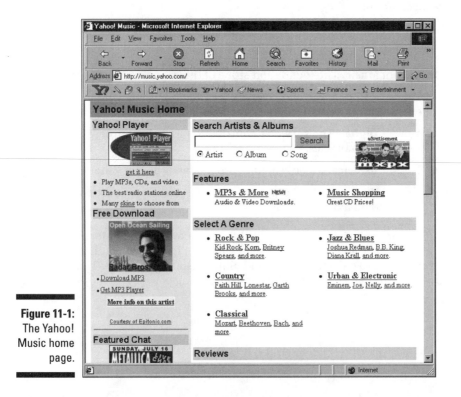

Figure 11-1:
The Yahoo!
Music home
page.

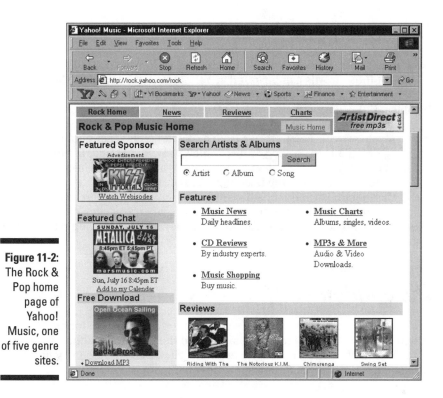

Figure 11-2:
The Rock &
Pop home
page of
Yahoo!
Music, one
of five genre
sites.

Each genre home page contains six major content headings:

✔ **Search Artists & Albums.** Use the radio buttons to select how to search (artist, album, or song), enter your keyword(s), and click the Search button.

✔ **Features.** This section is where you link to genre news, album reviews, CD shopping, charts, and MP3s of the genre. Some of these topics exist further down the home page in abbreviated form.

✔ **Reviews.** A handful of featured albums are linked directly from this section. Click the More Reviews link to see others.

✔ **Headlines.** About half a dozen headlines start you off. You can get a heavier dose of news by clicking the More Headlines link.

✔ **Charts.** One or two charts are included in the section for each genre, with a link to More Charts in some genres.

✔ **Today's Music Net Events.** This section contains a listing of live Internet events in all genres — the listing is identical in all five genre sites. The events range from Netcasts of music festivals and concerts to online chats with music celebrities.

The newsy stuff

Music might be a language unto itself, but a lot of words are used to describe it. Many of those words can be found at Yahoo! Music. To read the latest headlines about the music business, scroll down to the Headlines section of the Music Home page.

Yahoo! Music provides new stories from a handful of Internet publications, including CMJ, Launch, Rolling Stone, SonicNet, Wall of Sound, Down Beat Jazz, and Country.com. The news pages display timely stories from any or all of these sources. (Clicking the headline link keeps you within Yahoo! Music.) Notice that right next to the headline links are links to the sources themselves. However, you don't go to the source site when you click one of those links, but you do go to another Yahoo! Music news page featuring stories only from that source.

The opinion stuff

Music reviews are provided by the same sources as the news stories. For a limited selection of featured reviews, scroll to the Reviews heading. To see more reviews of country music, for example, click the more Country link or the similar link. Click similar links for the other genres.

The downloadable stuff

Downloadable music? Welcome to the 21st century. Yahoo! provides a directory to digital song files that exist on other sites. All music linked to Yahoo! Music is legal — Yahoo! avoids all bootleg sites, concentrating instead on MP3.com, eMusic, Liquid Audio and other sites that are in the business of licensing music and offering it in digital formats to visitors. Yahoo! itself does not store or provide any music. The service merely links to other storehouses.

 You need music playing software to hear your downloaded songs. The software you need depends on the file format you download. The latest versions (6.0 and later) of Windows Media Player, which many people running Windows computers own without knowing it, can play MP3 and Windows Media files. You need the Liquid Audio Player to hear Liquid Audio files. You need RealPlayer (which you may have as part of your browser) to hear RealAudio files.

The following steps walk you through a typical browse for downloadable music. In following along, you can get an idea of how the directory is structured.

1. **On the Yahoo! Music home page, click the MP3s & More link.**

2. **On the MP3s & More page, click the <u>Electronica/Dance</u> link.**

   Of course, you can click any genre you want. Indulge me as I pursue this path for the sake of illustration.

3. **On the subcategory page, click the <u>Techno</u> link.**

   The Techno page appears. At this point, you could bolt directly to an artist page, from the right-hand Most Popular sidebar, as shown in Figure 11-3.

4. **On the Techno page, click the letter M in the alphabetical directory.**

5. **On the directory page for the letter M, click the <u>6 Songs</u> link next to the artist Madsound Guy.**

   Each artist link shows how many songs can be found in the directory.

6. **On the Madsound Guy page, click the link of any song you'd like to download.**

   As you can see in Figure 11-4, the artist page lists songs in a chart that shows the available format and whether the song is free or pay-pre-download. Clicking any song link takes you to one more Yahoo! Music page. From there you link directly to the host site for that song and download it from there.

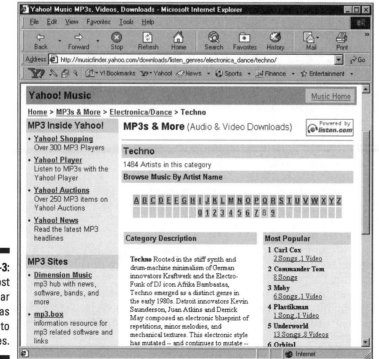

Figure 11-3:
The Most
Popular
section has
links to
artist pages.

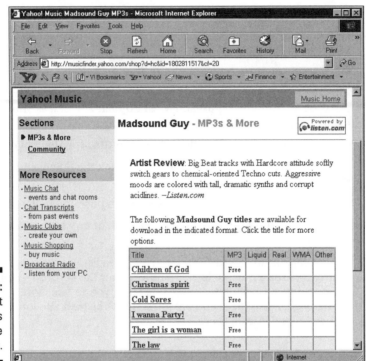

Figure 11-4:
Each artist
page lists
available
songs.

Download times depend on the size of the file (length of the song) and your connection speed. A typical 3 meg pop song might take as long as twenty minutes through a 28.8k dial-up modem or as brief as 20 seconds through a cable modem. Download conditions vary, too — sometimes delays occur during the download from excessive demand for that song.

Charting the hits

Charts are available only from the genre home pages, not from the Yahoo! Music home page. Click one of the genre selections as described previously to see charts.

Charts are organized pretty much the same way as news and CD reviews. Multiple sources are sometimes used for the sales charts: Billboard Magazine, CMJ, and Rick Dees Online for Rock & Pop charts, for example. Each source carries its own charts and compiles those charts using its own methods. Billboard and CMJ each feature nine music charts, ranging from Top 40 hits to blues albums to Internet retail bestsellers.

One of the best features of the Yahoo! Music charts is the way chart entries link to artist information in the Yahoo! Musicfinder database. Musicfinder is the source of search results in Yahoo! Music, which I describe in the next section. For an example of how this works, look at Figures 11-5 and 11-6. Figure 11-5 shows the Billboard Hot 100 Singles chart, with Matchbox Twenty perched in the number one spot. The band's name, along with most of the others, is a hyperlink. A click of that link takes you to Figure 11-6, the artist information page for the popular group.

Searching for music

In Yahoo! Music, searching has two results: information about recording artists (and their work) and invitations to buy CDs. The best place to begin a search is right on the Yahoo! Music home page. As you can see in Figure 11-1, the search form is front and center on the page. Proceed thusly:

1. **Using the radio buttons below the keyword-entry form, select whether you're searching for an artist, an album, or a song.**

2. **In the keyword field, type your keywords.**

3. **Click the Search button.**

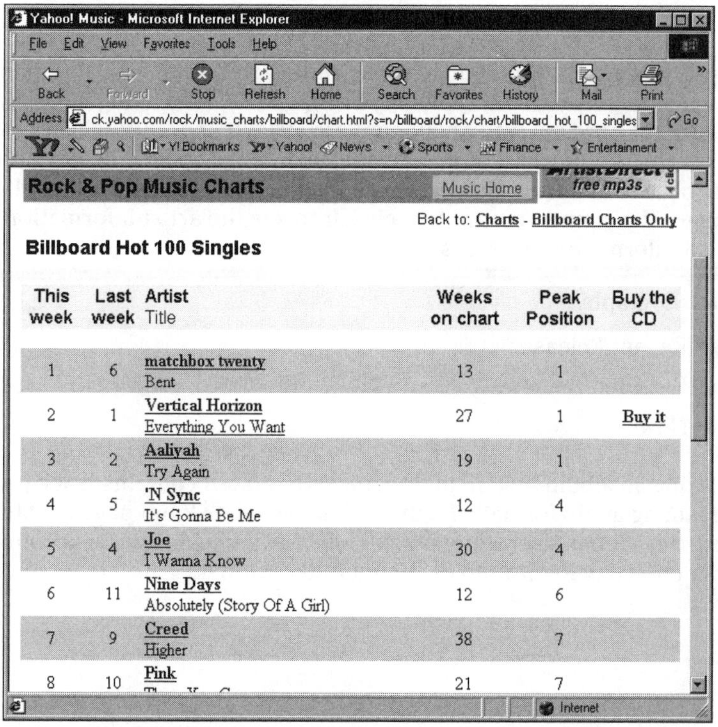

Figure 11-5: A Billboard hit chart, with links to artist information pages.

Yahoo! Music - Microsoft Internet Explorer
File Edit View Favorites Tools Help
Back Forward Stop Refresh Home Search Favorites History Mail Print
Address ck.yahoo.com/rock/music_charts/billboard/chart.html?s=n/billboard/rock/chart/billboard_hot_100_singles Go
Y! Bookmarks Yahoo! News Sports Finance Entertainment

Rock & Pop Music Charts   Music Home   ArtistDirect free mp3s

Back to: <u>Charts</u> - <u>Billboard Charts Only</u>

Billboard Hot 100 Singles

This week	Last week	Artist Title	Weeks on chart	Peak Position	Buy the CD
1	6	<u>matchbox twenty</u> Bent	13	1	
2	1	<u>Vertical Horizon</u> Everything You Want	27	1	<u>Buy it</u>
3	2	<u>Aaliyah</u> Try Again	19	1	
4	5	<u>'N Sync</u> It's Gonna Be Me	12	4	
5	4	<u>Joe</u> I Wanna Know	30	4	
6	11	<u>Nine Days</u> Absolutely (Story Of A Girl)	12	6	
7	9	<u>Creed</u> Higher	38	7	
8	10	<u>Pink</u> 	21	7	

Internet

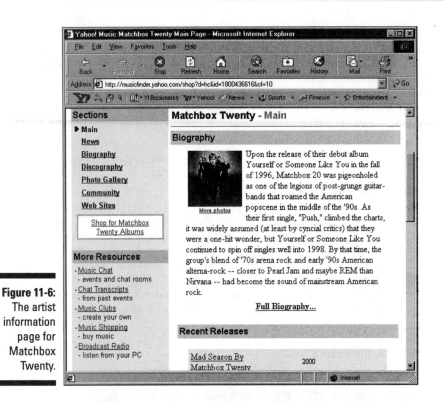

Figure 11-6:
The artist
information
page for
Matchbox
Twenty.

When you search for a music artist, the search results display all matches
that relate in any way to your keyword(s). The search engine assumes that
you might have entered an incomplete artist name, and delivers extensions of
that name if they exist. For example, searching on *sting* displays not only the
ex-Police lead singer, but also Paul Stinga, the Blue Stingrays, and other
names. If you find your match, click it to see the artist information page. The
artist information page has four parts:

- Biography
- Recent Releases
- Featured Reviews
- News

Clicking an album link displays a page that often contains track previews in
streaming audio formats. Figure 11-7 shows the album page for Sting's *Brand
New Day* album, each song of which is previewed with a 30-second excerpt in
your choice of RealAudio or Liquid Audio format.

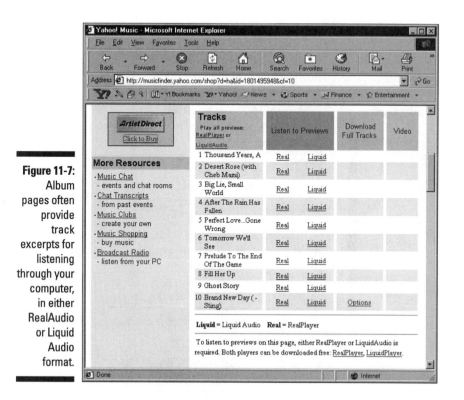

Figure 11-7:
Album pages often provide track excerpts for listening through your computer, in either RealAudio or Liquid Audio format.

Searching for an album or a song sidesteps the artist information page but otherwise is identical to searching for an artist. The search results skip right to links of album or song names, but you can always click the artist's name in parentheses to see that artist's info page.

In a buying mood

Like any self-respecting online service, Yahoo! provides plenty of ways to spend money. Yahoo! Music contains an entire Music Shopping section. To see the home page for that area, just click the Music Shopping link on the Yahoo! Music home page.

The Music Shopping home page delivers a mix of feature stories and shopping come-ons. Click any genre from the left-hand navigation sidebar or use the Search form. Either way, you eventually end up with an artist page listing all available albums for that group or artist. This is where things get interesting. Click any album to display the comparison shopping page (see Figure 11-8). On this page, the retail outlets carrying that CD are listed by price, enabling you to snap up the best bargain without visiting each store and searching for the CD.

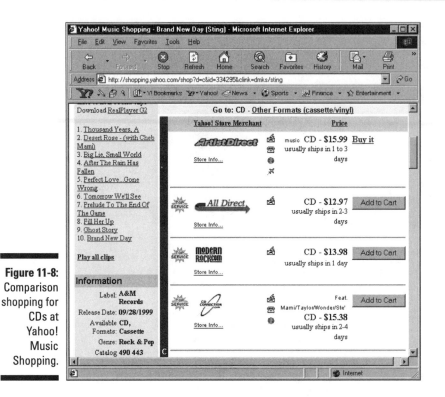

Figure 11-8: Comparison shopping for CDs at Yahoo! Music Shopping.

It's important to keep in mind that Yahoo! Music compares prices among the CD stores that have online shops within Yahoo! Shopping but no other online music stores. Fortunately, Yahoo! Shopping has a good selection of stores. But it's like comparing prices in a single mall. You might be accustomed to buying from other stores on the Net, but if you went to one of them you'd lose the convenience of the price comparison feature. Yahoo! Music currently hosts online shops for Tower Records, CDdiscounters.com, ModernRock.com, CDworld, and a few others. So the selection is good, but if you insist on buying all your entertainment from Amazon.com or CDNow, you must take the initiative to price the CD at those sites. (You can also try the Compare Price for this product on the Web link.)

My own price comparisons, broadened to include other online stores, indicate that the prices for music CDs at Yahoo! Shopping are excellent, routinely as much as $2.50 less for the same album at Amazon.com or CDNow. But if you insist on getting the best price every time, shop around yourself.

When it comes to buying, just click the Add to Cart button. All of Yahoo! Shopping uses the same online shopping cart screen (see Chapter 21). You may settle on a single product or continue shopping and adding things from other stores to the cart.

Listening to Yahoo! Radio

Yahoo! has recently added a radio player to its lineup. Some Internet radio programs play simple playlists of songs, not actual broadcast stations. Yahoo! Radio, however, gathers several broadcast stations of various styles, located all over the United States, and lets you choose among them.

You need both RealPlayer and Windows Media Player to get the most out of Yahoo! Radio. If your computer is so equipped, follow these steps to begin listening:

1. **Go to the Yahoo! Radio home page at the following URL:**

   ```
   radio.yahoo.com
   ```

2. **Scroll down the page and click the <u>Tune In and Start Listening</u> link.**

   A small browser window opens — this is the radio itself — and begins making noise. (See Figure 11-9.) The first sounds you hear are usually ads for Yahoo! Radio sponsors. Then one of the stations begins to play — whichever is currently the default station.

3. **Click one of the station links or preset buttons to hear a new station.**

   Expect the switch to take a little time — maybe up to 15 seconds.

4. **Use the Find more stations button to broaden your selection.**

   Clicking this button opens a browser window displaying a station directory. Click into the directory by genre and click any station link. The new browser window closes, and Yahoo! Radio stops, loads the new station, and begins streaming its audio.

5. **Use the small square Stop button to end Yahoo! Radio or the speaker icon to mute it without interrupting the stream.**

   You can leave the Yahoo! Radio window open even when the radio isn't playing.

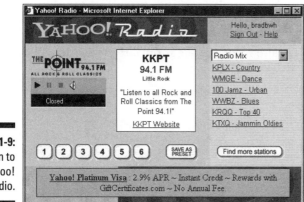

Figure 11-9:
Tune in to
Yahoo!
Radio.

Listening to Yahoo! Radio (or any streaming audio programming) might make it slower or more difficult to browse the Web when the music is playing, depending on your connection speed. If you use a telephone modem (28.8k, 33.6k, or 56k), you might run into difficulties — either the music stream is interrupted intermittently or Web pages load into your browser more slowly. If the slowdown gets too intense, just turn off Yahoo! Radio. Cable modem and DSL users shouldn't have any problem.

Music Goes Digital

Although the Yahoo! multiple-site strategy of delivering music makes for a lot of content, it's confusing. Perhaps in the future, Yahoo! will integrate its vast music-content service into a single coherent directory. For now, if you're a lover of online music (and who wouldn't be?), it's best to become familiar with Yahoo!'s separate directories.

Yahoo! Digital pulls together music from several partner sites, including eMusic, Liquid Audio, and the Internet Underground Music Archive (IUMA). The purpose of this site is to point you to song downloads at these other locations. Yahoo! Digital encompasses video as well, but video content isn't sprinkled around the Web nearly as much as audio content. Finally, Yahoo! Digital helps you locate and acquire the software tools you need to enjoy downloaded music.

You may be scratching your head at this point, remembering (as described earlier in this chapter) that the Yahoo! Music site has an MP3 directory. Doesn't Yahoo! Digital duplicate that effort? Well, no, actually — the idea is the same, but the directories are different. The artist I used earlier in the chapter, Madsound Guy, doesn't even show up in the Yahoo! Digital directory. So there's nothing for you to do but explore both directories. Each one lists music in several formats, not just MP3.

Go to the Yahoo! Digital home page at the following URL:

```
digital.yahoo.com
```

As you can see in Figure 11-10, the site is organized into the sections shown in the left-hand sidebar.

Figure 11-10:
The Yahoo!
Digital home
page.

Finding digital audio

Yahoo! Digital's core service is the music download directory. Like other
Yahoo! directories, this one is a multi-level affair. As you drill deeper into it,
you find more specific results until you finally link away from Yahoo! to a content site where the downloadable song resides. Follow these steps to get
started:

1. **On the Yahoo! Digital home page, click the <u>Audio</u> link in the left-hand
   sidebar.**

2. **Under the Music Archive heading, click a genre.**

   You can also click a letter of the alphabet — a good idea if you're looking
   for a particular artist. (There is no search form on this page.) The next
   step assumes that you clicked a genre, not a letter.

3. **On the next page, click any music group or musician.**

   Figure 11-11 shows the Blues directory page with several bands listed. Note
   that some music is located at IUMA and some at the Liquid Audio site.

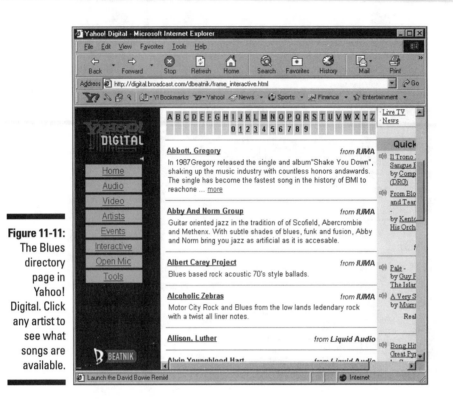

Figure 11-11:
The Blues directory page in Yahoo! Digital. Click any artist to see what songs are available.

4. **On the next page (see Figure 11-12), click the song and format you want to experience.**

   You never know what you might find on this page — many songs or just one, several formats or just one. In Figure 11-12, you see one song in two formats. Click the MP3 link to download the song or the RealAudio link to hear a streaming excerpt of the song.

Browsing the featured artists

The Artists section of Yahoo! Digital is the most newsy and chatty portion of the site. Here you find special content selections. In mid-2000, for example, Dave Matthews Band put four live recordings on the Internet at the official band site, and Yahoo! Digital promoted the event in the Artists section. You almost always find special download deals here.

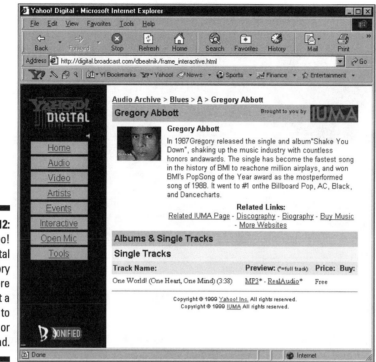

Figure 11-12:
The Yahoo!
Digital
directory
page where
you select a
song file to
hear or
download.

Remixing the music

Ready for a mind-blowing experience? All right. Click the Interactive link in the left-hand sidebar. It takes you to the Beatnik Interactive page. Nothing special right away, I realize. You must download and install the Beatnik Sonifier to have fun with this page.

Beatnik is an invisible browser enhancement that adds sound effects to the browsing experience whenever you're at a sonified site. The Interactive page is the only sonified part of Yahoo! Digital. Beyond making fun noises when your mouse moves across parts of the page, Beatnik lets you actually remix songs. You can raise the level of the drum track, eliminate the vocals, bring out the guitar — all by clicking on-screen buttons. (See Figure 11-13.) Then you can save your mix and send it to friends.

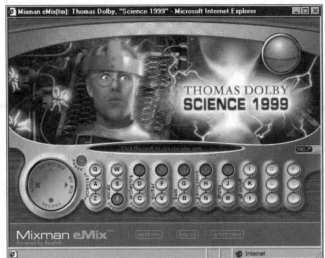

Figure 11-13:
Beatnik lets
you remix
selected
songs and
then save
your
personal
version.

The whole thing is more fun than a monkey at a fruit stand. Here's how to proceed:

1. **On the Yahoo! Digital home page, click the <u>Interactive</u> link on the left-hand sidebar.**

2. **On the Interactive page, click the Beatnik Download sign.**

   Follow the on-screen instructions for downloading and installing Beatnik.

3. **With Beatnik installed, open your browser.**

   You need to close the browser to install Beatnik. When you open it again, Beatnik is operational.

4. **Back on the Interactive page, click any of the Featured Interactive Remixes.**

   The Mixman window opens.

5. **Click the Let's Jam! Button.**

6. **In the Mixman window, click the buttons corresponding to the tune's tracks to emphasize or reduce the tracks.**

   This part takes some practice, but it's fun practice. Each Mixman window has a different graphic design, but they all work the same way. Click the Record button to save all your button-pushes. Click Send Mix if you want to e-mail your mix to a friend, who must have Beatnik to listen.

When mixing a song with Beatnik, don't surf away from the Interactive portion of the Yahoo! Digital site in your browser window. Even though the Mixman module of Beatnik opens in a separate window, it stops operating if you leave the Interactive page.

Calling all musicians

Yahoo! Digital runs an on-site program called Open Mic for independent musicians. If you or your band owns recordings of your work in MP3 or Liquid Audio digital format, Yahoo! invites you to upload the song(s) to the Open Mic directory. Click the Submit/Edit My Music Now link for uploading instructions.

For non-musicians, Open Mic is yet another music directory, this one containing music most people have never heard. Click the Open Mic link and scroll down the page to see the top level of the directory. Drill your way into it to see artist pages, which contain a link to the band's home page and another link for listening to the uploaded music.

Getting with the program

With all this digital music at your disposal, you need the software to listen to it. If you operate a Windows computer of fairly recent vintage, you probably already own Windows Media. If you run a modern browser, you might already have RealPlayer. Those two programs, by themselves, deliver a lot of music content. Yahoo! Digital dishes up many Liquid Audio files, and you must use the Liquid Audio Player to hear them.

Click the Tools link in the left-hand sidebar of Yahoo! Digital to download every program you need to hear music at the site. These are the programs that Yahoo! has partnered with — they don't represent all the digital music playback programs available on the Web, by any means.

Audio in Real Time

Yahoo! has been acquisitive in the past few years. One of the service's big acquisitions has been Broadcast.com, an Internet aggregator of streaming audio content. What the heck does that mean, you ask? It means Broadcast.com doesn't produce its own music or radio shows. It simply links to broadcasts at other sites. Furthermore, Broadcast.com made its mark years ago by assembling an online jukebox of complete CDs contributed by independent musicians looking for exposure.

This sort of wide-ranging linking is right up Yahoo!'s alley, and so it purchased Broadcast.com, which is now named Yahoo! Broadcast. Go to the home page at the following URL:

```
broadcast.yahoo.com
```

Yahoo! Broadcast is essentially a directory of listenable online programming. Most of the programs are formatted for either RealAudio or Windows Media. As you can see in Figure 11-14, the programming covers all kinds of topics. In this directory you can find music programs and plenty of talk-radio. Many sports events, such as Major League Baseball, are broadcast in real-time, making Yahoo! Broadcast a free, global tuner.

Check out the <u>CD Jukebox</u> link on the main Yahoo! Broadcast directory page. It leads to a genre directory of music types, and from there to a rich selection of complete CDs available for online listening. You can get lost in sound for days at a time. Many of the acts are unknown, but you can find familiar names in the stacks. A certain built-in quality filter exists here, as a participating group must have produced an entire CD. The CD Jukebox is a fine way to discover new music.

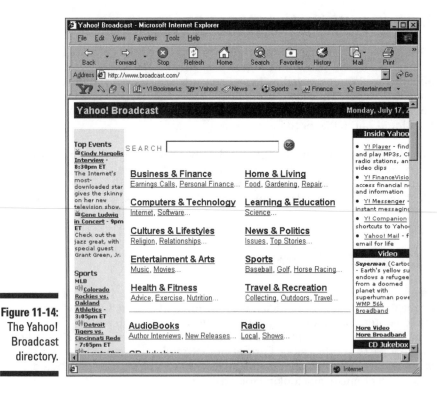

Figure 11-14:
The Yahoo!
Broadcast
directory.

The Yahoo! Player

After the first edition of this book was published, Yahoo! created a media player of its own to stand alongside Windows Media Player, Liquid Audio Player, RealJukebox, and other stand-alone music-playback programs. Yahoo! Player is a full-featured program, freely downloadable, that plays MP3, Windows Media, and other audio formats. The software bundles an Internet-radio tuner and an integrated Web browser. It's quite a package!

Yahoo! Player does not operate within the Web browser; you must download and install it. The integrated browser is Internet Explorer, and you must have a copy of that browser (Version 4.0 or later) on your hard drive. You also need to own Microsoft Windows Media Player. Both these elements are downloadable from the Yahoo! Radio home page. Of course, you need a sound card and speakers to hear anything.

To use Yahoo! Player, proceed as follows:

1. **Go to the Yahoo! Player home page at the following URL:**

   ```
   player.yahoo.com
   ```

2. **Click the <u>Download Yahoo! Player</u> link.**

   Be sure to read the system requirements just below the download link. Yahoo! Player is available only for Windows computers (as of this writing).

3. **Follow the on-screen instructions for downloading and installing Yahoo! Player.**

   The player operates as a stand-alone program, as shown in Figure 11-15, not a browser window. You boot it up like any other desktop program when you want to listen to digital music files or Internet radio stations.

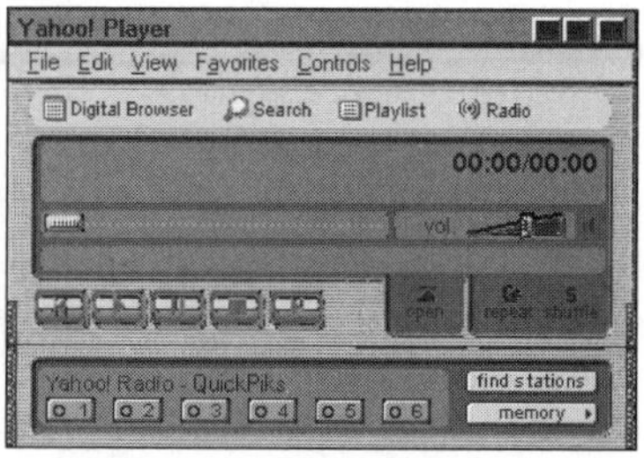

Figure 11-15: Yahoo! Player.

Like all such programs, Yahoo! Player seeks to become the default player for all media types that you store on your computer. (It can't play Liquid Audio files, though.) During the installation, and sometimes afterward, Yahoo! Player attempts to strong-arm you into agreeing to this default setup. If you use other programs to play certain media files — such as the popular Winamp to play MP3s — you might not want Yahoo! Player popping up at every turn. After installation, you can change the file associations by following these steps:

1. **In Yahoo! Player, click Edit ⇨ Preferences.**

2. **Click the Media Formats tab and then click the Details button.**

3. **Click the boxes next to formats you want Yahoo! Player to handle automatically and then click OK.**

4. **Back on the Media Formats tab, click the check box if you want Yahoo! Player to resist the attempts of other players to claim your chosen formats.**

   It's as if the software players are in a war with each other over your files! After you've selected the default formats for Yahoo! Player, it might be a good idea to click to add a checkmark to this box. You can always adjust these settings later.

Yahoo! Radio basically enables you to perform three functions:

- ✔ Listen to song files on your hard drive

- ✔ Listen to streaming audio from the Internet

- ✔ Search for Internet music, both streams and files

Following are tips for using Yahoo! Radio. The program's basic functions are also covered in this list:

- ✔ Click the Digital Browser button to open the integrated browser. Unlike your normal browsing program, the Yahoo! Player browser doesn't have a menu bar, and you can't access your Favorites (or Bookmarks) through it. This browser add-on is meant to be used with the player, to search for and download music.

- ✔ Click the Search button to display the Yahoo! Player Search page in the integrated browser. Here, you can scour Yahoo! Music for artists and songs.

- ✔ Click the Playlist button to open a new pane in the Player program, as shown in Figure 11-16. This window lists song titles that you load into Yahoo! Player. Use the buttons at the bottom of this pane to load and remove song files. The playlist pane opens attached to the side of Yahoo! Player, but you can drag it away from the main module.

- ✔ Click the Radio button to hide or display the radio buttons. The button is a toggle.

✔ Click any of the Yahoo! Radio Quick Piks to hear a radio station over the Internet. (You must be logged on to the Web to hear radio.)

✔ Click the find stations button to open the Yahoo! Radio station directory in the integrated browser.

✔ Click the memory button to select a different Channel Pack. Each Channel Pack contains six preset radio stations.

✔ Use the Play, Pause, and Stop buttons to control the playback of song files and radio stations.

Figure 11-16:
The playlist window of Yahoo! Player.

Chapter 12

Backgammon, Anyone?

In This Chapter

▶ Joining and watching games

▶ Creating your own game tables

***

Yahoo! isn't *all* fun and games, but one portion is devoted to pure interactive recreation, and that's Yahoo! Games. If you don't care for the violence of computer games, you have nothing to worry about. The most violent thing that transpires at Yahoo! Games is when a king gets checkmated. Yahoo! Games features board and card games that you can play with other Yahoo! members (or against the Yahoo! computer in some cases) in real time. This chapter walks you through one game, illustrating the basic gaming software common to most of the games. You don't need to install anything on your computer to play, as long as you have a Java-capable Web browser.

Rules of the Game

Yahoo! Games is the most heavily Java-dependent portion of the entire Yahoo! service. Other aspects of Yahoo! use Java, but not exclusively. For example, Java Messenger is just a supplement to the full-featured, downloadable Yahoo! Messenger. And the Java chat rooms are backed up by HTML chat rooms for computers that don't run Java easily.

Java is a software language that can be understood and used by different computer platforms. It's convenient primarily because it delivers applications to your computer by means of very quick downloads — usually just a minute or two, if that. Java is most often used to create a program or screen environment independent of your browser. Although Java runs on different computers — a facility known as *cross platform* — it can't overcome certain obstacles. Primarily, it needs a 32-bit operating system and a local hard drive to hold the Java program.

Because of Java's requirements, and because playing in Yahoo! Games is completely dependent on Java-readiness, certain home computer systems have trouble or are completely unable to participate in Yahoo! Games. They are

✔ **Windows 3.1.** Versions of the Windows operating system before Windows 95 are 16-bit systems and therefore cannot run Java.

✔ **WebTV.** WebTV systems (Classic and Plus) do not have local hard drives that can accept downloads of Java programs. WebTV users cannot play Yahoo! Games. (But they *can* play along with Jeopardy, unlike computer users.)

✔ **America Online.** The built-in AOL browser stumbles over many Web sites, and Yahoo! Games is no exception. AOL users should download a standard browser (Navigator or Internet Explorer) and use it rather than the default AOL browser.

After you have any Java problems squared away, Yahoo! Games provides really good playing environments for ten card games and five board games. Spades is the surprise popularity winner among the card games, but you can also play poker, gin, bridge, hearts, and a few others. Chess is the clear winner on the board side, but the backgammon and checkers rooms are usually bustling with activity as well.

The Yahoo! Games home page (see Figure 12-1) lists all available games and is the place to start meeting other people and playing a few games. Click the Games link on the Yahoo! home page or go directly to

```
games.yahoo.com
```

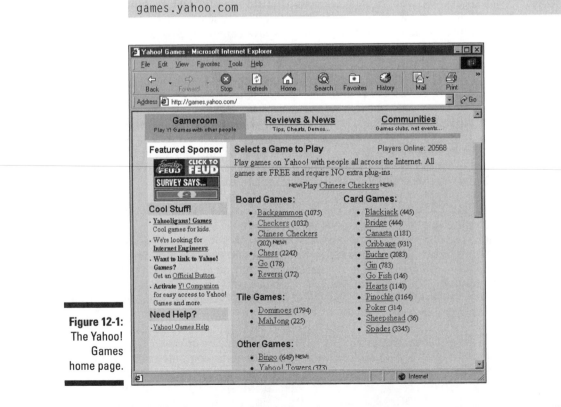

Figure 12-1:
The Yahoo!
Games
home page.

Playing a Game

Most Yahoo! games operate in basically the same way, with variations due to the different natures of the games themselves. Every game involves a Java download and a succession of windows. Using mouse clicks, you proceed from the game page in your browser to a room window that's part of a Java download, and from the room window to a game window, which is also part of the Java program. These three windows (browser window, room window, and game window) are independent and operate autonomously.

The following steps take you through the process of beginning a game of checkers (or watching a game without playing). Other games differ in cosmetic details, but the same basic windows apply to them all:

1. **On the Yahoo! Games home page, click the Checkers link.**

   The Checkers game page appears. Each game page lists several rooms you can enter immediately, usually in a lounge called Social. On some game pages, rooms are grouped by playing level: Beginner, Intermediate, and Advanced.

2. **Select a screen size.**

   The Screen Size box lists two options: 800 x 600 pixels (the default size) and 640 x 480 pixels (the smaller size).

3. **Click on a room or on a level of play.**

   A Java download starts, which might take a minute or two to complete through telephone modems or a few seconds through a cable modem. The next thing you see is a room window, independent of your browser window. Figure 12-2 shows the Checkers room window.

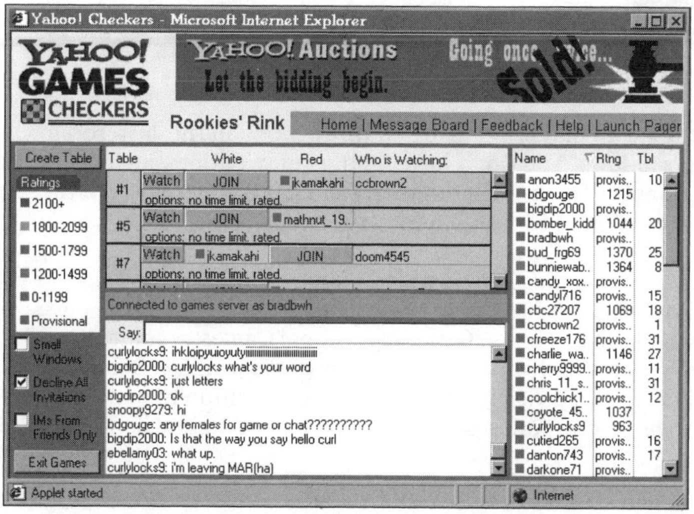

Figure 12-2: The Checkers room window, where you select a partner to play with or a game to watch.

4. Click any Watch button to observe a game in progress, or click any Join button to play.

A new window opens — the game window — independent of both the room window and your browser window. In two-person games, such as Checkers, clicking a Join button matches you with the listed opponent, and you begin the game by each clicking a Start button. In group games, such as Poker, the Join button gets you a seat at the table — you can also click the Watch button to observe the table and then Join from there. Figure 12-3 illustrates a checkers game window as a player sees it. I am red (the dark pieces) in this game. Note that I am losing miserably.

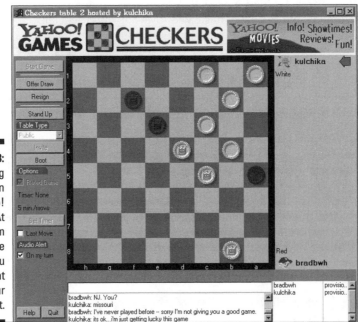

Figure 12-3: Playing Checkers in Yahoo! Games. At the bottom of the window, you can chat with your opponent.

Chatting with players is featured throughout all the Java room windows and game windows. You don't have all the fancy options included in Yahoo! Chat (see Chapter 13), but it's polite to say hi. If you're playing a timed game, chatting is often kept to a minimum.

Rules for the games can be found on most of the game pages in your browser window. I say *most* because, shockingly, at least one game page (poker) is missing a rules section. Generally, Yahoo! Games assumes a basic familiarity with the rules and with navigating the game window. Board games are played by clicking and dragging pieces from one position to another. The poker game window supplies preset buttons for calling, raising, and folding.

The room window contains the more complex set of features of the two Java windows. As you can see in Figure 12-2, the room window packs a busy screen into a small space. (You can resize the window.) Here are some important points about this window:

- ✔ The color-coded ratings in the left-hand sidebar are maintained automatically in Yahoo! Games. Whenever you enter a game room for the first time, you are given a provisional rating that moves up and down as you win and lose games. Notice how each name in the Name column has a rating color next to it.

- ✔ The Create Table button lets you establish a new playing station, which other people can join and to which you can invite anyone to play.

- ✔ Look at the Name, Rtng, and Tbl columns. A small arrow is next to one of these columns at all times. Click the header of any column to organize the names according to that column's criterion, and move the arrow next to the column header. This feature is especially helpful in listing potential players in order of their rankings.

- ✔ Check the Small Windows box to confine all game windows to the smaller 640 x 480 pixel size.

- ✔ Check the Decline All Invitations box to stanch the flow of Join invitations that's bound to arrive if you don't check it. (Keep reading to find out how to create a table and invite players.)

- ✔ Check the IMs From Friends Only box to receive Instant Messages from only your Yahoo! Messenger friends (see Chapter 15).

- ✔ All the items on the link menu near the top of the room window (except for Launch Messenger) open browser windows to various Yahoo! locations. Home goes to the Yahoo! Games home page; Message Board surfs your browser to the relevant board in Yahoo! Messages (see Chapter 14); Feedback displays an e-mail form with which you can write to Yahoo!; and Help takes you to an explanation page of many of the features of Yahoo! Games. The Launch Messenger link opens Java Messenger, not the full-featured Messenger (see Chapter 15).

- ✔ Double-click a player's name to pop open an options window (see Figure 12-4). That little window tells you the player's game history and rating. You can also send an Instant Message to that person. Check the Ignore box if you don't want to receive an Instant Message from that person. The Ping button send a data pulse to that person's server and back to your server — sort of Internet radar. The Ping test is for determining how much delay exists between two network points. Why have the Ping test in Yahoo! Games? Because when playing timed games, it's important that there be a quick network connection between the two players. If the Ping test results in a delay of more than a few seconds, frustrating lags might slow a game with that person. The Profile button opens a browser window displaying that person's Yahoo! Profile.

You can get involved in a game in two ways: Join someone's table or create your own table. Both are accomplished in the room window. Click the Join button of any room that needs a player, or click the Create Table button in the left sidebar to establish a new game.

Creating your own table is the only way to set the game timer (if one exists for that game) and invite particular players to join you. The following list continues in the Checkers windows, but the steps are essentially the same for the other games:

1. **In the room window, click the Create Table button.**

   A game window opens (see Figure 12-5). In some games, a pop-up box asking for timing and other settings precedes the game window.

2. **Using the drop-down menu, select the Table Type.**

   Public tables may be joined by anyone who wants to play and watched by anyone who wants to observe a game in progress. Protected tables may be watched by anyone, but players can join only by invitation. Private tables are invisible to other members and can be joined or observed only by invitation.

3. **Click the Set Timer button to establish a time limit for games.**

   The default timer setting for checkers is unlimited time for the complete game, with a limit of five minutes per move. (It takes deep strategic thinking to ponder a checkers move for five minutes. Falling asleep helps, too.) Clicking the Set Timer button pops open a Set Timer window (see Figure 12-6). The Initial time setting is an overall time limit for a game. The Increment is the number of seconds added to each player's clock after every move. (Called a *Fisher clock* in chess, this timing feature prevents a quick-moving player from ever running out of time.) Use the check box to set a five-minute per-move deadline. After entering your settings, click the OK button.

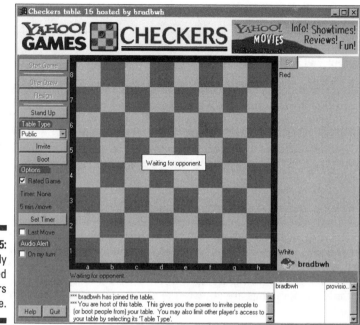

Figure 12-5:
A newly
created
Checkers
table.

4. **Check either or both audio alert boxes.**

   Actually, you can leave both boxes unchecked if you'd rather not be pestered by audio alerts. I find them convenient. You can get alerted when it's your turn or when your opponent has made a move.

5. **Use the Invite button to ask another player to your table.**

   A pop-up window appears with a list of players currently in the game room. As in the room window, you can sort the names by rank — just click the Rtng column header. If a player has a table number next to his or her name, that player might be engaged in a game. Click a player's name once and then click the Invite button. A pop-up window appears on that player's screen with an invitation to join you as well as Accept and Decline buttons.

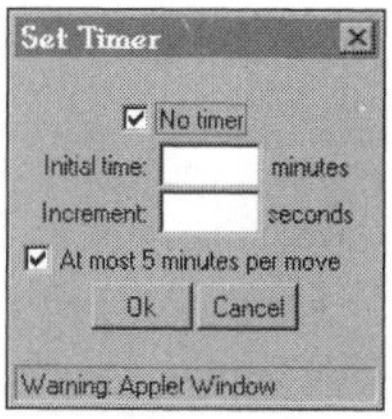

Figure 12-6:
The Set
Timer
window
places time
limits on
games.

6. **Click a Sit button to take your place at the table.**

   In checkers (and other board games) you get your choice of color. In multiplayer card games, you get your choice of position around the table. Click the Stand Up button to relinquish your place at the table.

The Boot button does not simulate your slamming a shoe on the table. It *does* give you the power to remove a player from your table. Click any player's name and click the Boot button to give that person the heave-ho. The expelled person receives a "You have been removed from the table" notice, and the game window disappears from that person's screen. Be careful! It's actually possible to boot yourself from your own table — an ego-bruising experience.

Throughout Yahoo! Games, you might see Ladder rooms. This new feature brings an element of competitiveness to the game rooms. Ladders are session rankings for people who want to see how they match against other players in the room. As you play games, Yahoo! moves you up and down the room ladder as you win and lose. It's a fun feature, especially if you plan to play several quick games during a single session. However, don't confuse Ladders with Rankings. Rankings are adjusted in all rooms and carry over from one session to another. Ladders exist only in marked rooms and apply to only a single session.

Feeling antisocial? Do you prefer solitary games? The Yahoo! Crossword (click the <u>Crossword</u> link on the Yahoo! Games home page) is a single-person game. Additionally, Hearts can be played against computerized opponents. From any Hearts room window, create a table with the Create Table button and invite three robots to play with you. Robots are identified as *~robot1, ~robot2,* and *~robot3.*

Scroll down the main games page to see more games you can play. Of particular interest is Baseball, which is a fantasy game based on statistics, in which you can join a league and let Yahoo! manage all the statistical accounting and bookkeeping for you.

Part IV

Meeting the
Yahoo! Community

The 5th Wave   **By Rich Tennant**

"No, Thomas Jefferson never did 'the Grind;' however, this does show how animation can be used to illustrate American history on the Web."

In this part . . .

Yahoo! is partly about information, partly about service, and partly about community. Part IV describes how to meet people and the best ways of staying in touch with them. Yahoo! Chat is a thriving real-time network of chat rooms, closely tied to Yahoo! Messenger, and both services get their own chapter here. The message boards are explained in Chapter 14, and another chapter walks you through creating and joining a Yahoo! Club. Finally, Chapter 17 shows you how to search for people by e-mail address or phone number.

Chapter 13

Introducing Yourself to Yahoo! Chat

In This Chapter

▶ Navigating the Yahoo! Chat home page

▶ Chatting the basic way with HTML

▶ Enhanced chatting with Java

▶ Finding rooms and creating rooms

*C*hatting has been on the cyberspace activity list for many years — since long before the Web was around. Online services such as CompuServe, America Online, and Prodigy provided virtual meeting rooms where people could talk through their keyboards in real time. Those early rooms were a nice alternative to discussions on message boards, which tend to be more literate, but also much more prolonged. Those ancient chat rooms, however, didn't have nearly the range of features found in modern virtual rooms. Besides, only members of the online service could use them. With Yahoo! Chat, anyone from the entire Internet population can easily join the party.

And what a party it is! People gather to talk about almost everything under the sun, and you can create your own chat room for special gatherings. Yahoo! makes it easy to see which of your online friends (as defined in Yahoo! Messenger — see Chapter 15) are currently chatting and also to view the Yahoo! Profile of any member in any room you enter. (Profiles are described in Chapter 1. My intent is to keep you flipping through the book until you're dizzy.)

Yahoo! Chat is an incredible way to meet people, and this chapter explains all the features that are at your command.

If chatting has a major downside, it's identity confusion. Almost everyone uses a chatting alias (or three or four), and you never have a guarantee that chatting partners bear any resemblance to the person they say they are. To put it plainly, men sometimes pretend to be women, and vice versa. People can pretend about their age when asked. Online identity can be slippery. Chat-room scandals that spill into the offline world are highly publicized, but it should be remembered that scandals are exceptions, not the rule. If you proceed with sensible caution, there's no reason not to make good, honest, and fun connections in public and private chat rooms.

Internet users must have a Java-compatible browser to use the Java Yahoo! Chat program. Earlier versions of browsers without Java implementation can use the HTML chatting program. (I describe the differences between the two and how to access both later in this chapter.) America Online members who are using the AOL browser must have Version 3.0 or later of the AOL program. WebTV users cannot use the Java version of Yahoo! Chat at all and must settle for the HTML program.

Yahoo! Chat Home Page

Yahoo! Chat is available to anyone with a Yahoo! ID (see Chapter 1). The place to begin your chatting experience is the Yahoo! Chat home page, which serves as a combination room menu and event guide. (See Figure 13-1.) Get there by clicking the Chat link on the Yahoo! home page or go directly to this URL:

```
chat.yahoo.com
```

Near the top of the Chat home page is a starter menu of chatting channel links, each leading to a selection of rooms. These rooms represent the very tip of the iceberg. It's a way to get started, but once inside the Yahoo! Chat empire you have your choice of hundreds of rooms, some of them created by other users. And you can make your own room.

Beneath the channel links are the imminent Live Events and ongoing Featured Rooms, which change depending on the time of day and what's going on in the news. The Featured Rooms are always open and set to automatically generate extra spillover rooms to handle large numbers of chatters. So when you select one of those rooms (StockWatch, for example) and enter the chat area, you might be deposited in the third version of the StockWatch room (StockWatch:3). From there you can navigate to other rooms, as I explain later in this chapter.

If you want to see a complete list of Yahoo! Chat rooms, click the Complete Room List link on the home page (scroll down if necessary to see the link). The entire list provides a good way to gain a quick overview of permanent chat rooms. User rooms, however, aren't on this list. User rooms provide some of the most interesting (and less crowded) chatting experiences on Yahoo!, so if you want to sample them, follow the procedure I describe later in this chapter.

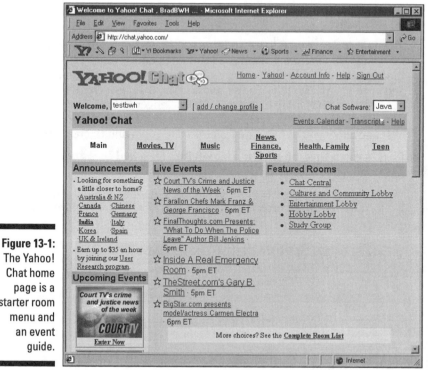

Figure 13-1:
The Yahoo!
Chat home
page is a
starter room
menu and
an event
guide.

The Live Events section of the home page advertises upcoming celebrity chats. Celebrity chats are a different and less social experience than free-for-all personal chatting. Still fun, though, in their own way. These formal chats are moderated, and the software controls who can speak at any moment.

Time to get started! Here's what to do first:

1. **On the Yahoo! Chat home page, use the upper drop-down menu to select a Yahoo! ID.**

   This menu contains all your IDs, if you have created more than one. Frankly, it's a good idea to have an ID (or two) just for chatting. Because everyone's ID is the changeable part of a Yahoo! e-mail address, it's a simple matter for anyone to roam through the chat area collecting e-mail addresses. If you chat often enough, you're bound to get some spam. Why not isolate it in its own e-mail box? Furthermore, it makes sense to create a Yahoo! Profile for your chatting ID that contains absolutely no personal information. Click the add/change profile link to do this, and refer to Chapter 1 for details about the Profile process.

2. **Use the Chat Software drop-down menu to choose Java chatting or HTML chatting.**

   The default selection is Java, and this is the best bet for anyone using a fairly modern computer, Windows 95 or later, and Version 3.0 or later of the Explorer or Navigator browsers. The next sections explain the pros and cons of each system. The simple story is that Java chatting is smoother and has more features but takes longer to load into your computer and occasionally crashes. Both methods have the same rooms available and allow you to navigate from room to room and to create rooms.

3. **Click a room link, or click a channel link followed by a room link.**

   Start anywhere you want. You can move around once you get inside. If you click a room from the more extensive Complete Room List, you're logged into the Java version of Yahoo! Chat, as shown in Figure 13-2.

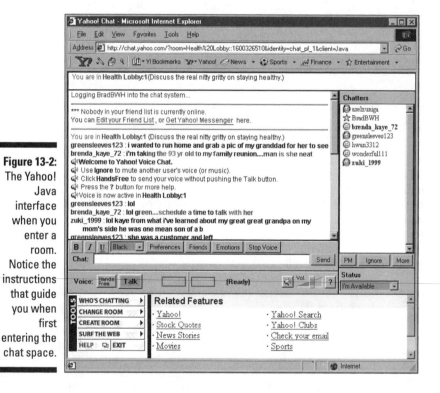

Figure 13-2:
The Yahoo!
Java
interface
when you
enter a
room.
Notice the
instructions
that guide
you when
first
entering the
chat space.

After you're in a chat room, you may stick around there and meet people or roam around the Yahoo! Chat landscape looking for the perfect room. The next two sections detail the features of HTML and Java chatting. The section after that explains how to find other rooms in either program.

Chatting and Messenger — joined at the hip

While you're using the Java chat program, Yahoo! Chat is closely integrated with Yahoo! Messenger (see Chapter 15). When you first enter a chat room in Java, the screen tells you which of your Messenger friends are currently online. They can also see you come online if their pagers are active, just as if you had booted up your Messenger instead of logging into a chat room. Don't be surprised if a message from one of those friends pops up in a separate window. By the same token, you can talk with any friend by clicking that ID and typing in the window that appears.

Down to Basics with HTML Chat

On the Internet at large, HTML chatting is generally considered to be primitive compared to Java chatting, but the HTML Yahoo! Chat program is pretty good. The biggest difference between HTML chatting and Java chatting lies in how smoothly the chatting streams onto your screen. With Java chat, the discussions flow seamlessly onto your main chat window. With HTML chat, the window must be updated (called *refreshing*) to see new lines of talk. The HTML program refreshes the window automatically every twenty seconds or so (and whenever you send a line of chat into the room). You can also click a Refresh button if you want more frequent updates. (Figure 13-3 shows an HTML chat room in action.)

HTML Yahoo! Chat has fewer features than the Java version but loads a little faster every time you enter a room and is more stable. (That means it doesn't crash your browser, which the Java chat program might do every once in a while.) Both chatting systems access the same rooms. The HTML program, however, doesn't hook into the Yahoo! Messenger the way the Java program does. (See the next section for details on that snazzy feature.)

When entering the chat space in HTML, you must reaffirm your HTML choice with the drop-down menu at every Web page displayed before you enter a room. Java is always the default chatting mode, even if you selected HTML on the preceding page. After you're in a chat room, your experience remains in the HTML realm without any action from you.

If no chatting appears on your screen for several seconds after entering an HTML chat room, just click the Send/Refresh button and the chat should appear. Or, if you don't feel like reaching for the mouse, just wait about twenty seconds for the automatic refresh.

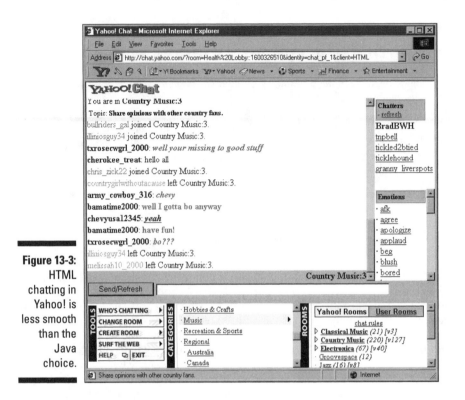

Figure 13-3:
HTML
chatting in
Yahoo! is
less smooth
than the
Java
choice.

You can participate in HTML chatting by typing a line in the text-entry field and then clicking the Send/Refresh button. (Using your keyboard's Enter key sends the line into the room also and is more convenient than clicking the on-screen button.)

Going Upscale with Java Chat

Yahoo!'s Java chat interface presents comfy rooms with lots of features. Chatting in this environment is sort of like visiting a friend's great apartment — the bar is stocked and he or she has a new home theater system. Improvements have been steady and productive for the past few years, and now Yahoo! can be proud of one of the slickest, most entertaining and workable text-chatting atmospheres on the Net. And integrated into the text environment is voice chatting. Figure 13-2 shows a Java chat room in action. You might want to refer to it as I describe the features, or even log onto a room online and follow along that way.

Participating in a Java chat room is as easy as typing a line in the Chat text-entry field and pressing the Enter key. (You can also use the on-screen Send

Decisions, decisions — HTML or Java?

You might think that Yahoo! is creating unnecessary confusion by providing two chat interfaces, HTML and Java. Especially because Yahoo! itself seems to want you to use the Java interface — in the drop-down selection menu on the home page, Java is the default choice.

So what gives? Why would anyone use the HTML version of Yahoo! Chat? Why is it even there?

In fact, there are good reasons to choose HTML chatting sometimes — and for some people, all the time. In particular, older Web browsers and computers can't accept Java *applets* (small programs written in the Java language), so people using older systems should definitely try HTML if Java chatting isn't working. That situation alone justifies the presence of the HTML system because it means no one is excluded from the popular chat realm of Yahoo!.

Under normal conditions, with a fairly modern computer, most people probably should choose Java chatting. Java is easier, smoother, and has more features.

If you fit into any of the following situations, however, HTML is preferable:

✔ If you use Windows 3.1 with any browser.

✔ If you use a Macintosh computer to run Internet Explorer or a version of Navigator before Version 3.0.

✔ If you access the Internet through WebTV.

✔ If you use an America Online version before Version 3.0 to access the Internet (probably on Windows 3.1).

✔ If you are accessing the Internet from behind a firewall, as is often the case with corporate office connections. (By the way, it's time to stop chatting and get back to work.)

✔ If you have many Yahoo! Messenger friends and want to avoid the distraction of being paged while chatting.

Fortunately for most people, it's easy to try both HTML and Java chatting. Whichever you're using, click the EXIT button to leave the chat room, and then enter the chatting area again from the Yahoo! Chat home page after selecting the other method from the drop-down menu.

Very few people choose HTML chatting over Java if they have a choice. HTML has no voice chatting; the features for meeting people are limited; and the manual refresh of the screen is a nuisance. If you're running a reasonably modern computer, go for the Java.

button, but it's less convenient when you're chatting quickly and sending many lines.) Later in this section, I describe features that change how your text lines appear in the public room.

Going private in Java

To the right of the main chat window is a narrower Chatters window that lists everyone in the room. Beneath the Chatters window are three buttons: PM (Private Message), Ignore, and More. Those buttons, together with a few other options, let you control and direct the flow of chatter and learn more about your fellow chatters.

Probably the most used function in the Chatters window is the Private Message button, which enables personal, side-of-the-room talking. You can engage in as many simultaneous private chats as you like. This type of interaction is extremely popular in Yahoo!. It's not too unusual to enter a room with 15 people in it and see nothing whatsoever in the main chat window — everyone is talking privately, and the PM windows are flying around behind the scenes.

It's perfectly acceptable to approach strangers with private greetings — but be polite. And remember that no one is obligated to talk with anyone else. If you don't receive a response to a private overture (fairly common), don't be offended and don't persist unless you know the person. A silent person might be busy, or have his or her hands full with other windows or might not understand Yahoo! Chat features well enough to reply. Just find someone else. The most sensible approach is to chat publicly for a while; you'll find a natural opportunity to extend a conversation in private mode.

To begin a private chat, just proceed as follows:

1. **In the Chatters window, click any name.**

2. **With that name highlighted, click the PM button beneath the Chatters window.**

   A small PM window pops open, as shown in Figure 13-4. You may also pop that window open by double-clicking any name in the Chatters window.

Figure 13-4: The Private Message (PM) window.

3. **In the text-entry form near the bottom of the window, type a message.**

   You may type as long a message as you want, but it's polite to keep it very brief.

4. **Click the Send button or use the Enter key on your keyboard.**

   Sending the message causes an identical window to pop open on the recipient's screen, with your words in the main, central portion. Your PM window stays open, with your words appearing in the main portion. If the person responds, the incoming line appears beneath your line, and you have a conversation going.

After you've established that private connection, it's an independent, autonomous stream of chatting. By that I mean the PM window stays open even if you move to another chat room. You may continue your private conversation as you move from room to room, for as long as you stay within Java chat.

Many people refer to the Personal Message (PM) window as the IM window and talk about private chatting as IM'ing. IM is a near-universal abbreviation for Instant Messaging, which is what private chatting is usually called.

More people things

Stay on that Chatters window because you can do more with it. First, note one cool feature that appears when you run your mouse cursor over the names in the Chatters window (don't click, just position the cursor over a name). A small pop-up message indicates how long, in minutes and seconds, that person has been idle — in other words, how long since that person typed anything in the main chat window. Also, if that person has changed his or her status (see the following section), that info appears.

The preceding section describes how to talk privately with a fellow chatter. A menu of options relate to other people in a chat room. Try this:

1. **In the Chatters window, click any name.**

   The name becomes highlighted. Be careful not to double-click — that just opens up a Private Message window.

2. **Click the More button below the Chatters window.**

   The Select Action window pops open, as shown in Figure 13-5. You can also make it appear by right-clicking any name in the Chatters window.

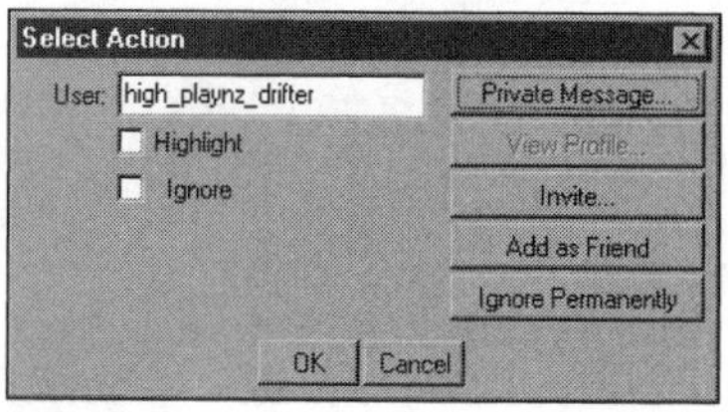

Figure 13-5:
The Select Action panel lets you find out about another chatter, or contact that person.

Select Action

User: high_playnz_drifter   Private Message...

☐ Highlight   View Profile...

☐ Ignore   Invite...

Add as Friend

Ignore Permanently

OK   Cancel

Here's what you can do with that Select Action window:

- **Click the Private Message button.** This is the third of three ways to open a Private Message window (see the preceding section).

- **Click the View Profile button.** This button opens a browser window that displays the Yahoo! Profile (see Chapter 1) for the selected ID.

- **Click the Invite button.** This function is unrelated to the name you've highlighted. The Invite button sends an on-screen invitation to another Yahoo! member to join you in your current chat room. Needless to say, all the names in the Chatters list *are already* in your current chat room, so the button might seem pointless. However, you may change the ID that appears in the Select Action window, substituting the ID of an acquaintance who isn't in the room. (Invites appear on the other person's screen as small windows with Yes and No buttons.)

- **Click the Add as Friend button.** This action places the currently selected ID in your Chat Friends list. If you don't have a group of friends called Chat Friends, Yahoo! automatically creates one for you. This way, new additions aren't mixed in with other Groups you might have already created. (See Chapter 15 for details about creating lists and Groups of Friends through Yahoo! Messenger.)

- **Check the Highlight box.** When the Highlight box is checked, the selected person's contributions to the main chat window are highlighted in bold type, on your screen only.

- **Check the Ignore box.** When the Ignore box is checked, the selected person's contributions to the main chat window do not appear on your screen (and your screen only).

- **Click the Ignore Permanently button.** Use this selection to place somebody's screen name on a permanent Ignore list for your ID. Then, whenever you use Yahoo! Chat with that ID, the ignored person's chat will never appear on your screen. This is a good option to use for chronic disrupters who prowls around spewing garbage into chat rooms. (Yes, such people exist and seem to take pleasure from that behavior.) If you make a point to throw those names onto your Ignore Permanently list, over time you can clean up your chat experience.

If you've checked either Highlight or Ignore (they can both be checked, but that's pointless because they conflict), click the OK button to put the changes in action.

You can do a quick Ignore on someone by using the Ignore button below the Chatters window. Just highlight a name and click the Ignore button. From then on, the Ignore button becomes an Ignore Off button when that person's ID is highlighted, so you can admit the person's chat back to your screen at any time.

Where are you?

In Figure 13-2, check out the Status menu below the Chatters window. The Status options are in a drop-down menu; when you select one, your chosen status appears once in the main chat window. These messages provide some preset explanations as to why you're being rude and not talking in the chat room. They are hooked into Yahoo! Messenger, and some are more appropriate to Messenger interaction than chat room socializing. However, the Be Right Back and On The Phone selections are good to use when your chat session is interrupted — in an environment where no one can see anyone else, it's polite to explain extended silences.

Just click once on any option in the drop-down Status menu and your status appears (once) in the main chat window, next to your name. Because chat text is continually scrolling upward, you might want to repeat the action if your phone call (or whatever) lasts a while. Note that your status also appears when you run your mouse cursor over your ID in the Chatters window.

Your status automatically reverts to I'm Available when you type anything into the main chat space.

Color your words

Yahoo! chat rooms are colorful places, mostly because any participant can distinguish his or her text lines by using colors and altered typefaces. Look at Figure 13-4 again and note the left-hand options above the Chat text-entry field. If you use a word processor, these items might be familiar. You can use them to change the appearance of your text in the main chat window. Here's how:

- ✔ Use the **B** button to make your words appear in **bold type.**
- ✔ Use the *I* button to make your words appear in *italics.*
- ✔ Use the <u>U</u> button to make your words appear <u>underlined</u>.
- ✔ Use the drop-down color menu to select a color for your words.

These selections are not only fun but also useful because they distinguish your "appearance" in the main chat window from everyone else's. Because multiple conversations are usually going on at once, it helps when the person you're talking to has a distinctive look.

One thing you don't want to do in a chat room (or on a message board, for that matter) is use all capital letters. In cyberspace, all caps LOOKS LIKE SHOUTING! From time to time, everyone accidentally presses the Caps Lock key of the keyboard; when that happens to you, you'll probably get a polite reminder to lower your voice. Heed the reminder and press the Caps Lock key again to turn them off before people start shouting back at you. Another piece of chat protocol to remember: Use the underline feature only occasionally, for emphasis.

Customizing the chat room

A number of options are available for adjusting what the main chat window looks like. These options are invaluable in creating a better chat experience and well worth finding out about. See the Preferences button above the text-entry field? That's where these features reside. Click it to open the Preferences window (see Figure 13-6), where you find these choices:

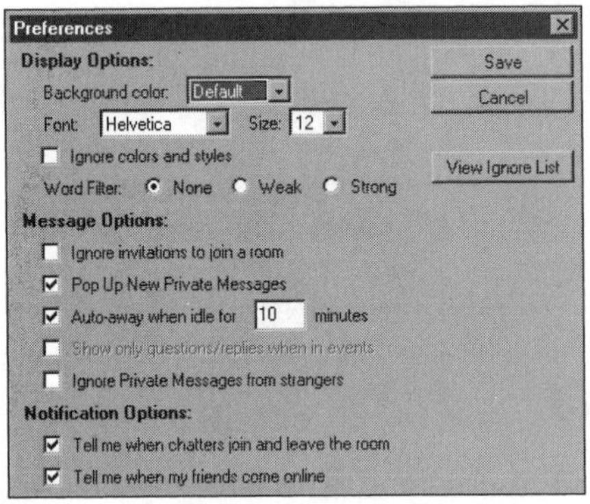

Figure 13-6: The Preferences window, where you can change the way chatting appears on your screen.

- ✔ **Font** and **Size.** This is where you set the typeface and font size of all the lines scrolling up the main chat window. Don't confuse this with the color, bold, italic, and underline setting for *your* lines, as described in the preceding section. Use Display Options for selecting the typeface and font size for *everyone's* words. Individual choices about color, boldness, italics, and underlining will still appear on your screen. If you prefer large type, choose a larger Size from the drop-down menu. If you prefer squeezing as much chat as possible in the window, choose a smaller font size.

- ✔ **Background color.** This selection defines the color against which all chatting appears. The background color appears only in the main chatting window, not in the entire browser window.

- ✔ **Ignore colors and styles.** Check this box to make everyone's text look the same in the main chat window. Your selected Display Options still have effect.

- ✔ **Word Filter.** Yahoo! maintains a database of words generally considered obscene or offensive. Yahoo! doesn't divulge the contents of its lists, but you can apply a general filter to words by selecting Weak or Strong. Use None if your language sensibility is robust.

✔ **Ignore invitations to join a room.** Checking this box suppresses pop-up invitations. Anyone inviting you receives a message that you're not accepting invitations.

✔ **Pop Up New Private Messages.** If you don't want to miss any whispers from fellow chatters, check this box to ensure that new Private Message windows are displayed on top of your chat window, where you can't miss them.

✔ **Auto-away when idle.** You may select this to make your status change if you don't say anything for a while. This feature is good for talkative chatters and not so good for people who like to listen quietly. Verbose chatters can leave their computers for a few minutes without having to remember to manually change their status. Silent types, however, will find their status unexpectedly changing even while they're happily (and demurely) watching the action — and may not receive any Private Messages if Auto-away kicks in.

✔ **Tell me when chatters join and leave the room.** This option is checked by default, but you might uncheck it when visiting high-traffic rooms. Busy rooms with lots of talk and plenty of people coming and going are hard to keep up with when the screen fills up with notices of arrivals and departures. Sometimes, the text can scroll so quickly upward to accommodate the chatter and the notices that it's hard to read. Slow things down and clear away the clutter by getting rid of the announcements.

✔ **Tell me when my friends come online.** This is a nice feature if you're waiting for someone in your Friends list to log on.

Keeping track of friends

Yahoo! has a buddy system called Friends that links people through the Yahoo! Messenger (see Chapter 1). Because the Messenger and Yahoo! Chat are an integrated set of features, your Friends can find you in the chat realm

---

Jazzing up Yahoo! Chat

If you spend some time in Yahoo! chat rooms, you can't help noticing that some people have jazzier text colors than most folks. In most cases, they're using CheetaChat, a free program that interfaces with Yahoo! Chat and adds new features. The most common identifying feature of a CheetaChat user is rainbow text that fades from one color to another, letter by letter. The program includes an integrated Web browser, customizable chat-room interface, file-sharing tools, and various other perks. CheetaChat can be downloaded free of charge; there is never a shareware fee. You can learn more at the CheetaChat site, located at the following URL:

www.cheetachat.com

even if they are using only the Messenger, and you can likewise contact them from either program. The only requirement is that both sides of the conversation be logged into *either* Yahoo! Messenger *or* Yahoo! Chat.

When you're in a Java chat room, you can adjust your Friends list and access your Friends by using the Friends button just above the text-entry field. Clicking it displays a message in the main chat window, notifying you who among your designated Friends is online (through Chat or Messenger) and linking you to your Friends list. You can do two things at this point:

- Click the ID of any friend who is online to open a Private Message window and talk to that person. Your friend need not be in the chat room with you or even in Yahoo! Chat — but if your friend isn't in Yahoo! Chat, he or she must be using Yahoo! Messenger. (That person's name wouldn't appear if he or she weren't available for a private chat.)

- Click the Edit your Friend List link to open a new browser window showing your groups of friends. Whatever adjustments you make on this page are saved for your Messenger settings and your Chat settings.

Emoting, Java style

The same range of emotional declarations is available in Java chat as in HTML chat. Just click the Emotions button above the text-entry field to pop open a windowed list of all options. You must double-click any emotion to display it in the main chat window, but that's all you need to do. No typing is required.

Voice chatting

Beneath the Chat text-entry field is the Voice bar, containing controls for chatting audibly with other participants in the room. You need speakers attached to your computer to hear voice chats emanating from the room you're in, and you need an attached microphone or headset to put your own voice into the space.

Voice chatting transpires simultaneously with, an independent of, text chatting. The voices you hear do not correspond to the text chats you see in the room, and you can be saying one thing into your microphone while typing something else into the chat window. (Assuming you're remarkably coordinated.)

Voice chatting works essentially the same way as it does in Yahoo! Messenger (see Chapter 15). Only one person in any room can talk at any moment. Click and hold the Talk button when you want to say something. Alternately, you can click the Hands Free button, and the Talk button activates whenever you say anything (as long as no one else is talking). The Hands Free button is best used when background noise around you is minimal; otherwise, the Talk button could be activated unintentionally, preventing others in the room from talking.

Voice chatting can be an unnerving feature. There you are during a quiet evening, text-chatting away, when suddenly a voice speaks as if someone were in the room. I've been startled many a time by this feature. Fortunately, there are ways to turn it off when you want to stick to text only. To the right of the Voice bar is a small box with a speaker pictured in it; click that to mute the sound of voice chatting in the room. You can also click the Stop Voice button above the Voice bar to disable the feature entirely; the entire Voice bar disappears.

Tools of the Chat Trade

Beneath the main chat window in both the HTML and Java rooms is a TOOLS box with several buttons that help you navigate among rooms and people. These buttons work identically in both chat systems, so I've grouped the explanation about them in this section.

Finding individual chatters

You can search for, or browse among, all Yahoo! IDs currently chatting in all the rooms. Just follow these steps:

1. **In the bottom-left panel, click the WHO'S CHATTING button.**

2. **Click a letter in the displayed alphabet. Or type a Yahoo! ID in the search-entry form and then click the Search button.**

   Going the alphabet route lets you browse among all current chatters, as shown in Figure 13-7. This option has little point unless you don't quite remember a person's ID but do remember its first letter. Otherwise, you're rummaging through a gigantic list of screen aliases. Use the search-entry form if you know a person's ID and want to see whether he or she is chatting.

3. **In the list of names, click a name, the GOTO link, or the INVITE link.**

   Clicking a name opens a new browser window and shows you that person's Yahoo! Profile. The GOTO link shifts you into the chat room that person is currently occupying. The INVITE link sends an invitation to join your current room. It could be a room you created or any room at all. In

HTML chat, the invitation appears on the person's main chat screen with a <u>Yes</u> link that, if clicked, shifts that person into your room. In Java chat, the invitation appears as a pop-up box with Yes and No buttons.

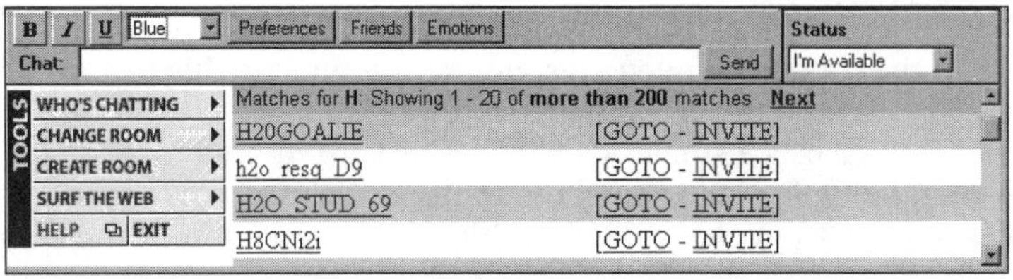

Figure 13-7:
Browsing among current chatters, below the main chat window.

After you get into the same room with someone (either that person's current room through GOTO or your own through an accepted INVITE), you may pursue further conversation on the main chat screen or with a private message.

Finding new rooms

Chat room surfing is just as much fun as Web surfing. Yahoo! has what you might call house rooms, provided by the service and always open, and User Rooms, which anyone can create.

You can't search for a room by name, unfortunately, but you may browse among all created rooms:

1. In the bottom panel, click the CHANGE ROOM button.

The CATEGORIES window appears.

2. Click any category.

The ROOMS window appears.

3. Select either Yahoo! Rooms or User Rooms.

Unsurprisingly, Yahoo! rooms are created by the service and remain open all the time. (See Figure 13-8.) Any room on this list might overflow into replicated rooms if there's a big crowd. User rooms are temporary (and don't overflow), but any that appear on the list are currently open. User rooms are often more interesting than Yahoo! rooms, are less crowded, and are dedicated to quirkier topics.

4. **In the ROOMS window, click any room.**

You're automatically shifted into that room and your Chatters list changes to list the people in that room.

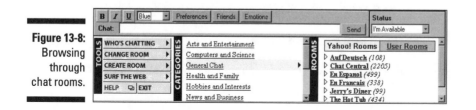

Figure 13-8:
Browsing through chat rooms.

In the ROOMS window, individual rooms are listed by order of popularity, with the busiest rooms at the top of the list. This is good to remember, because if you specifically want a more intimate chat in a less crowded room, you should scroll down toward the bottom of the list.

In the CATEGORIES window, you might notice an <u>Adult</u> link. That's where the sex-oriented rooms are stored. There's no getting around it — explicit sex is one of the most popular topics in Yahoo! Chat. Clicking the <u>Adult</u> link displays a warning and states the age requirement of 18 years or older to enter the area. However, there is no software block or verification routine in place to stop someone of any age from entering. So, parents, beware.

When you enter the Adult Chat area, the function of the CHANGE ROOM button changes. The CATEGORIES window is eliminated and the whole lower panel is dedicated to the Adult Chat category. The extra space is used to display Yahoo! Rooms and User Rooms at the same time.

Making your own space

Throwing together your own room is uniquely satisfying and a good way to provide a space into which you can invite others. Here's how to get started:

1. **In the bottom panel, click the CREATE ROOM button.**

2. **In the CREATE ROOM window, type a room name and a welcome message.**

It's a good idea to keep the room name fairly short, or it won't fit well in the User Rooms list. (Three or four words usually fit without trouble.) The welcome message appears in the main chat window when people enter your room.

3. **Select whether your room will be Public, Private, or Secured.**

   Public rooms are open to anyone to enter at any time. Private rooms are not listed in the User Rooms list, but people can still enter them by using the <u>GOTO</u> link next to anyone who is in your private room. Secured rooms also do not appear in the User Rooms list, and no one can enter them unless you invite them with the Invite feature.

4. **Click the Create my room button.**

Many people create rooms that, over time, become regular hangouts for groups of virtual friends. It's worth a try.

Chapter 14

The Thread of Discussion: Yahoo! Message Boards

Message boards have a curious but profound appeal. I have a long-standing affection for them, because message-board communities were the first aspect of cyberspace I became addicted to, in the pre-Web online services. A good messaging community provides a unique forum for human acquaintance in a few ways:

✔ Message board discussions transpire outside real time. You might post a message during your lunch hour, which someone might reply to while you're in an afternoon meeting. A few more people might chip in while you're commuting home, and by the time you log on in the evening, you have five messages to reply to. Yet the cumulative effect somehow blends together into a coherent, flowing discussion.

✔ Friendships on message boards develop independent of physical proximity and time-zone differences. As a result, you might find yourself meeting people from all over the world, as if they were neighbors. Message boards emphasize that everyone is a neighbor in cyberspace.

✔ Message-board discussions tend to be deeper than chat-room discussions.

✔ Getting to know someone in a message discussion eliminates the physical clues by which we tend to judge each other in person. On the board, people get to know each other from the inside out. Ideas and their articulation become paramount.

A totally satisfying message board community is ideal, but of course your actual experience might vary. There is as much variety in the quality of message boards as there is with chat rooms. And since Yahoo! is so large and international, its boards encompass the full range of possibility: the good, the bad, and the ugly.

Yahoo! message boards are popular. As I describe in this chapter, the underlying software that manages message *threads* is not as advanced in Yahoo! as in some other discussion forums. However, the simple interface keeps pages moving quickly, which is important when you're reading lots of messages, each on its own page. This chapter explains how the boards work for those who prefer to read only and then for those who want to post a message or create a new thread topic.

Getting in the Fray

Yahoo! Message Boards is organized in typical directory style — similarly to the Yahoo! directory, as you might expect. Instead of directory pages to Web sites, browsing yields directory pages to Yahoo!-created message boards with user-created message topics on them.

Browsing for a discussion

The place to start is the Yahoo! Message Boards home page, which is shown in Figure 14-1. Click the <u>Message Boards</u> link near the bottom of the Yahoo! home page or go directly to the message section with this URL:

```
messages.yahoo.com
```

The main part of the Message Boards home page is the Categories directory, which contains links to every message board in Yahoo! and every discussion thread on those boards. The following steps drill into the Health section of the directory, by way of illustrating how it is designed:

1. **On the Yahoo! Message Boards home page, click the <u>Health & Wellness</u> directory category.**

   The Health & Wellness directory page appears, as shown in Figure 14-2. This is a second-level directory page and includes both subtopics in the Health & Wellness category and, below the subtopics, specific message boards. Clicking a subtopic drills you deeper into the directory, and the third-level pages usually include nothing but specific message boards, with no further subtopics. Specific message boards are subtopical in nature, and lead to discussion threads called Topics. Follow on to the next step.

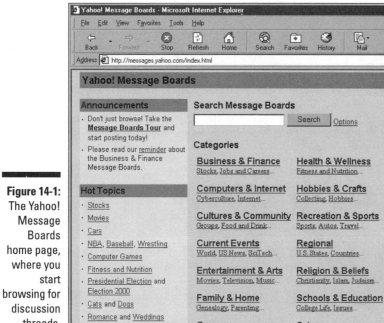

Figure 14-1:
The Yahoo!
Message
Boards
home page,
where you
start
browsing for
discussion
threads.

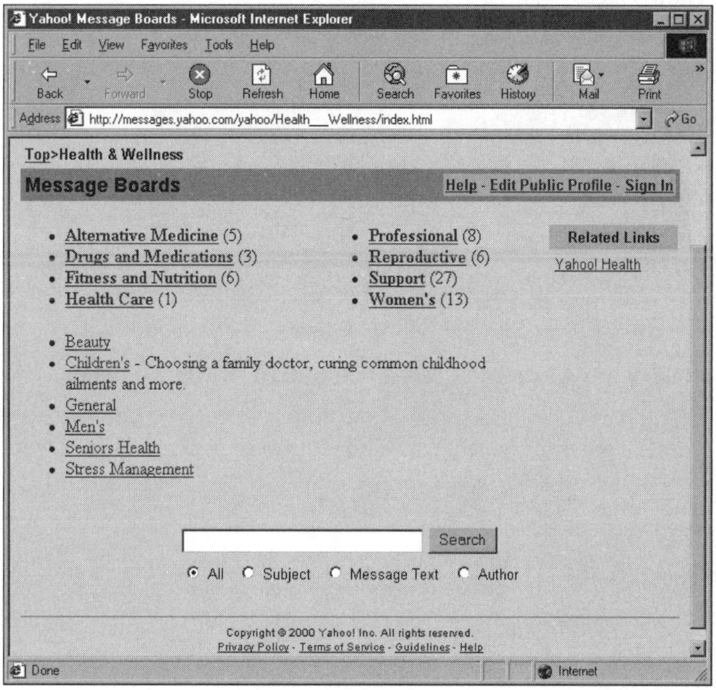

Figure 14-2:
Click a
subtopic (on
top) or
message
board
(below).

2. Click any message board link (<u>Children's</u> for this example).

The Children's message boards page appears, as shown in Figure 14-3. Note that discussions are listed chronologically, with the discussion that has the most recent message contribution placed on top (as you can see in the Last Post column of dates). You can switch the view by clicking the <u>Msgs</u> link to see the discussions ordered by how many messages they contain, with the most popular discussion atop the list. Likewise, click the <u>Topic</u> header to arrange the discussions alphabetically. The alphabetical list is useful if you're trying to locate a particular topic you've seen before.

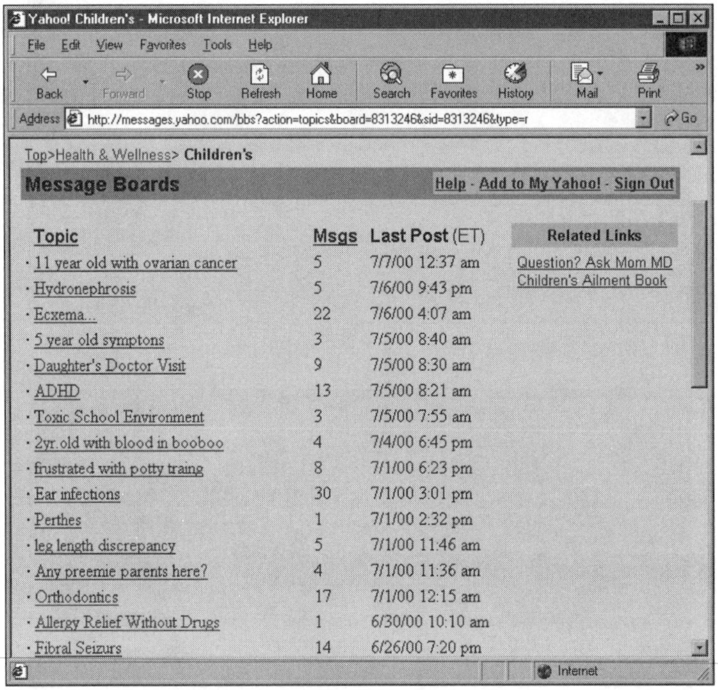

Figure 14-3: On this page, you can arrange the list of discussions in three ways by clicking the column headings.

3. Click any discussion thread (topic) to see its messages.

The message page appears, as shown in Figure 14-4. You get the thread's initial message plus a list of subsequent messages listed from most recent to oldest.

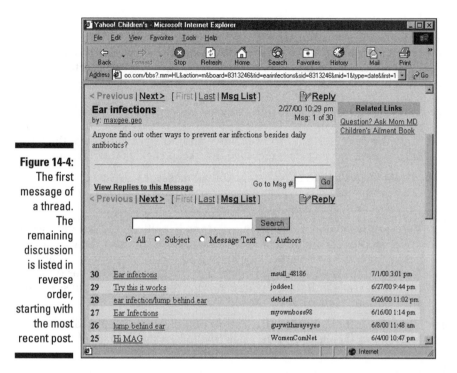

Figure 14-4:
The first
message of
a thread.
The
remaining
discussion
is listed in
reverse
order,
starting with
the most
recent post.

4. **Read the original message of the thread, reply to it, browse other messages in the thread, or search the message board by keyword.**

   I explain replying to messages and creating original messages (new threads) later in this chapter. In Figure 14-4, notice that the thread, which at the time of this screen shot contained thirty messages, lists those messages in reverse order — most recent first, from number 30 backwards.

All the navigation options (Previous, Next, First, Last, Msg List) are available when viewing any message in any discussion thread — not only when viewing the originating message, as in Figure 14-4. In that illustration, you can see that Previous and First are grayed out and unavailable as links because you are viewing the thread's first message.

Navigating a message thread

Unlike Usenet newsgroup readers such as Outlook Express and Netscape Messenger, Yahoo! Message Boards does not use a *graphical threading* system. Dedicated messaging programs like those two can arrange discussion threads using indents to show visually which message are responses to which other messages. Such a system is convenient because you can tell at a glance how the discussion is flowing and who is responding to whom. Other well-known and popular message-board systems, including Yahoo!'s, work more like a traditional cork message board, on which everyone posts messages and hopes for the best. Yahoo! Message Boards provides certain features that help you make sense of the message thread structure.

The following options are available on every message page:

- ✔ **View the next message.** You can move chronologically through the message thread, viewing each message. Just keep clicking the <u>Next</u> link.

- ✔ **List messages in order.** Normally, thread messages are listed in reverse order, with more recent postings near the top. You can see a chronological list of messages by clicking the <u>Msg List</u> link.

- ✔ **View replies to any message.** In any thread, multiple discussions spring up as people respond to different messages. You can sort the various conversations by using the <u>View Replies to this Message</u> link. (If the link is not present beneath any message, that's because nobody has replied to that message or because you're viewing the thread's first message, to which *all* subsequent posts are replies.)

- ✔ **View the author's profile.** The author of the message is linked immediately below the message title. Click that link to see the Yahoo! profile for that ID.

- ✔ **Reply to the message.** Using the <u>Reply</u> link gets you started on a reply to the message. I discuss replying to and creating message threads later in this chapter.

Following discussion threads is all the trickier in Yahoo! because a response does not necessarily have the same message title as the original message. (Big mistake in my opinion. But did Yahoo! ask for my advice when designing this software? Nooo.) In fact, because the Reply feature asks for a title rather than supplying the original title, in most cases responses *are* titled differently. For this reason, using the <u>View Replies to this Message</u> link often really helps you follow along.

Message boards can be just as unruly as chat rooms. In fact, I've noticed much more hostility in Yahoo! Message Boards than in Yahoo! Chat. You're more likely to run into sexual language and erotic flirting in a chat room, but the boards are full of irascibility over the most trivial subjects. You might have trouble believing (but I hope are at least somewhat entertained by) the level of ire vented on the message boards when people argue over a new movie. If you feel moved to report outright abuse, racism, or some other socially unacceptable message-board behavior to Yahoo!, use the following URL:

```
add.yahoo.com/fast/help/mb/cgi_feedback
```

Cut to the chase

Browsing is a good way to get acquainted with the overall scope of Yahoo!
Message Boards, but when it comes to finding a specific topic, thank good-
ness for search engines. The Yahoo! search engine is woven throughout the
Yahoo! Message Boards sections and is accessible from virtually any page
you're on.

Message searching works similarly to directory searching (see Chapter 7).
You type one or more keywords, and the search engine returns matches that
lead to message boards or individual messages or both.

You may begin a message search from any part of Yahoo! Message Boards.
For illustration, the following steps walk you through a search beginning on
the Yahoo! Message Boards home page.

1. **On the Yahoo! Message Boards home page (refer to Figure 14-1), type
   one or more keywords into the search field above the directory
   categories.**

2. **Click the Search button.**

The search engine looks for matches to your keyword(s) in message titles,
author IDs, and message texts. Because the engine doesn't automatically
treat multiple keywords as an unbreakable phrase, and because matches can
occur in the text, title, or author ID, you might get more results (and less relevant results) than you want.

To force the search engine to recognize your keywords as a phrase, place
quotation marks around the words. An example is the keyword phrase *call
options*. Without the quotation marks, the keywords match with every
instance of *call* and *options* in every message and title in the system. Using
"call options" narrows the results beautifully, returning matches to discussions about investment strategies using call options.

Figure 14-5 shows a typical results page in Yahoo! Message Boards, in this case
for a search on the word *option*. Two types of keyword matches show up:

  ✔ **Board matches.** Board matches occur when one of your keywords
    matches a message board (subcategory) title. A board match indicates
    that your search query is solidly matched to a broad subject with many
    possibly relevant discussion threads.

  ✔ **Message matches.** Message matches occur when at least one of your
    keywords matches within a message, a message title, or an author ID.
    Note that some message matches display part of the actual message,
    helping you determine whether it's worth clicking over to read the
    whole thing.

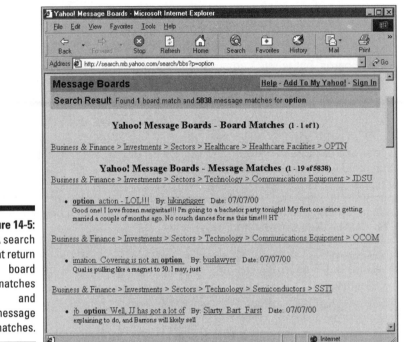

Figure 14-5:
A search
might return
board
matches
and
message
matches.

Board matches and message matches provide a similar distinction that category matches and site matches do in the main Yahoo! directory (see Chapter 7 to understand what the heck I'm talking about).

To gain access to more advanced search options, click the <u>Options</u> link next to the Search button on the Yahoo! Message Boards home page. The options aren't fancy. Simply click the radio button next to the message element you'd like to search. Here are a few hints for using these options:

- ✔ There's no point using the All option. If you want to search everything, stick to the main keyword-entry form on the Yahoo! Message Boards home page.

- ✔ Use the Titles option when you want to narrow in quickly on extremely relevant messages. When used with a keyword phrase or a name, such as *"sean connery"*, the Titles option provides a laser-quick way of getting to discussions on well-defined topics.

- ✔ Use the Message Text option when you have time to pore over lots of results. Narrow your hits by using more keywords or enclosing a phrase in quotes.

- ✔ Use the Authors option when you know someone's ID (or part of the ID), and you're looking for that person's messages.

Join in the Fun

It's not necessary to ever post a message, and many people enjoy message boards in *lurker* mode — silently reading messages without speaking up in a thread. However, even the most steadfast lurker can be tempted out of the closet with a provocative discussion or an opinion that just must be expressed. This section explains how to post a message and create a new topic (thread).

Adding your two cents

As I explain in a previous section, every message has a <u>Reply</u> link attached to it. Clicking that link takes you to a series of forms you use to formulate a reply, title it, and post it on the message board, as shown in Figure 14-6. Proceed as follows:

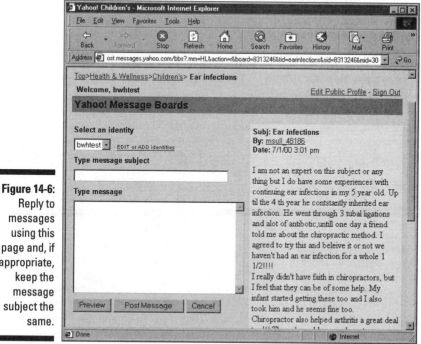

Figure 14-6: Reply to messages using this page and, if appropriate, keep the message subject the same.

1. **Select an identity from among your Yahoo! profiles.**

   See Chapter 1 for instructions on creating a Yahoo! profile. If you have created only one, you may either use it as your public profile on the message boards or create a specialized one for messaging. Click the EDIT or ADD identities link to create a new profile.

2. **In the Type message subject field, type a title for your message.**

   It helps other visitors to the thread if you make your title similar to, identical to, or at least vaguely reminiscent of the title of the message you're responding to. The original message subject is displayed in the Subj: heading to the right. No matter what, keep the title fairly short.

3. **Type your message.**

   Yahoo! messages accept URLs as part of messages and turn them into live links that anyone can use. So feel free to add a link to your Web page beneath your signature or link readers to a Web site that's relevant to your message.

   To see what your message looks like before committing it to the message board, click the Preview button. From that page, you may edit your message or go ahead and post it.

4. **Click the Post Message button.**

Notice that the message you're replying to is placed on this page, but it doesn't appear in your message unless you manually copy and paste portions of it into the Enter your message here field.

What is e-mail verification, and why do we need it?

You must be a registered Yahoo! user to post a message. That simply means you must own a Yahoo! ID. (See Chapter 1.) Yahoo! puts you through an extra step before you post your first message by requiring e-mail verification of your *true* identity. This extra step was added to tighten security in a realm where identity is fluid, at best. If someone posts material that is flagrantly illegal, Yahoo! (and legal authorities) have a handle on tracking the real person down. So, for the sake of security, everyone must proceed through the e-mail verification procedure — but only once.

When you attempt to post your first message, Yahoo! displays a screen asking for your non-Yahoo! e-mail address. That's the one that comes with your online access account. It could be an address from America Online, AT&T, Earthlink, or whatever provider you use. No sooner do you enter an address than Yahoo! sends a verification note to *that* address, with instructions for proceeding. In most cases, you simply click a link to another Web page, type your Yahoo! password, and you're verified.

Starting up a conversation

The next level of active participation after replying to messages is creating new message threads. You may create the first message of a new thread on most boards that are at the bottom of their directory levels. This means, for example, that you *cannot* create a new thread at the directory level where all the major league baseball teams are listed. Yahoo! has sensibly created a board for each team, and users cannot create duplicate or irrelevant boards at that level. However, you *may* create a new thread on the board of your favorite team. The upshot is that you can create a thread on the message board, but you can't create the message board itself.

On any message board page, the <u>Create A Topic</u> link is for starting a new thread. It leads to a page virtually identical to the Reply page, but without any reference to an original message because you are creating the thread's first message. Just choose your profile, as before, and then type a title and your message. Click the Create Topic button when you're finished or the Preview before Posting button to see what you did before committing it to the board.

You might notice that not every thread board uses the <u>Create A Topic</u> link. That's because each board has a certain amount of room, though Yahoo! does not divulge how much or how the space is measured. You may create a topic wherever that link exists. If there's no link, you're out of luck for the time being, pure and simple. A recent upgrade of the entire Yahoo! Message system has improved what used to be a somewhat frustrating situation. When you can't create a new thread, simply start a new topic using the Reply feature and create a very different message title. That method gets the discussion going just as well.

Chapter 15

Your Messenger Is Knocking

*L*et me state it right up front. Yahoo! Messenger is one of the great features of cyberspace. For Yahoo! users, it's an invaluable software gadget that centralizes much of the Yahoo! experience. Messenger is free, small, and doesn't take much screen space, but this powerful little module keeps you in contact with friends, lets you search the Web, delivers e-mail alerts, tracks your stock portfolio, updates sports scores, and integrates beautifully with your browser.

Messenger is Yahoo!'s answer to the online passion for *instant messaging,* which is one-to-one chatting and file sharing. You can exchange messages and files with anyone else running Messenger and even get groups together for chatting.

Yahoo! has designed Messenger to stay running all the time, and while that might seem excessive, I've found that it's exactly what works best for me. It's the first thing I boot up when I go online, and I never turn it off.

The Double Life of a Messenger

Yahoo! provides two working versions of Messenger. One is a Java applet that you can activate from the Yahoo! Messenger Web page. The other, more complete version is a distinct program that must be downloaded and installed on your computer's hard drive. The full version has far more features, and you should definitely choose it to get the full Messenger experience. Both versions are available from the following URL:

```
messenger.yahoo.com
```

Both versions of Yahoo! Messenger are free. The full, downloadable version contains conferencing, voice chat, file sharing, hooks into My Yahoo! and Yahoo! Finance, News, Sports, Mail, Personals, and Web directory, as well as a search engine that can rummage through just about any portion of the whole service.

The Java version of Messenger is convenient as a tester and for computer systems that can't run the full version (including Macintosh operating systems before version 8.5, UNIX, and Windows 3.x). The Java applet is somewhat less stable than its full-featured counterpart, causing occasional browser crashes.

With Yahoo! Messenger, you can

- ✔ Chat with individuals or small groups outside Yahoo! Chat and integrate some features into Yahoo! Chat when you go into chat rooms.

- ✔ Create groups of friends (called, amazingly, Friends) and set up alerts for when your Friends connect through Yahoo! Messenger or Yahoo! Chat.

- ✔ Work in tandem with your browser to quickly link to news stories, financial information, Yahoo! e-mail, search results, and many other portions of Yahoo!.

- ✔ Exchange pictures and other computer files with anyone else running Messenger.

- ✔ Talk — really talk, with your voice (if you have a microphone and speakers attached to your computer) — with people all over the world, free of charge.

Getting the Full Messenger Experience

The free, downloadable Yahoo! Messenger program is built for Windows (95, 98, 2000, NT) and Macintosh 8.5 or later. Your computer must be running one of those operating systems to use Messenger. Early Mac-version users and early Windows (pre-95) users can have fun with the Java version of Messenger (see the preceding section).

Messenger is also available for Windows CE (version 2.11 or later) and Palm portable devices. And a mobile phone version is in development. These mobile versions of Messenger let you log on and chat with other Messenger users from anywhere, as long as you have an Internet-capable, wireless hand-held device.

Downloading Messenger to a desktop or a laptop computer and connecting to Yahoo! through it, isn't very hard and is definitely worthwhile. The file is less than 1 megabyte — far smaller than many program downloads. The download takes a few minutes through a 28.8K modem and is even faster through speedier modems. Just follow these steps to get started with a Windows computer:

1. **On the Yahoo! home page, click the <u>Messenger</u> link.**

2. **Click the <u>Windows</u> (or <u>Macintosh</u>, if you use a Mac) link under the Quick Download header.**

   The Windows File Download window appears for Windows users.

3. **Select Save this program to disk and then click the OK button.**

   The Save As window appears.

4. **Select where on your hard drive you want to place the file.**

   Saving the file to your desktop makes it easy to find in the next step, but use whatever download location you're comfortable with.

5. **When the download is complete, find the downloaded file and double-click it.**

   Double-clicking the file begins the installation procedure.

6. **Follow the installation instructions that appear on your screen.**

7. **When installation is complete, click Yahoo! Messenger in your Start menu to launch the program.**

   When Messenger launches, as shown in Figure 15-1, it automatically attempts to connect with Yahoo!. If you're already logged on to the Internet, Messenger recognizes that and simply connects with the Yahoo! server and begins locating any Friends you've assigned to your ID.

Messenger starts as a small window, but you may resize it to any dimension you like. It's convenient to keep it compact for viewing online friends and chatting, but widening the window is helpful when using the information features described in this section.

When Yahoo! Messenger first launches and connects, it lists any Friends who are online. Offline friends are not listed. However, you can change this display to include all friends, with a lit-up icon to distinguish those who are connected. Just pull down the Messenger menu and then choose Show All Friends. To switch back, choose Show Only Online Friends.

Figure 15-1:
Yahoo!
Messenger
as it first
appears
after
logging on.
Members of
your Friends
list are
displayed.

Getting Messenger for your Palm

To use the Palm version of Messenger, shown in Figure 15-2, remember that you must be able to log on to the Internet with your Palm-based device. You need not only the PDA but also a modem that is either built into it or can be attached to it. The Palm VII has built-in connectivity; the Palm III and Palm V can be enhanced with OmniSky service or another modem add-on (such as PalmModem) with connection service. The handspring Visor can take add-on modems to give it Internet connectivity.

You also need a Palm-based browser, which may or may not be included with your device or connection service. If your Palm device doesn't have a browser, you can download one from one of many download sites for PDAs on the Web.

Figure 15-2:
Yahoo!
Messenger
as it
appears
in a Palm
handheld
device.

To acquire and install the Palm version of Messenger, start by downloading the program to your desktop or laptop and then move it into your Palm using HotSync. Just follow these steps:

1. **On the Yahoo! Messenger home page, click the __Palm__ link under the Quick Download header.**

2. **On the Palm OS Version page, click the __Download for PalmOS__ link.**

3. **Save the download file to your computer desktop or some other location.**

4. **Run the Install Tool, which is most likely located in the Palm Desktop directory of your computer.**

5. **Click Add in your Palm to set up the downloaded file (messenger.prc) to your HotSync list.**

6. **Place the Palm in its HotSync cradle and HotSync it.**

When you're ready to use Messenger in your Palm, click the Y! icon.

Getting Messenger for your Windows CE handheld

Yahoo! Messenger is now available for Internet-connected handheld devices running the Windows CE operating system, as shown in Figure 15-3. To use Messenger, you need a CE-based PDA running version 2.11 or later of the Windows CE operating system. Such devices are available from diverse manufacturers such as Casio, Compaq, Hewlett-Packard, Sharp, NEC, IBM, Hitachi, and others.

Figure 15-3:
Yahoo!
Messenger
as it
appears in a
Windows
CE portable
device. It
looks similar
to the
Windows
version.

As with the Palm version, CE users need to own a connection option for their handheld devices, and a CE-based Web browser must be installed.

To download the CE version of Messenger to your desktop or laptop computer and then transfer the program to your PDA, follow these steps:

1. **On the Yahoo! Messenger home page, click the <u>Windows CE</u> link under the Quick Download header.**

2. **On the Windows CE page, click the appropriate <u>Download</u> link.**

   Two download possibilities exist — one for Windows Pocket PC devices and one for Windows CE version 2.11 devices, including older Pocket PCs. Whichever path you choose, save the download file to your desktop or some other location.

3. **Double-click the downloaded file to begin installation.**

   Unlike the Palm version of Messenger, the CE version must undergo an installation process while still in your desktop or laptop.

4. **Synchronize your handheld Windows CE device.**

When you're ready to run Messenger on your CE device, choose Start ⇨ Programs, and then Yahoo! Messenger.

You can download the CE version of Messenger directly to your connected PDA, without passing the download file through a computer first. The exact process for doing so varies slightly depending on your device, and Yahoo! spells out the instructions online Using your connected PDA, here's how to download Messenger directly:

1. **On the Yahoo! Messenger home page, click the <u>Windows CE</u> link under the Quick Download header.**

2. **On the Windows CE page, click the <u>download directly to your device</u> link.**

3. **On the next page, click the link that corresponds to your device.**

4. **Double-click the downloaded file to begin installation.**

When you're ready to run Messenger, choose Start ⇨ Programs ⇨ Yahoo! Messenger.

Training Messenger

You can make Messenger behave properly when you turn on your computer and appear the way you want while you're using it. To do so, choose Edit menu ⇨ Preferences and then click the General tab. On the General tab of the

Preferences dialog box, seven check boxes are related to basic operating selections, as shown in Figure 15-4. Use the check boxes to do the following:

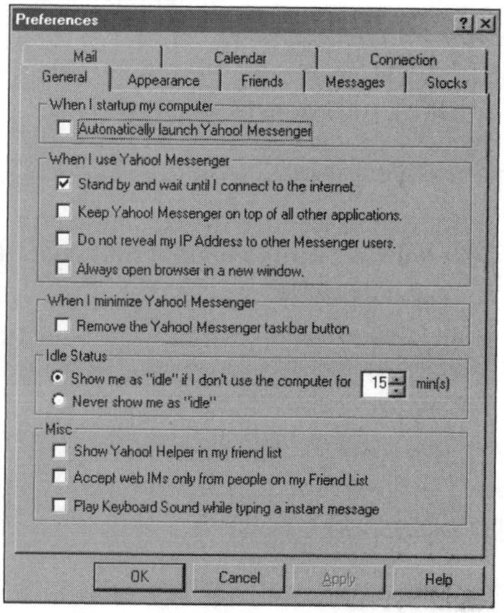

Figure 15-4:
General
Preferences
determine
how
Messenger
behaves
when
started.

✔ **Automatically launch Yahoo! Messenger.** Checking this selection puts Messenger in your startup folder, from which it boots automatically when you turn on your computer and load Windows.

✔ **Stand by and wait until I connect to the internet.** Whether you set Messenger to launch automatically or not, this setting determines whether Messenger attempts to connect with Yahoo! even if your computer is not yet online. Check the box to put the brakes on, forcing Messenger to wait until you manually connect with the Internet.

✔ **Keep Yahoo! Messenger on top of all other applications.** Check this box if you want Messenger to be visible on your screen at all times. If you find running in this mode inconvenient (it blocks your view of other on-screen windows), you may uncheck it at any time.

✔ **Do not reveal my IP Address to other Messenger users.** For most people, it's a good idea for security reasons to check this box. The IP address reveals your exact log-on path to the Internet.

✔ **Always open browser in a new window.** I like to check this box. When Messenger uses your browser for something — getting news stories or sports scores, for example — this selection ensures that a fresh browser pops open so that you don't lose whatever you're looking at in the current browser window.

✔ **Remove the Yahoo! Messenger taskbar button.** This selection takes effect when you minimize the Messenger window. I prefer showing Messenger in the taskbar at all times, so I leave it unchecked.

✔ **Show me as "idle."** Use this selection to automate how you appear to other Messenger users when you don't send a message for a certain period of time. You can turn the feature off entirely by selecting the Never show me as "idle" radio button. I find it convenient to leave the feature on, set for fifteen minutes, so friends don't think I'm ignoring them if I step away from the computer.

✔ **Show Yahoo! Helper in my friend list.** Yahoo! Helper is an automated Help feature that accepts and responds to Instant Messages. If you use it often, it makes sense to keep it visible as a "Friend."

✔ **Accept web IMs only from people on my Friend list.** Selecting this feature prohibits messages from strangers — anyone who wants to chat with you must be added to your Friends list first.

✔ **Play Keyboard Sound while typing an instant message.** Turn on this selection to hear a clacking typewriter sound when you type in Messenger. It drives me crazy, so I leave it off.

If you're not sure what you did and want to start again from scratch, click Cancel to close the Preferences window, open it again, and begin anew. When you've made your selections, click the OK button.

Five of the other Preferences tabs ask you to select an audio sound to play when certain things happen. I've found that the sounds are useful for getting my attention, and they eliminate the need for me to keep Messenger visible on my screen. I often like to know when friends come online and log off and when something comes into my Yahoo! e-mail box. Here's how it works:

✔ **Flash the taskbar "tray" icon.** This is the most inconspicuous type of alert because you see it only when you happen to glance at the Windows tray. (The tray is the right-hand portion of the Windows taskbar with the tiny icons.)

✔ **Display a dialog box.** The dialog box is a tiny window that appears atop your screen, in active mode. If you're working in another application (such as typing a book chapter in a word processor), you might be surprised to get jolted out of one window and placed in another. Still, I keep this function selected so that I know what the alert is about.

✔ **Play a sound.** This feature is great. Default sounds download with the Messenger package and are loaded into all the alerts. You may audition the sounds by clicking the ear button, and select new ones to audition by using the Browse button.

Use the preceding selections to get notified when friends come and go (Friends tab in the Preferences window); when you receive an Instant Message (Messages tab); when it's time for an event listed on your Yahoo! Calendar (Calendar tab); when you receive something in your Yahoo! e-mail box (Mail tab); and when you receive a stock alert (Stocks tab).

Making Friends and Chatting

Yahoo! Messenger began as a chat module, pure and simple. It was a social program. Information pieces have been added to Messenger, but many people still use it primarily as a way of meeting people online and chatting with them.

Friends are at the heart of Yahoo! Messenger. You may use Messenger to search for new friends and of course to get to know current friends better. All four buttons beneath the menu bar (refer to Figure 15-3) contain functions related to friends and communication. Some of those functions are duplicated when you right-click a friend's name. Furthermore, the Messenger menu puts all the functions in one place. In other words, Yahoo! Messenger tries to make it as easy and intuitive as possible to talk to people.

The following sections explore the two basic social functions in Yahoo! Messenger: finding and talking to friends.

Finding and adding friends

If you're completely new to Yahoo!, the best way to begin meeting people is to participate in Yahoo! Chat, which I explain in Chapter 13. From there, it's easy to throw a new friend directly into your Friends list. However, that process is somewhat hit-or-miss if you're looking for friends who share particular interests. Here's another way is to use the Friends button on Messenger:

1. **With Yahoo! Messenger connected, click the Friends button.**

   The Search For Friends window opens, as shown in Figure 15-5.

2. **In the first drop-down menu, select whether to search by keyword, name, or Yahoo! ID.**

3. **In the blank field next to the Search button, type a name, an ID, or a keyword.**

4. **In the Gender drop-down menu, select Male, Female, or no preference.**

5. **In the Age ranges fields, specify an age range within which to search.**

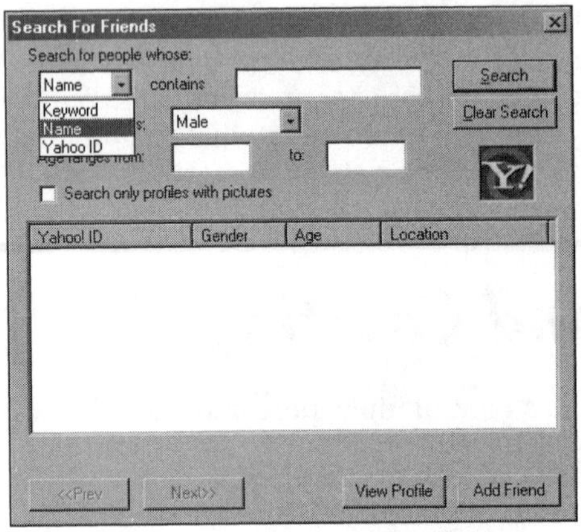

Figure 15-5:
The Search
For Friends
window
allows you
to search by
keyword,
Yahoo! ID,
or real name
and to
specify a
gender.

6. **If you want to eliminate results that don't have pictures, click the Search only profiles with pictures check box.**

7. **Click the Search button.**

    Your search results (see Figure 15-6) are displayed in the main portion of the Search For Friends window — the entire search process transpires within the panel, without appropriating a browser window. Right-click any name in the results list to add that person as a friend, send an instant message, or view the person's Yahoo! Profile. (Viewing the Profile does open a browser window.)

Of course, you may use Messenger's Add button to include friends in your group after meeting them in some other fashion. You can also encourage friends you know outside Yahoo! to get Messenger and join the party. Just click the Friends button, select Invite a friend to get Messenger, fill out the Web page that appears in your browser, and click the Invite Friend button. If your friend takes you up on the offer, he or she will need to download Messenger and install it or use Java Messenger.

The time is bound to come when you want to remove a friend from your group. It's not necessarily an insult (though if a fellow Trekker called you a Denubian slime devil, you should dump that person immediately) — sometimes a Friend link goes unused because the other person is rarely online. Whatever reason motivates the removal of a friend, it's easily accomplished:

1. **When Yahoo! Messenger is connected, right-click the name of any friend.**

    If Messenger is set to display only friends who are currently connected, pull down the Messenger menu and select Show All Friends.

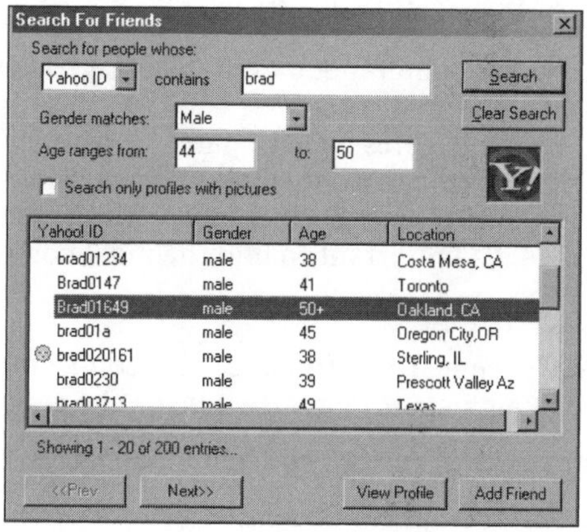

Figure 15-6:
Results of a
search for
friends.
Right-click
any name to
view the
Yahoo!
profile, add
that person
as a friend,
or send a
message.

2. **Right-click the ID you intend to remove from your group.**

3. **Click the Delete Friend selection.**

   A small window opens, asking whether you're sure you want to delete this person. Be sure! Yahoo! IDs are often obscure, and it can be hard to find someone again.

4. **Click the OK button.**

   After a second, the deleted name disappears from your list of friends.

Chatting with friends

You can chat with other Messenger users in four ways:

✔ **Online text chatting.** This is traditional chatting, using an Instant Message window to trade lines of typed text with another connected user.

✔ **Offline text chatting.** You may send an Instant Message to anyone on your Friends list, even if that person is not presently connected. If your friend is unconnected, the message is stored until he or she next connects to Messenger.

✔ **Online voice chatting.** Yahoo! added real-time voice chatting to Messenger in May, 1999. To use this feature, both participants must be using a version of Messenger released after that time. Not sure whether your Messenger is recent enough? Pull down the Messenger menu. If one of the selections is Start a Voice Chat, you're in business. If not, download a new Messenger (it's free), as described previously in this chapter.

✔ **Online group chatting (text or voice).** You can pull more than one friend into a chat, which is then called a Conference. Conferences operate in both text and voice mode simultaneously. It is outrageously cool.

The most typical way of beginning a Messenger chat is to send an Instant Message to a connected friend. You can do this in five ways, which reveals how important chatting is to the Messenger lineup of features. I'm spelling out the five methods because it's important to find the most comfortable way to begin chatting:

✔ Double-click any friend's name. (The friend can be connected or unconnected but don't expect an instant response if he or she is not online.)

✔ Right-click a friend's name and select Send Instant Message.

✔ Click a friend's name and then press Ctrl+S.

✔ Click a friend's name, click the Messages button, and then choose Send Instant Message.

✔ Click a friend's name and then choose Edit ⇨ Send a Message.

Whichever way you open an Instant Message window, Figure 15-7 illustrates what it looks like. The Instant Message window is easy enough to use — at the most basic level, you just type a message and click the Send button. However, the full-featured Messenger also incorporates some fancy text perks that are missing from Java Messenger:

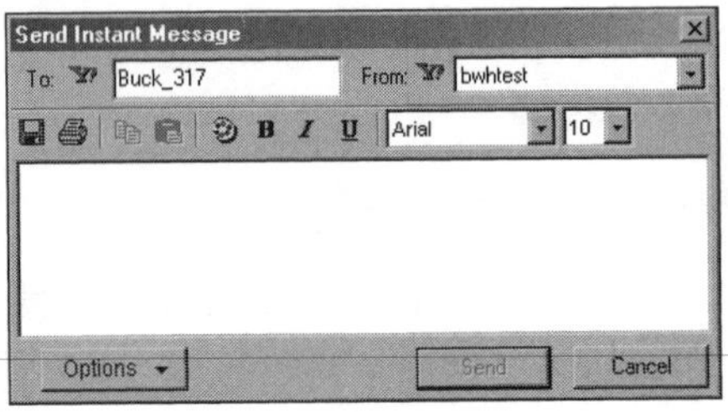

Figure 15-7: The Send Instant Message window, where chats are initiated.

✔ The floppy disk icon is for saving a chat to your hard drive. The save should be performed after a chat is complete but before you close the Instant Message window. Yahoo! Messenger *does not* save the chat as it proceeds — in other words, you can't save it at the beginning and end up with the whole chat later, unless you save it again at the end.

✔ The printer icon lets you print a chat session.

✔ Click the color palette icon to choose a color for your text. Colored text appears colored both on your screen and the other person's.

✔ Use the **Bold,** *Italic,* and <u>Underline</u> icons to change your text. You may use any or all of these in combination with text color.

When you first send an Instant Message, the window disappears from your screen. This might be disconcerting if you're accustomed to chat systems that leave the window open. You can change this default setting in the Preferences window (press Ctrl+P) under the Messages tab. Just click the check box next to Keep message window open and then click the OK button. I also find it useful, under the same Messages tab, to set the Enter key to send the message rather than insert a carriage return. Most chatting involves a series of short lines — rambling dissertations are unusual, and besides, Yahoo! automatically wraps long lines of text to the recipient's window size. So carriage returns aren't necessary unless you chat in verse.

Begin a voice chat by following these steps:

1. **When Yahoo! Messenger is connected, right-click the name of any Friend on your list.**

2. **Select Start a Voice Chat or Start a Conference.**

3. **In the Invite Friends to a Voice Chat (or Invite Friends to a Conference) window, click the name of the friend you want to invite.**

   Only connected friends are listed in this window. If you'd like to invite a Yahoo! ID not on your Friends list, type the ID in the Add field and click the Add button.

4. **Click the Add>> button.**

5. **When you have selected and added everyone you want in the chat, click the Invite button.**

   Everyone on your list receives an invitation window, and clicks a Yes button to accept or a No button to decline. (Nothing personal; it's just that the last time you spent four hours talking about your ingrown toenail.)

When you send your invitation, a new window opens on your screen, as shown in Figure 15-8. The Voice Chat window is where you manage voice and conference chats. Notice that all the Instant Message features are incorporated near the bottom of the window. Conveniently, text chatting is fully available during voice chats. It's especially convenient because the voice feature works for only one person at a time.

When you want to talk in a voice chat, click and hold the Press to Talk button and then speak into your microphone. Your partner (or all your partners in a conference) hears your words almost as you speak them — the transmission speed is about as fast as a phone call. People chatting from far-off points of the globe experience a slight delay.

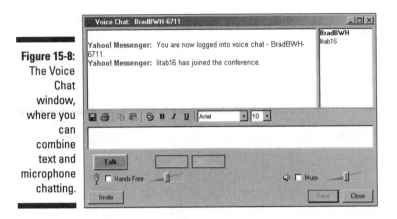

Figure 15-8:
The Voice
Chat
window,
where you
can
combine
text and
microphone
chatting.

You can avoid the annoying need to press the Talk button repeatedly by using the Hands Free option. When you click the Hands Free check box, the Talk button is automatically activated when you speak. This feature works best when using a headset rather than a free-standing microphone. Also, minimal background noise is helpful.

Only one person can use the Press to Talk button at a time or, using Hands Free, can talk at any moment. When a person is speaking, his or her ID is highlighted in the list of people attending. This system gets a bit frustrating in a group chat but works well enough one-to-one. Remember that you can continue typing while people are speaking into their microphones.

The Messenger Control Center

Although many people are satisfied with Yahoo! Messenger as a social tool, it's far more than just a mobile chat room. Five tabs at the bottom, plus a hidden search engine, unlock its information resources. The tabs are not identified with text but divulge their identities when you run your mouse cursor over them. Here's what those five tabs do:

- ✔ **Friends.** The left tab opens the window described in most of the previous sections of this chapter. This is where your Friends groups appear and where you initiate Instant Messages and voice chat sessions.

- ✔ **Stocks.** The Stocks tab, second from the left, displays the stock prices you selected in the Stock Portfolios of My Yahoo!. (It doesn't display the more advanced portfolios from Yahoo! Finance.) If you haven't created a stock portfolio in My Yahoo!, this tab displays a simple default selection of stock prices. To adjust your portfolio, visit your My Yahoo! page and click the Edit button in the Portfolios module (see Chapter 2).

✔ **News.** As with the Stocks tab, the News section links to your settings in My Yahoo! and displays the same headline links. In this tab, an Edit button is provided for making alterations, which get applied to both My Yahoo! and Yahoo! Messenger. When you click a headline link in Messenger, your browser displays the full story.

✔ **Sports.** Again, the Sports tab follows your My Yahoo! settings. An Edit button lets you change those settings, hooking into your browser window. An added twist in this tab is that clicking anywhere in the main window space connects your browser to Yahoo! Sports. It's a nice feature, though unexpected and startling at first. This feature might be added to the Stock and News tabs by the time you read this.

✔ **Alerts.** The right-hand tab provides a recap of what's happening in your account. The list, which is shown in Figure 15-9, notifies you of new e-mail that's arrived at your Yahoo! address, new messages in your Yahoo! Personals mailbox, alerts from your Yahoo! Calendar settings, stock alerts if you've established alert parameters in your My Yahoo! portfolio, and a Friends Online summary.

Figure 15-9:
The Alerts
tab sum-
marizes
your Yahoo!
account.

Note the small magnifying glass icon in the lower-right corner of Messenger. Clicking that icon reveals the hidden keyword-entry form for searching. More convenient even than searching within Yahoo!'s Web pages, this powerful search engine can be told to rummage around in almost any portion of the entire Yahoo! service.

To conduct a Messenger search, follow these steps:

1. **With Messenger connected, click the magnifying glass icon to reveal the keyword-entry form.**

2. **Click the small arrow next to the keyword form to pop open a menu list.**

3. **From the menu, select any item.**

4. **Click your mouse in the keyword-entry field and then type one or more keywords.**

5. **Press the Enter key on your keyboard.**

    Messenger takes control of your browser and displays the search results in a browser window.

The New Messenger

Just as this book was going to the printer, Yahoo! released a test version of a new Messenger upgrade. Often, software upgrades don't amount to much. In this case, though, the new Messenger is a dramatic improvement. So the wheels of publishing were halted with a screech and the book extracted from the printer's clutches so I could point out a few important new features.

The new Messenger is available, at this writing, only for Windows users. By the time you read this, the upgrade may be ready for Macintosh and Unix users also, and it might be the default download for all three computer types. That doesn't mean that veteran Messenger users need to upgrade, though — you must download the new version to see these new features on your screen.

An easier way to chat

The big change in the new Messenger? A much tighter integration with Yahoo! Chat. Previous versions force you to get into Yahoo! Chat through your Web browser, as described in Chapter 13. Now, you can select and enter chat rooms straight through Messenger. Here's how:

1. **In the main Messenger panel, click the Chat icon.**

    This is a new icon that appears only in the new Messenger. The Change Room window pops open. (See Figure 15-10.)

2. **In the Change Room window, select a chat-topic category from the left directory pane.**

3. **Double-click any chat room from the center (Yahoo! Rooms) or right-hand (User Rooms) panes.**

    The chat room opens in a new window (see Figure 15-11), and the Change Room window disappears. Voila! This process is much faster than logging into Yahoo! Chat through your browser.

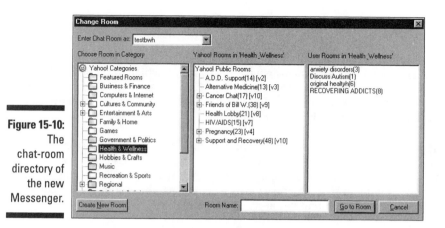

Figure 15-10:
The
chat-room
directory of
the new
Messenger.

Although the directory of Yahoo! Chat rooms looks quite different through the new Messenger compared to the browser interface (see Chapter 13), it directs you to the same rooms. Use the Create New Room button to . . . well, to create a new room.

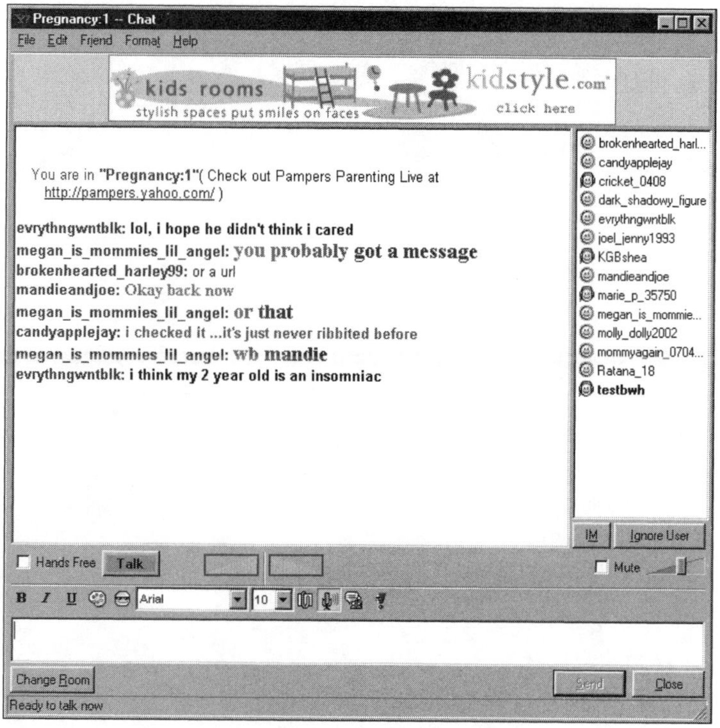

Figure 15-11:
A chat room
as viewed
through
the new
Messenger.

Using your headset in the new Messenger

Another big improvement of the new Messenger is that voice chatting is easier. The new instant messaging panel, through which you talk to friends, sports a new microphone icon. Click that icon to begin a voice conversation — remembering that your chat partner must have a microphone and speakers, or a headset, plugged in to participate.

The new version of Messenger is not compatible with older versions in some ways, notably when it comes to voice chatting. Even if your partner is using a headset, that person cannot voice chat with you when using an older Messenger, if you have the new version. However, chat room participants can talk freely using different versions of Messenger.

Chapter 16

Virtual Treehouses: Yahoo! Clubs

· ·

In This Chapter

▶ Browsing and searching for Yahoo! Clubs

▶ Joining someone else's club and uploading pictures

▶ Creating and configuring your own club

· ·

*I*magine creating your own Web site, dedicated to a subject of interest —
perhaps music, movies, sports, genealogy, current events, or meeting people.
Now imagine the site complete with a message board for posted discussions
and a chat room for real-time talking. Creating a feature-rich site like that,
from scratch, would take more knowledge and skill than most people have
time to acquire.

Yahoo! Clubs are an alternative to building a site from scratch. Think of clubs
as site-building kits. Just follow the easy instructions and all the features get
plugged in automatically, arranged in the site as neatly as a sectional couch.
Yahoo! offers a simple trade: You get ease in exchange for customization. In
other words, all Yahoo! Clubs look pretty much the same (see Figure 16-1), so
you're not going to make a personal visual statement with one. But setting up
clubs is a snap and they work well.

Although Yahoo! Clubs are great for enterprising people who want their own
site, you don't need to be ambitious to enjoy them. They're also fine for visiting
and joining. Clubs are meeting places for people with a shared interest.

This chapter goes into detail about how to search for Yahoo! Clubs, use their
features, and create your own club.

Finding and Joining Clubs

You can get started with Yahoo! Clubs by proceeding directly to the Yahoo!
Clubs directory at the following URL. Browse among the clubs, visit any in
the directory, and join clubs you might want to return to later:

```
clubs.yahoo.com
```

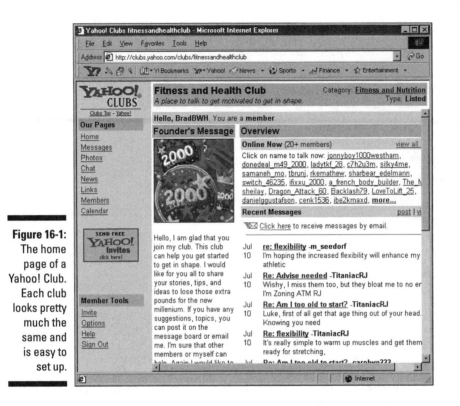

Figure 16-1:
The home
page of a
Yahoo! Club.
Each club
looks pretty
much the
same and
is easy to
set up.

Feel free to poke around the directory and explore individual clubs. You might get the hang of it quickly, through trial and error. The following sections walk you through browsing, searching, and joining clubs.

Club-hopping

The Yahoo! Clubs directory and search engine work similarly to the main Yahoo! Web directory described in Chapter 7. On the main directory page, you see 16 main directory topics, each listed with a handful of subcategory links. (See Figure 16-2 for a partial view of the directory page.) Click any directory link to begin drilling down to a topic of interest.

If you join any Yahoo! Clubs, those clubs are listed in the left-hand sidebar of the main Yahoo! Clubs directory. It makes it easy to reach your clubs, though creating bookmarks for them in your browser makes reaching them even easier.

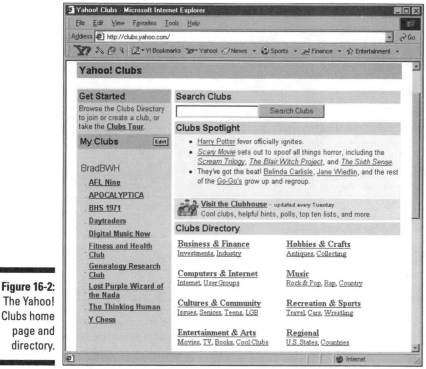

Figure 16-2:
The Yahoo!
Clubs home
page and
directory.

Each page of the Yahoo! Clubs directory presents links to individual clubs and — in all but the lowest directory levels — subcategory links leading to other clubs in more specific topics. The second-level directory pages list the most popular clubs (by membership count) in *all* the subcategories of that directory topic. Figure 16-3 illustrates how the listing is arranged. The figure shows the Computers & Internet directory category. First come the links to subcategories and then the most popular clubs for the whole Computers & Internet category.

Lower subcategories continue to list the most popular clubs but only within the subcategory. In many cases, too many clubs exist to list them all on one page, so you need to use the A-Z Index link to sort through them all.

Popularity breeds popularity, especially when Yahoo! places the high-membership clubs so visibly in the directory. The result of this system is that the clubs with big memberships tend to get even bigger, while less visible clubs remain anonymous. How does a club get more members in the first place? In many cases, a club gets members simply by being one of the first clubs in a certain subcategory. If you want to find hidden gems (worth searching for in many cases), you need to take the path less traveled. Dig down into the directory using the A-Z Index link or by simply exploring lower directory levels. Best of all, use keywords to search the directory.

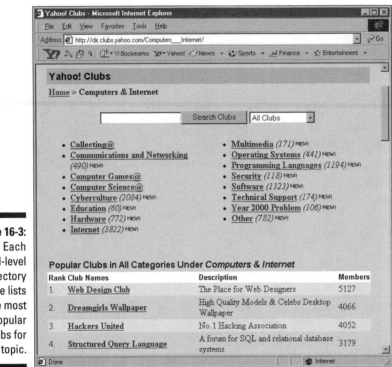

Figure 16-3:
Each
second-level
directory
page lists
the most
popular
clubs for
that topic.

Finding the right club

At any time while browsing, you may crank your investigation to the next level by searching the Yahoo! Clubs directory with keywords. The process is nearly identical to searching the main Yahoo! Web directory, described in Chapter 5. Just follow these steps:

1. **On any Yahoo! Clubs directory page, type a keyword (or more than one) in the keyword-entry form.**

2. **If you're in any directory page except the top one, use the drop-down menu to select whether to search All Clubs or In This Category.**

3. **Click the Search Clubs button.**

Just as in the main Yahoo! Web directory (see Chapter 7), your search results might contain both category matches and site matches (called clubs site matches in this directory). This arrangement occurs when you search with broad keywords, especially single keywords. The category match links you to the subcategory directory page for MP3 clubs, where you can browse all relevant clubs whether or not they contain the term *mp3* in their club name. The list of clubs site matches represents all clubs with *mp3* in their names.

Joining in

As you find interesting clubs, you might want to join up with some of them. Yahoo! places no limit on the number of clubs you can join. However, your patience might have a limit as you begin receiving e-mail communications from all your new clubs. Fortunately, it's easy to get out of clubs. (I describe how a bit later.)

You can explore any club to some extent without joining. But until you're a member, you can't do the following:

- ✔ View member-uploaded photos (and upload your own)
- ✔ Post messages on the message board
- ✔ Place items on the calendar
- ✔ Be included in the club's member listing
- ✔ View the News page

So limited observation is possible as a nonmember but participation requires membership. Joining is easy. On the home page of any club you visit, do the following:

1. **Click the <u>Join this club</u> link (upper-right corner of the page).**

   The Join *Clubname* page appears.

2. **Select the Yahoo! ID you'd like to use in this club.**

   If you have just one Yahoo! ID, it's an easy choice.

3. **Type a comment if you'd like one to appear next to your name in the member list.**

4. **You may review the Terms of Service agreement at this time by clicking that link.**

   I discuss the Terms of Service later in this chapter. It's a standard legal document, and you don't need to review it every time you join a club.

5. **Click the Yes! I Accept button.**

   You just joined! The next thing you see is the club home page, and all club features are now available to you.

You must have a Yahoo! ID to join a club. Chapter 1 describes how to make an ID.

Being an Active Member

After you join a club (which takes about ten seconds; see the preceding section), all its features are open to you. The clubs are very interactive. Yahoo! Clubs all contain the same basic features, which are linked in the left-hand sidebar. The following sections walk you through the various rooms and hallways of your new club.

Welcome home

The first page a visitor or member sees when visiting the club is its home page. This is where you find the purpose of the club according to the Founder's Message. Here's what else you find on the home page:

- ✔ The Overview section has two portions. First, under the Online Now heading, you see a list of club members who are currently logged on with a Yahoo! ID. These folks are not necessarily visiting the club at the same time you are, but they are engaged in some Yahoo! activity (perhaps chatting or using Messenger) that enables them to receive messages from other Yahoo! members. Click any ID to send a message to that person — a browser window opens with a Java version of Messenger.

- ✔ The second portion of the Overview area shows several of the most recently posted messages, with links. You may read any one of them or click the view all link to — you guessed it — see a complete list of messages. The post link is a shortcut to putting something up on the message board. Use the post link to start a new discussion topic. If you're responding to someone else's message, use the Reply function on the message screen.

- ✔ Under Stats, you see how many members the club has and how many page views the club has displayed to all members. (A questionably useful statistic.) It also gives the date the club was founded, for those of an historical bent. A daily log of the past few days shows how busy the club has been.

- ✔ The Contact section contains an e-mail link for contacting the club founders. The link displays a page with a text-entry form for typing a message and a Send Mail button. The e-mail is automatically addressed to the club founders — you don't need to look up an address.

- ✔ The Chat Room section displays how many members (if any) are currently logged on to the chat room. The <u>enter</u> link takes you there.

- ✔ The left-hand navigation bar has all the main club links. It provides the easiest way to access the message board, chat room, photo area, News page, and other standard features.

Notice the links under Member Tools. They give you a few more things to do:

- ✔ **Invite.** Click this link for a fill-in form that allows you to send a standard club invitation to any e-mail address.

- ✔ **Options.** Options are always good, but these particular options don't have much to do with your presence in the club. Clicking the <u>Options</u> link opens up the following possibilities: sending an e-mail to the club founders, editing the list of clubs you've joined, editing your Yahoo! Profile (see Chapter 1), or searching the database of Yahoo! Profiles (see Chapter 1 again).

- ✔ **Help.** Clicking the <u>Help</u> link delivers some pages of explanation about how everything works. Obviously, considering the immortal quality of the prose you're holding in your hand right now, you don't need the Help section.

- ✔ **Sign Out.** Talk about a negative Member Tool. Use this link when you want to quit your Yahoo! ID. Doing so launches you right out of the club, and you need to sign in again (which you can do from many locations in Yahoo!) before visiting any of your clubs as a member.

When you're navigating around a Yahoo! Club, you don't need to use your Back button very much, if at all. That's because the main navigation sidebar is enclosed in an autonomous *frame,* and it doesn't change when you click a link. So, for example, you may travel from the Home page to the message board and then to the News page, all without using your Back button to get at the navigation links again. The links stay in place while you're surfing.

Tacking up a message

The message board is where most club conversations take place. The most recent messages are linked to the main portion of the home page, or you can click the <u>Messages</u> link to see a complete list, as shown in Figure 16-4. The Messages page is full of links. You may, of course, click any message link to see the message. Clicking the Member ID of the message's author pops open a new browser window displaying that person's Yahoo! profile.

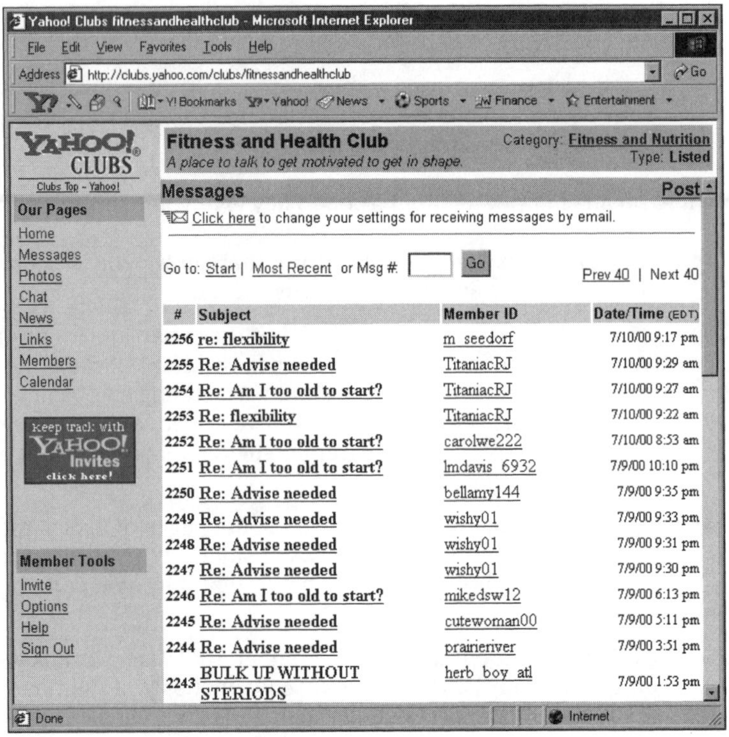

Figure 16-4:
The
Messages
page of a
Yahoo! Club.
You can
rummage for
messages
and view
member
profiles.

> Yahoo! Clubs fitnessandhealthclub - Microsoft Internet Explorer
>
> File Edit View Favorites Tools Help
>
> Address http://clubs.yahoo.com/clubs/fitnessandhealthclub   ⏎ Go
>
> Y! ⚲ 🖊 ⚲ ▥ ▾Y! Bookmarks Y!▾ Yahoo! News ▾   Sports ▾ Finance ▾ Entertainment ▾
>
> **YAHOO! CLUBS**®   **Fitness and Health Club**   Category: **Fitness and Nutrition**
> Clubs Top - Yahoo!   *A place to talk to get motivated to get in shape.*   Type: **Listed**
>
> **Our Pages**   **Messages**   **Post**▴
> Home
> Messages   ✉ Click here to change your settings for receiving messages by email.
> Photos
> Chat   Go to: Start | Most Recent or Msg # [   ] Go   Prev 40 | Next 40
> News
> Links   **# Subject**   **Member ID**   **Date/Time** (EDT)
> Members   2256 re: flexibility   m_seedorf   7/10/00 9:17 pm
> Calendar   2255 Re: Advise needed   TitaniacRJ   7/10/00 9:29 am
>   2254 Re: Am I too old to start?   TitaniacRJ   7/10/00 9:27 am
> keep track with   2253 Re: flexibility   TitaniacRJ   7/10/00 9:22 am
> **YAHOO!**   2252 Re: Am I too old to start?   carolwe222   7/10/00 8:53 am
> **Invites**   2251 Re: Am I too old to start?   lmdavis_6932   7/9/00 10:10 pm
> click here!   2250 Re: Advise needed   bellamy144   7/9/00 9:35 pm
>   2249 Re: Advise needed   wishy01   7/9/00 9:33 pm
> **Member Tools**   2248 Re: Advise needed   wishy01   7/9/00 9:31 pm
>   2247 Re: Advise needed   wishy01   7/9/00 9:30 pm
> Invite   2246 Re: Am I too old to start?   mikedsw12   7/9/00 6:13 pm
> Options   2245 Re: Advise needed   cutewoman00   7/9/00 5:11 pm
> Help   2244 Re: Advise needed   prairieriver   7/9/00 3:51 pm
> Sign Out   2243 BULK UP WITHOUT   herb_boy_atl   7/9/00 1:53 pm
>   STERIODS
>
> Done   Internet

The messages are displayed in chronological order, with most recent postings at the top. So as you cast your eye down the screen, you're looking back in time, seeing the discussions in reverse order. The messages are not threaded in an indented style as you might be accustomed to from a Usenet newsgroup reader or some other message boards on the Web. Still, you can follow the discussions pretty well by watching the message titles, because replies to messages keep the same title. Also, when viewing any message that has had replies posted to it, you may see those replies by clicking the View Replies to this Message link, as shown in Figure 16-5. Create a reply yourself by clicking the Reply link. (I'm not sure you needed me to tell you that.)

Don't be fooled by the <-Previous and Next-> links. Those links refer to the previous and next messages *chronologically,* not necessarily the parent message and reply to the message you're reading. Usually, many conversations on several topics are transpiring on the message board simultaneously. Always use the View Replies to this Message link to follow a single discussion.

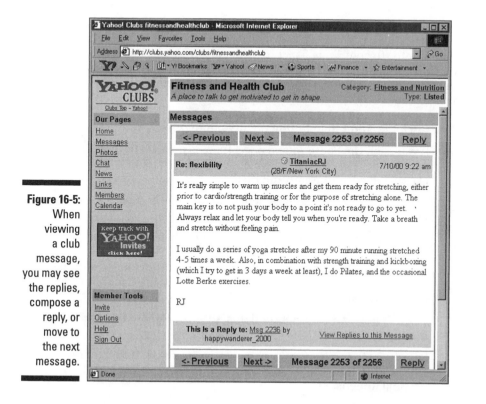

Showing yourself off

The Photos section really makes the clubs more personable by encouraging members to upload pictures of themselves or anything that relates to the club's topic of interest. Whether you upload a picture or not, you may browse the photos of other members:

1. **Click the <u>Photos</u> link in the left-hand navigation bar.**

   The Photo Album page is displayed.

2. **Click any of the photo album links.**

   The page for that album is displayed, with links to individual photos.

3. **Click any little camera icon or the name of the photo to see that photo.**

   A new page appears, and in a second or two the photo appears.

Members are entitled to create photo albums or upload individual photos into preexisting photo albums. You always have a Default Club Album to upload into. To contribute a picture, you must have one digitized and residing on your computer's hard drive. It helps (very much) to know where on the hard drive the picture is located. Given those requirements, here's what you do:

1. **Click the Add Photo button on any photo page.**

   If you're on the Photo Album page, there is no such button. Use the <u>Add Album</u> link to make a photo album, or click the album to which you'd like to upload your photo and then click that Add Photo button.

2. **On the Adding a Photo page, click the Browse button to locate your photo.**

   The Browse button opens a file locator, which you can use to look for the picture in your hard drive files. Use the <u>on the web</u> link to use a picture stored somewhere on the Web. Note that linking to someone else's graphic without permission is considered unethical and could even be illegal.

3. **In the Name and Description fields, title your photo and type a short description.**

4. **Select whether you want your photo resized and, if so, by how much. Or click the Don't resize selection option to leave your photo in its original dimensions.**

   Resizing is a bit tricky. If your photo is very big, you should resize it so that other members don't have their systems tied up by downloading a large graphics file. (Also, club photo areas are limited in size, so everyone use small files to make room for others.)

   Yahoo! Clubs have three default photo sizes: Large, Medium, and Small. The large size is *very* large (640 pixels for your picture's largest dimension). Fellow members might get a bit upset if you use that size. I recommend Medium or Small. Keep in mind that club photos can't be enlarged, only reduced. So if your picture is already on the small side (no more than four inches wide or long), there's no point in resizing it. (Resizing affects your picture's reproduction in the club, not its size on your hard drive.)

5. **If you are resizing your picture, click the Preview button to see the result.**

6. **Click the Upload button to finish the process.**

Ch-ch-ch-chatting

Talking in real-time with other members is a distinct pleasure of club membership. The chatting atmosphere is usually less "noisy" and the screen is less cluttered than in the main Yahoo! Chat area. (See Chapter 13.) Furthermore, conversations tend to stay on topic better in a club.

In other respects, club chatting is similar to general Yahoo! chatting. If you've tried one, you're likely to get your bearings quickly in the other. The software for the two areas is the same. When you click the Chat link on the home page, your browser downloads the Java chat program — it doesn't take long. (If you're using a Windows computer, a panel might appear asking your permission to download the Java elements. There are two such elements, so there may be two panels. Click the Yes button to both.) After the chat program is in place, you can see who else is in the room and begin chatting, as shown in Figure 16-6.

You might come to grips with the chatting interface (the room) fairly quickly through experimentation. Feel free to click buttons, type lines into the room, change the color of your text, send Personal Messages, and so on. If you'd like a detailed walk-through of the Yahoo! Chat program, please refer to Chapter 13, where I hold forth on the subject well into the night.

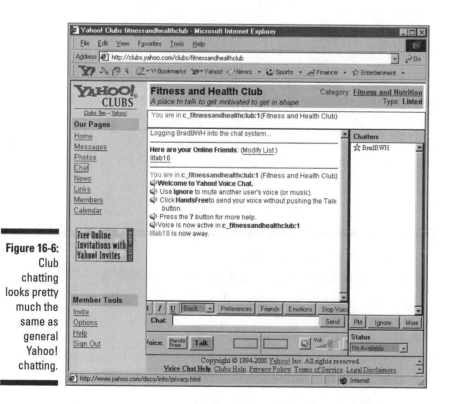

Figure 16-6:
Club
chatting
looks pretty
much the
same as
general
Yahoo!
chatting.

The Java chat download happens only once — then you can use it repeatedly. As long as you keep your browser open, you may hop in and out of clubs, chatting away, without suffering the delay of downloading the chat program over and over.

No news is bad news

If you click the <u>News</u> link to view the News page, you might notice that it looks similar to a My Yahoo! page. In fact, it is a My Yahoo! page — but in this case, it's a Founder's Yahoo! page because the club's founders have control over what appears on it. They have the same options that you do when you create your own personalized Yahoo! page (which I describe how to do in Chapter 2).

If the News page doesn't contain the content you'd like to see, I suggest writing to the club founders with a request.

Shared links

The Links page is for contributing Web links to sites related to the club topic. Any links you add should be of general club interest — as opposed, say, to your personal Web page (unless your site is relevant to the club).

Clicking any link on the Links page opens a new browser window to display the site, so you don't have to worry about losing your view of the Yahoo! Club while you're surfing elsewhere. (Perhaps you weren't really chewing your fingernails over that prospect anyway.)

To add a link, follow these short and simple steps:

1. **On the Links page, click the <u>Add A Link</u> link.**

   The Add A Link page appears.

2. **Type the Web address of the site you're contributing.**

   Note that the *http://* portion of the address is already present, so just add the rest of the URL.

3. **Type a short comment about the site.**

   The comment will appear on the Links page next to the site link.

4. **Click the Add Link button.**

   Your link contribution is added, and the Links page is again displayed. Notice that your link is now at the bottom of the list. (It's at the bottom because it's the most recent, not because it's inferior in any way.) Note also the Edit and Delete icons next to your link. Use the Edit icon if you've made a typing mistake and want to correct it. Use the Delete icon if the whole thing was a horrifying error and you want to remove all the evidence.

Making first contact

The Contacts page is where all the club's members are listed, starting with the founders and moving methodically (and alphabetically) through everyone else. Unfortunately, you can't search for members by Yahoo! ID — a much hoped-for feature for the future. (A future feature creature.) Each member link, if clicked, opens a new browser window with that person's Yahoo! profile displayed.

You may change the comment associated with your listing (or add a comment if you didn't before) by clicking the Edit My Comments link. You might notice that the page doesn't allow much room for comments, so keep it very short or risk being cut off in mid-profundity.

Mark your calendar

The calendar is a nifty part of the clubs. Click the Calendar link to see it. Each club founder decides how the calendar is displayed when you first link to it, but you can change it on your screen.

Calendars are used by the founders to schedule club events and mark dates of significance to club interests. However, *any* member can add an event to the calendar. You might think this would be chaotic, and it could be, but my observation is that most members stay away from controlling the calendar, perhaps because they don't realize how much control they have. If that's the case, I might be doing a disservice to club owners everywhere by spilling the beans, but here goes.

Look at Figure 16-7 to see the monthly view of a club calendar. A few dates are marked for club meetings. Note the Add links. Click one of those to add an event to that day. (You can also use the Add Event button to schedule an event for any day.) The calendar works similarly to the general Yahoo! Calendar, which I elucidate in Chapter 25. The main difference here is that you may send e-mail invitations to any event you place on the club calendar, as shown in Figure 16-8. The invitation is a form letter sent to your addressees. The Address Book link connects you with your Yahoo! Address Book, which I describe in Chapter 3.

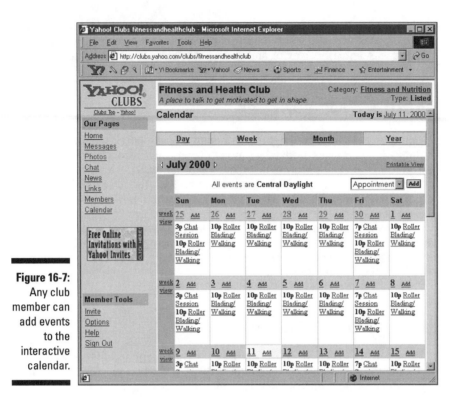

Figure 16-7:
Any club
member can
add events
to the
interactive
calendar.

Be cautious in placing an event on the club calendar. Look through a few
weeks or months to see how the club uses this feature. If the membership
enjoys celebrating individual birthdays and other personal events, add away
along those lines. But if the calendar adheres more strictly to club event
scheduling, it's best not to add personal holidays.

Building Your Own Clubhouse

Visiting other people's clubs or even just browsing through the Yahoo! Clubs
directory can inspire a desire to create your own. Not a problem — Yahoo!
makes it easy. You don't design or implement the message board, chat room,
uploading procedure, calendar, or any of the other standard club features.
Those things are prebuilt and incorporated in your club automatically.

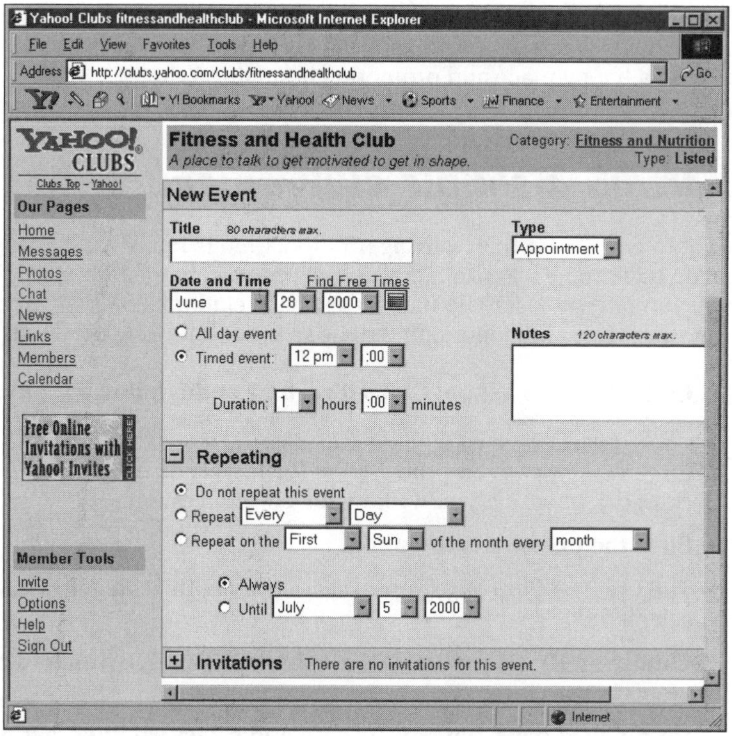

Figure 16-8:
The New Event page provides date and time settings, plus an invitation form. You can add one-time and repeating events.

Creating a Yahoo! Club is one of the easiest ways to have your own Web site. You get less flexibility than building a cyberhome at GeoCities or some other virtual community that offers page templates and the freedom to add your own HTML code. The tradeoff for the diminished flexibility is the enhanced ease. With Yahoo! Clubs, you just answer a few questions and you're in business — your club is online, live, and ready to accept members. You may customize it somewhat, with a picture, with an introductory message, by determining what goes on the News page, and in some other small ways. But basically, Yahoo! Clubs are like housing developments — each structure looks pretty much the same.

Let me clarify something in case you're scratching your head over the *HTML code* I mentioned in the preceding paragraph. HTML stands for HyperText Markup Language, the underlying code of all Web pages. You can create a Web page in four basic ways. The most difficult is to write the HTML code by hand, which requires knowledge and a willingness to stay up most of the night correcting mistakes. You can also use an HTML editor, which facilitates the coding process. Next, you may use an online template such as the ones provided by GeoCities and other page-building communities. Finally, and easiest of all, is to plug yourself into a prefab site such as Yahoo! Clubs.

This section gets you started with your own Yahoo! Club and walks you through the various options at your disposal. I also throw in a few tips about making the club a happy place and promoting it outside Yahoo!.

Starting a simple club quickly

I want to emphasize that starting a Yahoo! Club is really easy. Really. Easy. You do have some ways to fancy up the process, but Yahoo! doesn't insist on them and offers a laser-fast path to getting a club up and live quickly. You can get a very basic club functioning right away by following these steps:

1. **Go to the main Yahoo! Clubs directory at the following URL:**

   `clubs.yahoo.com`

2. **Click your way to any third-level (or lower) directory page, choosing a category in which you'd like your club to reside.**

3. **Click the Create a club button.**

   The Create a Club page appears, confirming the category you've selected.

4. **Choose an ID (if you have more than one) under which to create your club.**

5. **On the next page, name your club and select whether you want the club listed or unlisted in the Yahoo! Clubs directory.**

   Naming the club is important. Think of a title that conveys the gist of your topic concisely. At the same time, get imaginative. I've noticed that some of the most successful clubs have intriguing names that almost force the casual browser to investigate. Whether you choose a cryptic title or a plainly descriptive one, keep it short.

   As far as the listing is concerned, most clubs are listed. Usually, you would have no reason to avoid a listing. However, if you're setting up a family club, a work-related club, or any club whose members will all be personally invited to join, select Unlisted.

   You may also enter the geographic location of the club, which would probably be your residence. Unless your club's topic is related to its geographical location, there's not much point in filling it in.

6. **On the same page as Step 5, review the Terms of Service agreement by clicking the <u>Yahoo! Clubs Terms of Service</u> link and then click the Yes! I accept button.**

   After you click the acceptance button, your club is created.

The next page gives you a link to the new club and a link for setting more club options. The club is in the Yahoo! Clubs directory at this point (unless you chose to make it private in Step 5 above), and you can start inviting friends to join it, using the <u>Invite friends</u> link. (You may access the same invitation page at any time using the link under Member Tools, as described previously in this chapter.)

You need a Yahoo! ID to create a club or even to participate in them. If you don't currently have one, please perform 74 penitential push-ups. Then go to Chapter 1 where I explain how to create a Yahoo! ID. It's easy.

Customizing your club

Yahoo! Clubs all look pretty much the same (which is an advantage when you're club-hopping), but you can do a few things to make yours unique. After you've created the basic club (following the steps in the preceding section), click the <u>Fix it up</u> link to customize your club. The Adjust Club Settings page gives you the following options:

- ✔ **Describe Your Club.** You get only eight words, so make the most of them.

- ✔ **Founder's Message.** This message, usually a few sentences long, appears on the main club page. Use it to expound on the brief club description, or say a few words about yourself, or set up a chat schedule.

- ✔ **Your Home Page Address.** You can fill this in if you have a Web page or site. You don't need to divulge your URL, though. Some people supplement a Web page at another location by using a Yahoo! Club because it adds built-in messaging, chat, and calendar features. You might decide to link to your Web page even if it's unrelated to the topic of your club — the option is yours.

- ✔ **Picture URL.** This is where you may place the Web location of a picture, which will appear on the main club page. It's just about the only way you can give your club page a distinctive graphics appearance, but — like the other customization options — it isn't required. You may use a photo of yourself or any graphic you think will enliven your club's subject.

- ✔ **Listed or Unlisted.** By this point, you have already chosen whether to list your club in the Yahoo! Clubs directory or leave it out. This option gives you a chance to reverse your decision.

Note that if you make your club unlisted at this point, you will not be able to list it again in the Yahoo! Clubs directory.

The trickiest option is placing a picture on your club page. Keep three points in mind:

- ✔ You cannot upload the picture to Yahoo!. To the contrary, you point club visitors to your graphic. You must know the URL of the graphic, and when you enter it, Yahoo! automatically creates the code that displays the graphic on your club page.

- ✔ The process works with the two most common graphic file formats — GIF and JPEG (sometimes called JPG) — but no others. Make sure your picture is in one of those formats before entering the URL. You know the format is correct if the very final portion of the URL is .gif or .jpg.

- ✔ The space for the picture on your club page is rather small, to put it generously. Specifically, the picture gets squeezed to a size of 150 pixels high and 150 pixels wide. The closer to that size your picture is, the better it will look. Pictures that exceed one or both of those dimensions will get distorted when they appear on a club page.

After you set all the options you chose to adjust, click the Submit Changes button.

Using the Administrative Tools

As founder of a Yahoo! Club, you have awesome power. Perhaps *awesome* is something of an overstatement. At any rate, you have some control over your membership and the settings for club options. This control is located in a series of links called Admin Tools, located in the left-hand sidebar of any club you founded. (Non-founding members can't see the Admin Tools links.)

As a club founder, you can perform four main control tasks:

- ✔ Remove a member or make him or her a founder
- ✔ Send e-mail to members
- ✔ Edit the settings for your club page
- ✔ Change the settings of your club's calendar

Editing members

The Edit Members page displays a list of your club's founder(s) and members and provides two actions you can perform on them. Clicking the <u>Delete</u> link removes a member from the club, never to return. Clicking the <u>Make Founder</u> link turns a regular member into a founding member and gives that person access to the Admin Tools.

Think twice before exercising your stunning power to delete a member or make someone a founder. Kicking someone out of your club is permanent, and that Yahoo! ID will never be able to join again. It's stiff punishment and should probably be used only in cases of severe disruption, such as posting obscene material to your club or harassing other members. Conversely, turning someone into a founder makes that person invulnerable to deletion, so make wise choices. This option is mostly used when a group decides to open a club together — one person creates the club, the others join, and the first person makes them all founders right away.

Sending e-mail

Clicking the <u>Send Email</u> link displays the Send Email to the Club page, where you can contact all your members at once. This is a great feature but should not be overused. If your members start complaining to Yahoo! that you're contacting them too much, your club might get nuked.

This page is easy to use and doesn't require keeping an address book. Just type your e-mail message into the form and click the Send Mail button.

This feature should be used (in moderation) to notify your members of scheduled club events, for periodic updates of your personal news, or to inform your membership of developments in the subject of your club. For example, members of a club about Web animation might be interested to know about a new animated cartoon site. But you can also use the message board for such announcements, and that's probably what your members would prefer.

How much mail is too much mail? Forget about daily circulars to your members — that's way too much in most cases. A weekly bulletin is borderline acceptable to most people. Less frequent communications are acceptable. Remember that your members can't opt in and out of your mailing list. All members are automatically on the list and receive everything you send from the Send Email to the Club page.

One idea that makes greater use of the Send Email administrative tool is to create a club expressly for the purpose of generating a mailing list. For example, you might write a weekly Cool Site tip and desire to distribute it to people by means of an e-mail list. You could create a Weekly Cool Site club and make it clear that members will receive an e-mail every week. In this case, the message board and chat room are less important features than receiving the weekly e-mail, though of course they can still be used. This idea is a quick, easy, and free way to build a mailing list.

Editing settings

The <u>Edit Settings</u> link provides a continuous opportunity to alter the basic settings you might have adjusted when you created the club. If you didn't set these options at that time, or if you did and you want to change them, it's not a problem. Use the input forms on this page to describe the club in eight words or less, write a brief Founder's message, list your Web page address if you have one, link the club's main page to a picture URL, and de-list your club from the Yahoo! Clubs directory.

Proceed cautiously if you're considering removing your club from the directory. After you unlist it, you can never list it again. (Another one of those irrevocable decisions so commonplace in life.)

Calendar options

The Calendar page is where you, as a founder, can alter the default settings of the club's interactive calendar. Using the drop-down menus and radio buttons, select the following options:

- **Default View.** This is where you decide if your calendar will automatically display one week, a month, a day, or a year at a time.

- **Default Day View.** Your choices here are List and Graphical, referring to how the calendar page is laid out. I prefer Graphical, but try them both and see which looks best to you.

- **Time Zone.** Select your local time zone from the drop-down menu of global time zones.

- **Daylight Savings Time.** For most of the United States, it's best to set this option to Automatic. Everyone else should select On or Off.

- **Working Hours.** This option sets at what hour each calendar day begins and ends.

When you're finished with the settings, click the Save button to see your new calendar. Remember, you can alter these settings at any time.

Chapter 17

The Great People Quest

*T*he Internet might seem like a galaxy of colorful Web pages (billboard heaven?) but actually it's all about people. What started out as the information highway has a more personal destiny than merely feeding data faster and more overwhelmingly than ever before. Ultimately, the Net will fulfill its potential only if it brings people closer together. It is already stepping into that destiny in a few ways.

E-mail, for all its seeming impersonality, is actually the servant of closer relationships. And I know from personal experience that e-mail has the power to bridge the chasms of time, geography, and neglect. Have you ever thought of tracking down an old friend through e-mail? This chapter explains Yahoo!'s contribution to that goal.

Personal ads also thrive on the Internet. This fact might make the Web seem like nothing more than a digitized meat market. But the truth is that information databasing, when applied to the problem of human loneliness, can improve the human condition. (Didn't think we'd get quite this deep in a ...*For Dummies* book, did you? Keep your head — I'll emerge from the philosophical mist soon.) Yahoo! Personals opens up one of the most popular meeting places for people looking for companionship of all sorts, and we go there in this chapter. Keep reading to see how your Yahoo! account helps you find old friends and make new ones.

Finding an E-Mail Address

To find regular folks, look in the phone book; to find a business, look in the Yellow Pages. To find an e-mail address, what can you do? The Web has several e-mail directories, and one of them is in Yahoo!.

Keeping an e-mail directory is a thorny challenge for a few reasons. First, people increasingly have multiple addresses. Office e-mail, home e-mail, Web-based e-mail. In the early days of the Internet, a single e-mail address defined a person's virtual location — like a street address in the offline world. The contemporary online scene, however, doesn't have a single, irrefutable identifier. People are spread among many addresses.

The second reason e-mail directories are problematic is that even though many people might have a main address, it's liable to be changed fairly often. Every time your long-lost high-school buddy switches Internet providers, the e-mail address changes. Directories try to keep up, but not one of them provides a really stellar, reliable service.

Yahoo! People Search offers e-mail address searching but from a different angle. The idea is not to attempt a database of all current e-mail addresses. Instead, the service is a registry of information about people who *want to be found.* This idea was originated by a company called Four11, and Yahoo! liked it enough to buy Four11 and recast it as Yahoo! People Search. This directory finds *only* those people who have registered a free listing in the directory. As such, it's not a general-purpose e-mail White Pages. People Search is designed to help people find old friends and invites everyone to include a bit of personal history to help past acquaintances locate them.

If you've been on the Internet for a while, you might have registered with the old Four11. If you did so before September 1, 1998 — surprise! Your listing no longer exists. Follow the directions in the following section for creating a new listing.

To begin searching for e-mail addresses, click the <u>People Search</u> link on the Yahoo! home page or go directly to

```
people.yahoo.com
```

Figure 17-1 illustrates the People Search page. Follow these steps:

1. On the Yahoo! People Search page, under the Email Search banner, fill in the Name fields.

Either field is optional, but filling in both (first and last name) makes it easier to find someone. Entering only a first name is likely to overwhelm you with results. The Reset button clears both fields of any text.

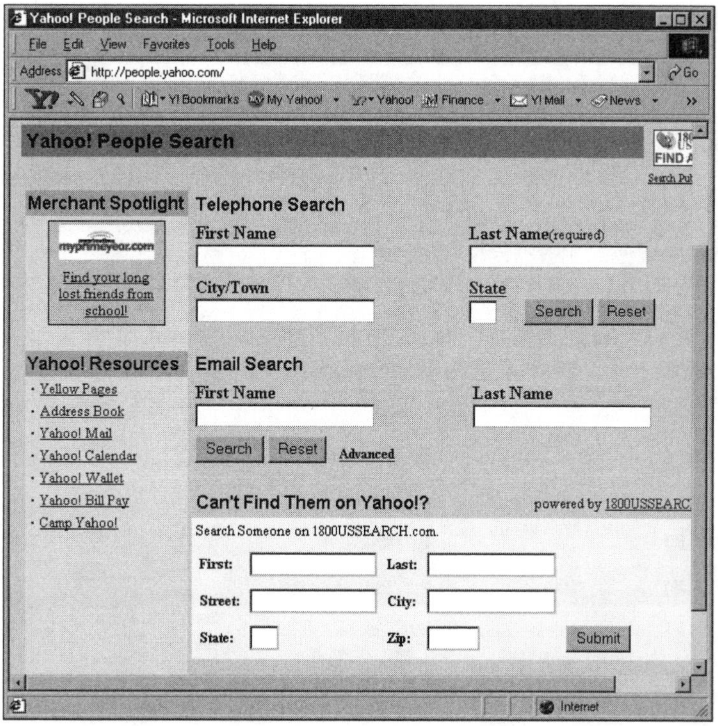

Figure 17-1:
The People
Search
page, from
which you
can find
e-mail
addresses
and phone
numbers.

2. **Click the Search button.**

   The Email Basic Search Results page appears, as shown in Figure 17-2.

3. **Click any link in the Name column or the Email column.**

   Email links open up a window of your default e-mail program, ready to
   send a note to the selected address. Name links provide as much information about that person as he or she provided to the database.

The right column on the E-mail Basic Search Results page shows the Search
Public Records on 1800USSEARCH link. This link leads to a commercial service
through which you can really find out about somebody, including information
about bankruptcies, civil judgments, and previous addresses. This detective
work, provided by 1800USSEARCH.com, is a fee-based service not provided
by Yahoo! but linked by Yahoo!.

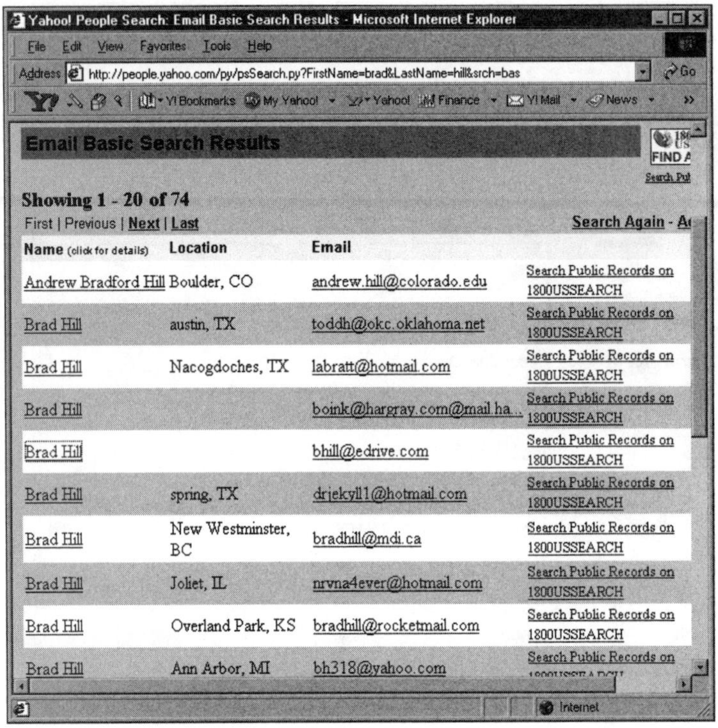

Figure 17-2:
Results of
an e-mail
search.
Click a
name to
see more
information
or an
address to
send an
e-mail.

If you're simply looking for an e-mail address, you can end your search on the Email Basic Search Results page. But if you click a name link to proceed to a person's information page, a few conveniences await you:

✔ Click the Address Book link to add the e-mail address to your Yahoo! Address Book (see Chapter 3 for more on Yahoo! Mail).

✔ Click the Try Phone Search link (if one exists for the person you've found) in hope of finding your person's phone number. However, the search engine isn't the sharpest knife in the drawer when it comes to this particular function. It gathers the name and state information, disregarding a more detailed address if present, and delivers more phone-number search results than you want. Aren't computers supposed to make things more convenient? Oh well. Try calling directory assistance.

✔ Click vCard if you have an e-mail program that supports the vCard format. That's about as helpful as mud, right? Here's the story — vCards are just a format for storing address book information. Outlook Express, Netscape Messenger, and other mail programs accept vCard entries, though they use different systems for getting a vCard entry into their address books. Look at your Help files or program documentation for information about vCards. Clicking the vCard link initiates a download of a person's address book information.

A somewhat more advanced form of e-mail searching lurks on the other side of the <u>Advanced</u> link on the People Search page. The Advanced Email Search page, which is shown in Figure 17-3, invites you to ask for matches to specific aspects of the People Search directory, including an old e-mail address (very handy) and an organization name.

The results of an advanced search depend very much on just how divulging your target person was when registering at People Search or the old Four11. But it's worth a try. Fill in as many of the fields as you can and then click the Search button full of hope.

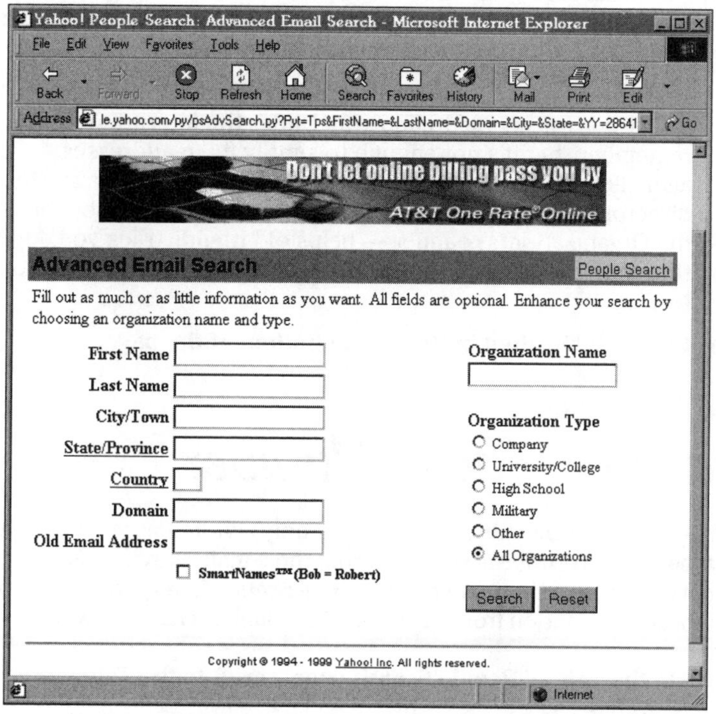

Figure 17-3:
The
Advanced
Email
Search
page.

Getting Yourself Registered

As long as you're using People Search, why not participate in both directions? That is to say, instead of just searching in the database, register yourself so people can find *you*. Here's how:

1. **On the Yahoo! People Search page, click the <u>Edit/Create My Listing</u> link.**

2. **On the next page, read the Terms of Service Agreements and then click the I Accept button at the bottom of the page.**

   This agreement is a standard legal morass in which you promise to provide accurate information and absolve Yahoo! of any legal responsibility should you be harmed through the use of People Search. (Like if your keyboard starts biting back at your hands or if the old college friend you track down makes you pay, with interest, that 100 dollars you've owed him for 20 years.) One important agreement is that you won't duplicate the listings or use them for any commercial purposes, such as bulk e-mailings.

3. **On the Create your Yahoo! People Search Listing (could they have thought of a longer page name?), fill in your name and any other info you want to add to the searchable database.**

   Text-entry fields are optional, but the more information you plug in, the easier it is for people to find you. Under the Internet Address(es) banner, remember that it's not enough to simply fill in addresses — you must also click the radio button next to any address you want added to the directory. Filling out the High School and University sections — under the Organization(s) banner — helps old friends track you down. Whether that thought inspires you to add the information or leave it out is up to you.

4. **Click the Finished button at the bottom of the page.**

Looking Up a Phone Number

Yahoo! has a nationwide (United States only) White Pages for looking up phone numbers. This service is separate from the e-mail search, even though you initiate both from the same page. No registration is required — Yahoo! gets its database information from the phone companies. Here's how to find a number:

1. **On the Yahoo! People Search page, scroll to the Telephone Search area.**

2. **In the Last Name field, enter a name.**

   The Last Name field is the only required field, but the more information you can provide in the other fields, the better.

3. **Click the Search button.**

That was easy, and the results are probably a good deal more satisfying than in the Email Search section. Figure 17-4 shows a Phone Search Results page. You might be wondering what happens when you click a phone-number link. You get a download page for Net2Phone, a free software product that lets you make phone calls over your computer. (The calls aren't free, but the software is.) If you have a Windows computer with speakers and a microphone, you might want to investigate Net2Phone. The download is a no-risk, no-obligation affair, and you can test out the on-screen phone by making real calls to toll-free 800 numbers before opening an account to make toll calls with the program.

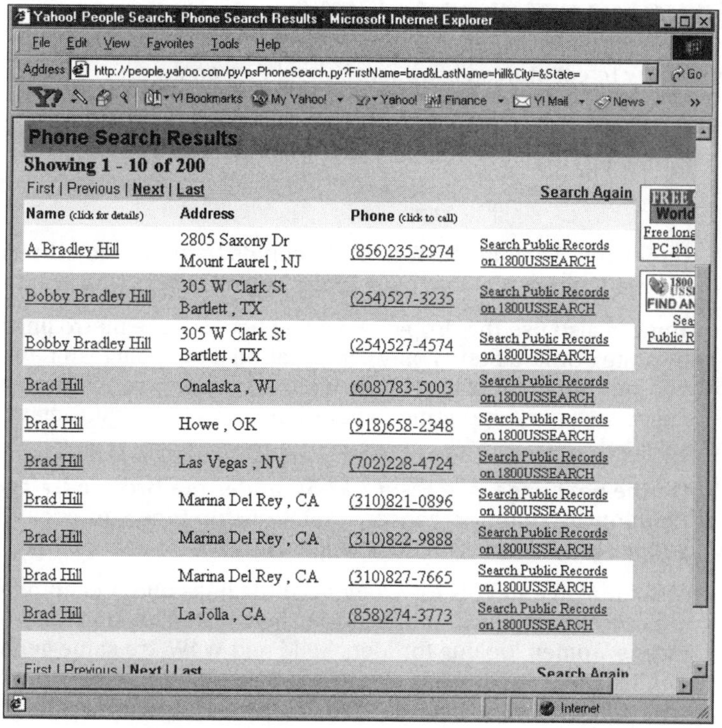

Figure 17-4:
The Phone Search Results page. None of these Brad Hills is I.

Getting Personal

All well and good, but searching for love is the thing. Yahoo! runs one of the most popular personal classified services on the Web. The classified service is only moderately sophisticated, but it has two great advantages over slick competing online personals sites. First, it's free. Putting up an ad, browsing, contacting someone — it's all free of charge. Second, it's fast. You can cover a lot of ground in your search for Mr. or Ms. Right without spending all night at it. After all, what you *really* want to spend all night doing is getting to know someone, not searching for his or her e-mail address. Yahoo! lubricates the process (so to speak).

Yahoo! Personals is part of Yahoo! Classifieds, which I dutifully explore in Chapter 23. I've separated the Personals section because personal ads are all about meeting people, whereas the other categories in Yahoo! Classifieds are about selling things.

Browsing personal ads

Here's how to get started browsing Yahoo! Personals:

1. **Click the Personals link on the Yahoo! home page or go directly to the following URL:**

   ```
   personals.yahoo.com
   ```

2. **Under the Welcome to Yahoo! Personals banner, click the metro area closest to your residence (or to the region where you want to browse).**

   You can also use the drop-down menu beneath the metro links to browse by state (United States only). International browsing isn't available. If you surf into Yahoo! Personals while logged into your Yahoo! ID, the metro area corresponding to your home location is automatically selected.

3. **On the next page (see Figure 17-5), under the Browse By Type of Relationship banner, choose a relationship type and click the gender-preference code that appeals to you.**

   M is for Men and W is for Women, so the links under each relationship are cryptic but decipherable. M4W means Men looking for Women. W4M means Women looking for Men. M4M and W4W are same-gender ads. I don't know if anyone has ever clicked the All link, except perhaps androgynous folks with very broad tastes. However, for the purpose of unbiased illustration, I'm clicking it in this example.

   Note that you can also search for ads by keyword. Use the drop-down menus the select your gender preference.

4. **On the Search Results page, begin reading ads or consider searching with keywords.**

   Figure 17-6 shows the page containing personal ads (10 to a page), plus the search fields in the left sidebar. The search options are on every page of ads, and I describe how to use them in the next section.

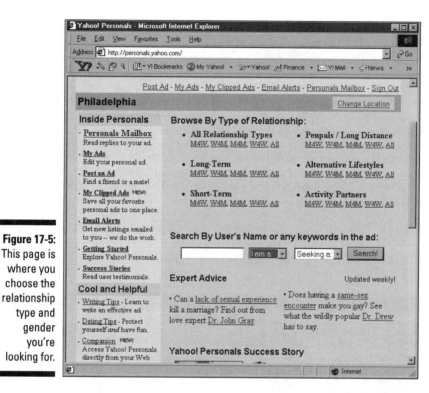

Figure 17-5:
This page is
where you
choose the
relationship
type and
gender
you're
looking for.

As you can see from Figure 17-6, each personal ad consists of three parts:

✔ A header, which includes the age and town of the person posting the ad, the advertiser's screen name, and the date of the ad's posting.

✔ A description makes up the body of the notice.

✔ A More button is presented at the bottom. The More button links to another page with the remainder of long-winded ads, plus more information about the advertiser. On the detailed page, click the Clip This Ad link to add the advertisement to a personal clipping folder of favorite ads. You can access that folder from the Yahoo! Personals home page (when you are logged in with your ID), by clicking the My Clipped Ads link.

Getting picky

Use the NARROW MY SEARCH sidebar options to weed out elements you don't want to see in a classified ad. You can't determine in advance whether a new romantic interest will criticize your haircut. (Life is dangerous.) But you can force the search engine to find ads from people of a particular ethnicity, religious inclination, and age. You can eliminate smokers or non-smokers. You can sort the messages by date or age of the advertiser. And you can filter older ads, which is usually a good idea.

The KEYWORDS field searches not only the Description part of the ad but the Yahoo! ID as well. If you want to match a phrase, put quotation marks around it.

If the standard search options aren't delivering your soulmate to the front door, you can try the Advanced Search page, which is shown in Figure 17-7. Although the Advanced Search page has an impressive layout (the figure shows only part of the page), it adds only a few features to the standard search options. For example, you can distinguish between drinkers and non-drinkers and people of different body types.

Yahoo! Personals sets up a special Personals Mailbox for you, distinct from your Yahoo! Mail account. Personals mail is *not* mixed in with your regular Yahoo! mail, unless you give someone your Yahoo! Mail address.

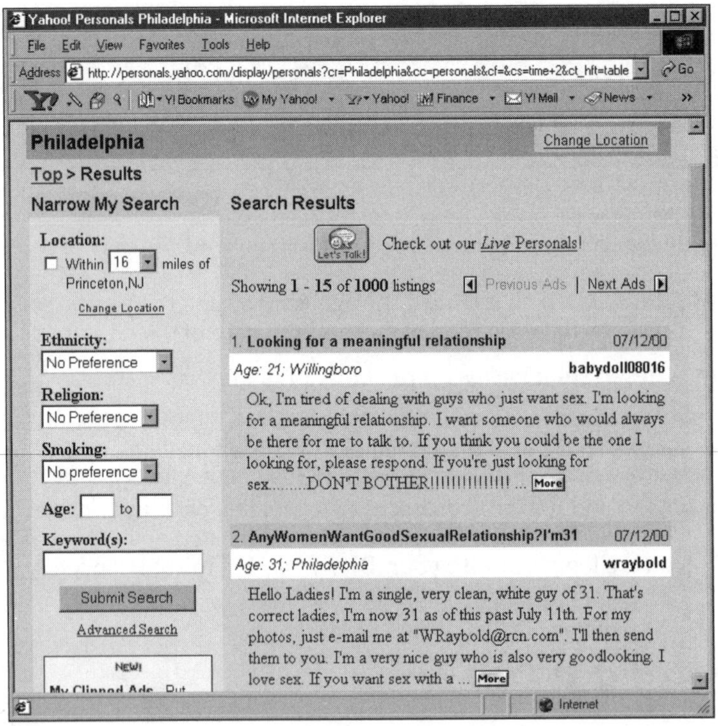

Figure 17-6: Yahoo! personal ads. Search options are available on each page.

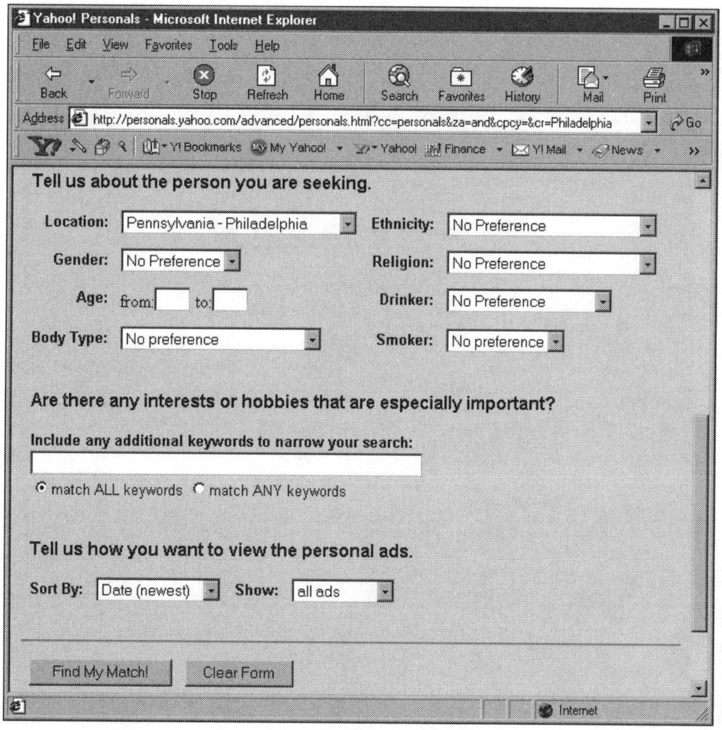

Figure 17-7:
Use
Advanced
Search to
match up
with a
person's
character-
istics and
interests.

Placing a personal ad

Browsing, writing responses to ads, hoping for replies — all is well and good, but you can cut to the chase with a more assertive approach. Consider placing your own Yahoo! personal. Here's how:

1. **On the Yahoo! Personals home page, click the Post Ad link.**

   The link takes you to the general submission page for Yahoo! Classifieds.

2. **Click the Personals link.**

3. **On the submission page (see Figure 17-8), fill in all required informa- tion fields, plus whatever optional information you want to share.**

4. **In the large text field (scroll down to see it), write your message.**

5. **Click the Submit entry button near the bottom of the page.**

   Your ad is automatically positioned in the geographical directory that best matches your zip code.

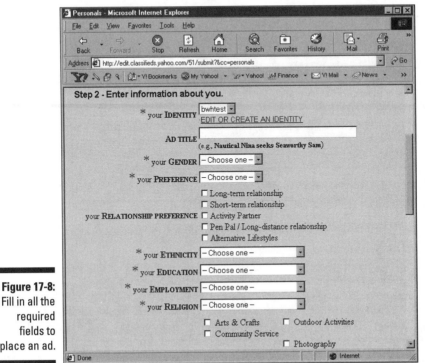

Figure 17-8:
Fill in all the
required
fields to
place an ad.

Responses to your personal ads go directly and automatically to your Personals Mailbox. They are not mixed with your Yahoo! Mail. Some people set up a separate Yahoo! ID for Personals communications, to assure that all Personals correspondence remains separate from other letters. Your Personals Mailbox is accessed in a few different ways, including from My Yahoo! (if you choose the link to appear there) and from Yahoo! Messenger. You may also click the <u>Personals Mailbox</u> link on the Yahoo! Personals home page (refer to Figure 17-6). Of course, at any time, you can shift a correspondence from your Personals Mailbox to another address by giving someone another of your e-mail addresses.

Letting the ads come to you

Yahoo! Personals has a new feature since the last edition of the book, and it's one that caters to computer potatoes. Tired of going to the trouble of browsing personals? Set up a profile of your desired person and let Yahoo! send matching ads to you as they are posted. Here is how to do it:

1. **On the Yahoo! Personals home page, click the <u>Email Alerts</u> link.**

2. **On the Yahoo! Personals - Alerts page, click the <u>Create An Alert</u> link.**

3. **On the next page, fill in all the required fields and as many of the optional fields as you choose.**

   This is where you describe the type of ad you want to receive. Make sure you specify the e-mail address at which you want to receive the alerts. At the bottom of the page, you can determine two delivery times per day.

4. **Click the Finished button.**

Part V
At Your Service, Yahoo! Style

The 5th Wave   By Rich Tennant

"NOW, THAT WOULD SHOW HOW IMPORTANT IT IS TO DISTINGUISH 'FERTILIZING PRACTICES' FROM 'FERTILITY PRACTICES' WHEN DOWNLOADING A VIDEO FILE FROM THE INTERNET."

In this part . . .

The service aspect of Yahoo! gets full play in these three chapters, which focus on travel and on researching major purchases such as cars and real estate. Pay particular attention to Chapter 20, which describes the invaluable Yahoo! Companion.

Chapter 18

Non-Computer Destinations

In This Chapter

▶ Imagining travel destinations with Yahoo!'s help

▶ Planning a trip and booking tickets

*Y*ahoo! Travel is a double-faceted travel site, incorporating destination info with reservation and ticketing services. As such, it's appealing to armchair travelers and also useful for determined ticket-buyers. The destination content is wonderfully literate and interesting — great text and minimal pictures. The ticket-reservation service operates much like others on the Web, finding the least expensive options automatically and enabling online purchases of plane tickets, hotel reservations, and rental-car reservations.

Get to the right portion of Yahoo! by clicking the <u>Travel Agent</u> link on the home page or by entering this URL in your browser:

```
travel.yahoo.com
```

The Yahoo! Travel home page, which is shown in Figure 18-1, links to both the destination content and the reservation service. This chapter explains the high points of each.

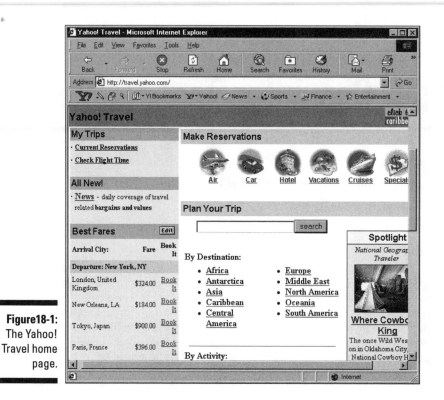

Figure18-1:
The Yahoo!
Travel home
page.

Armchair Traveling

I don't know about you, but I like reading about foreign places and imagining I'm visiting them. (I try not to imagine cramped train seats, unpalatable food, vexing language problems, and bewildering currency exchanges, though.) Yahoo! Travel features great travel writing, especially when it comes to the history and culture of a place, and also preparatory information for soon-to-be travelers. Following is the best way to dive into this part of Yahoo! Travel:

1. **On the Yahoo! Travel home page, click any <u>By Destination:</u> link.**

   Don't be fooled by the search form above the links — it leads only to Yahoo! directory pages, not to travel destination pages. You could search on the keyword *computer,* but that's not what you came to Yahoo! Travel to accomplish.

2. **On the next page, click any <u>Featured Countries</u> link.**

   Not many countries are left off these lists; the destination section is gratifyingly complete. You may also use the map in the left sidebar. Click on the map to display a larger version, which is interactive. On the larger map, click any country to proceed.

3. **On the country destination page, which is shown in Figure 18-2, begin your exploration of that country's cities, weather, attractions, and culture.**

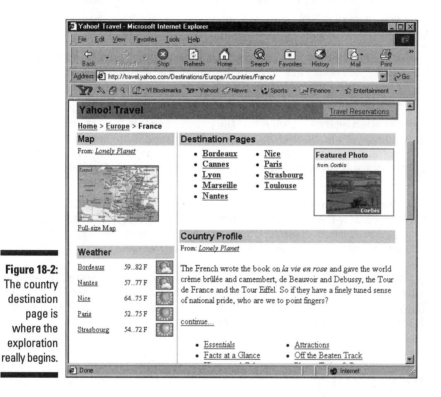

Figure 18-2:
The country
destination
page is
where the
exploration
really begins.

The country destination page is an information hub that you might want to bookmark if you're involved with ongoing research about a destination. Most country pages include the following sections:

✔ **Destination Pages.** Some countries feature pages dedicated to cities or regions. Each of those pages presents information for travelers about dining, transportation, nightlife, local attractions, and other points of interest. Usually, a featured article from *National Geographic Traveler* or *Kroll Travel Watch* helps convey the flavor of a destination.

✔ **Country Profile.** The Traveler's Info links, provided by the Lonely Planet travel site, are an incredible, valuable resource. This is where armchair traveling gets really satisfying. I've lost myself in this section, learning about the cultures of far-off places. All editorial content behind these links is composed with style and humor. The Facts at a Glance page is a dry political and economic cheat sheet, but the other sections bring countries to life with rich descriptions of history and current atmosphere. The History and Culture page is a definite keeper — I've hopped from country to country in Yahoo! Travel just reading that page.

✔ **Map.** The tiny map in the left sidebar expands with a click, but it's not interactive. It's nice to see a country's layout, though.

✔ **Weather.** Nothing brings a place to life like knowing what the weather is doing *right now.* Click any city link under the Weather banner to get a five-day forecast, including the present moment, so you can plan your imaginary residence in a foreign land.

✔ **Vacation Search.** Scroll down the page to see this feature, in the left sidebar. It's positioned on each country destination page, but it has nothing to do with the country. It's a generic Yahoo! Travel feature that allows you to search for tour packages according to destination, price, and duration.

✔ **Currency Converter.** This interactive puppy is convenient. See at a glance how the destination country's national currency stacks up against German, British, American, and Japanese monetary units or use a drop-down menu to convert other currencies.

At any point in your exploration of destinations, if you feel inspired to actually travel somewhere (you have to get out of that armchair sometime), click the Travel Reservations link on the Yahoo! Travel banner to shift over to the ticket-buying portion of Yahoo! Travel.

The Real Thing

Time to get out of your imagination and into a real airplane? Yahoo! Travel has you covered when dreaming turns to reality with an online reservation service that covers plane travel, hotel stays, and car rentals. Other sections specialize in vacations, cruises, and bargain travel packages.

Buying plane tickets online is safe, convenient, and empowering. I dumped my human travel agent years ago. I liked him, and he did a good job, but you can't beat the ease and flexibility of researching your own options and making the purchase from home.

As with other e-commerce, you buy plane tickets with a credit card. Yahoo! transfers your personal information from your Yahoo! ID account and then asks you for your credit card number at the "point of purchase" — on the screen where you actually buy the tickets. You can have a Yahoo! Travel account, however, without having a Yahoo! ID. It's just that if you have the ID, opening the travel account is a little easier.

As of this writing, the Yahoo! Travel reservation service is available for American and Canadian residents only. This restriction will probably change — that's my personal prediction, not the Yahoo! company line. Personal predictions are offered free of charge.

Reserving a plane trip is somewhat complicated but not difficult. You just need to persevere through a number of screens. You may bail out of the process at any time by clicking a Cancel button if one appears on the page, by surfing your browser elsewhere, by logging off the Internet, or by throwing your computer out the window. (The last option is an act of desperation and should be reserved for moments of pure despair.) Seriously, you're in no danger of becoming inextricably involved in the reservation process or unwittingly buying a ticket until the final purchase page, which I mark clearly in Step 10. Here's what to do:

1. **On the Yahoo! Travel home page, click the <u>Air</u> link.**

   The Roundtrip Flight Search page appears, as shown in Figure 18-3.

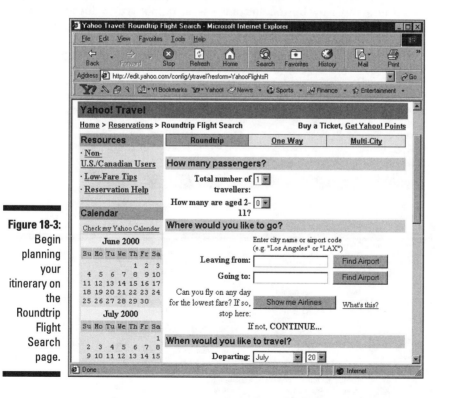

Figure 18-3: Begin planning your itinerary on the Roundtrip Flight Search page.

2. **Fill in all the information fields.**

   The important thing to remember on this complex page is that you can't make any bad mistakes. If you leave something out, Yahoo! tells you about it and prompts a correction before proceeding. Throughout the planning of an itinerary, you have the ever-present option of returning to this page and changing your settings — so don't agonize over whether to leave in the morning or the afternoon. If you're planning something more elaborate than a simple roundtrip excursion, click the <u>Multi-City</u> link. Skip over the Show me Airlines button for now — it's a diversion that I discuss right after this instruction list.

The <u>Terms and Conditions</u> link directly above the Show me available Flights button regurgitates standard legal language about the use and abuse of the flight reservation service. (Smoking the service is considered abuse.) Clicking the button is, legally, your acknowledgment of the Terms and Conditions, so you might want to glance at them.

3. Click the Show me available Flights button.

The Select a Flight page appears, as shown in Figure 18-4. Don't panic — clicking the Buy Now button doesn't charge your credit card. You can still back out. The Buy Later option usually lets you reserve an itinerary for 24 hours. If you're ready to buy tickets during this session, proceed with the Buy Now button. In some cases, Yahoo! Travel doesn't present complete roundtrip itineraries at this stage — when this happens, you are asked to choose an outgoing flight by clicking the Select button. The next page asks that you do the same for the returning flight.

Figure 18-4:
Select your
itinerary
from this
page.

4. **Click the Buy Now button or the Buy Later button to continue planning your trip.**

   The Review the ticket price information page appears.

5. **Click the Rules button for either leg of your trip to review the ticket restrictions and requirements.**

6. **Click the I Agree button — unless you're having second thoughts, in which case it would be a good time to click the Cancel button.**

   The Ticket Delivery Options page appears. E-Tickets are convenient but don't offer the tactile reassurance of a physical ticket. The E-Ticket eliminates the possibility of the stomach-dropping experience of arriving at the gate and realizing you forgot your tickets.

   The lower portion of this page describes general rules and conditions of traveling. It explains that flights are sometimes deliberately overbooked, that you should show up early, and other details that are second nature to experienced travelers.

7. **Select whether you'd like an E-Ticket, normal mail delivery of a paper ticket, or FedEx (fast) delivery of the ticket by clicking the button of choice.**

   The Complete the passenger information page appears.

8. **Adjust any fields that are inaccurate and then click the Information Is Correct button.**

9. **On the next two Choose your seats pages, select seats from the airplane diagram and then click the Continue button. Or if this is getting too complex, click one of the radio buttons and then click the Bypass Seat Maps button.**

   The Enter billing and delivery information page appears. This is the do-or-die page. If you continue past here, you're going on a trip. Or, at least, your credit card will be billed, whether you go or not. So be careful. You may have come this far just to see how the system works, but this is where the safe exploration ends. Don't let your mouse cursor anywhere near the Continue button unless you intend to buy these plane tickets.

10. **Type your credit card information, billing address, and delivery address and then click the Continue button.**

    If you don't want to buy tickets, the safest way to back out is to click the Cancel button.

Reserving an airplane flight is the most complicated procedure in Yahoo! Travel. Reserving a car or a hotel requires filling out the same sort of information (city, date, time, credit card payment) and using the same sort of drop-down menus and text-entry fields. You may use the Car and Hotel links from the Yahoo! Travel home page to get started with those reservations, even if you already have plane tickets purchased through Yahoo! Travel or elsewhere.

Chapter 19

What's This, the Real World?

I remember the real world, though it's been a long time since I ventured into it. Bright light emanating from the giant flame ball in the sky, fresh air, changing seasons almost as pretty as my screensaver. Large metallic contraptions that move people around, gigantic shelters made of wood and plaster, and places to go where people give you money to perform tasks. I don't remember the real names for these things, but I do know Yahoo! helps you obtain them.

This chapter illuminates Yahoo!'s contribution to bridging the online and offline worlds when it comes to job hunting, house shopping, and car buying.

Getting a Job

I don't know if the entire job-hunting odyssey will ever be replaced by online services. It's hard to imagine an effective job interview being conducted without a face-to-face meeting. But when it comes to resume sharing and sorting through local or national listings, nothing beats the data-crunching power of computers or the networking facility of the Internet. Online job searches are a big deal, for employers and employees both.

Yahoo! Careers (see Figure 19-1), has links to editorial and database content that helps you learn about and pursue careers. The first step is to surf to the following URL or click the <u>Careers</u> link from the Yahoo! home page next to Guides:

```
careers.yahoo.com
```

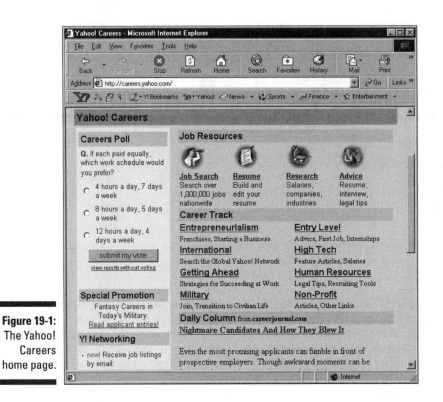

Figure 19-1:
The Yahoo!
Careers
home page.

Most people who enter Yahoo! Careers are looking for a job. You can get a fast start by clicking the Job Search link under the Job Resources heading. Then follow these steps:

1. **On the search page, use the drop-down menus and text-entry fields to describe the location and job type you're looking for.**

   This form gets company-specific if you want, though you don't need to fill in any of the text-entry fields. The Keywords field might be the most crucial to an effective search. Use that field to enter a job specialty, such as *information technology,* so you can define your expertise more specifically than the Function drop-down menu allows. Another option is to use keywords to specify a location within a state — a city, for example. Basically, use the Keywords field to search for any helpful matches that may occur in the text of a job listing.

   Note that if you enter Yahoo! Careers while signed in to a Yahoo! ID, this page automatically defaults to the location listed in your profile. Use the Change Location link to . . . well, change the location.

2. **Click the Find Jobs button.**

   The Search Results page appears, as shown in Figure 19-2.

3. **Browse your results and click the More Detail button to see details about any job.**

   If you'd rather browse than search, use the Job Listings directory beneath the search form.

TIP

You can adjust your search on any results page, using the Modify Your Search table at the bottom of the page. Click the DATE, COMPANY, or FUNCTION link to sort your results chronologically or alphabetically according to that column. (Sorting by date gives you a jump on new listings.)

Clicking the More Detail button displays an in-depth job listing. This page contains a job description and contact information.

The flip side of cruising job listings is distributing your resume. In other words, instead of finding a company, let the companies find you. Yahoo! Careers provides a resume database, which may or may not prove effective. The service is certainly flexible, allowing you to make the resume public or private, and you can attach it to responses to listings.

Yahoo! Careers - Listings - Microsoft Internet Explorer
File Edit View Favorites Tools Help
Back Forward Stop Refresh Home Search Favorites History Mail Print
Address _jtrm=&cpo=&cpj=&ck=&cc=employment&za=and&cr=Philadelphia&cs=time+2&cf=1&ct_hft=table
Go Links
Y! Bookmarks Yahoo! News Sports Finance Entertainment
Philadelphia
Change Location
Top > Classifieds > Search > Results
Showing 1 - 15 of over 1000 listings
Previous Ads | Next Ads
DATE COMPANY FUNCTION TERM TITLE LOCATION FULL LISTING
07/19/00 Top Echelon Network of Recruiters Service Salary LASER FIELD SERVICE Philadelphia, PA More Detail
07/19/00 Top Echelon Network of Recruiters Other / Not Specified Salary Oracle DBA Wilmington, DE More Detail
07/19/00 Top Echelon Network of Recruiters Other / Not Specified Salary Architecture Practice Manager Philadelphia, PA More Detail
07/19/00 Top Echelon Network of Recruiters Service Salary Regional Professional Service Manager Philadelphia, PA More Detail
07/19/00 Education Online Sales Work At Home Educational Marketer Philadelphia, PA More Detail
07/19/00 Education Online Marketing Work At Home Educational Marketer Philadelphia, PA More Detail
07/19/00 Job Sleuth Service Salary Free..Easy..Internet-Wide Job Detection Philadelphia, PA More Detail
Internet

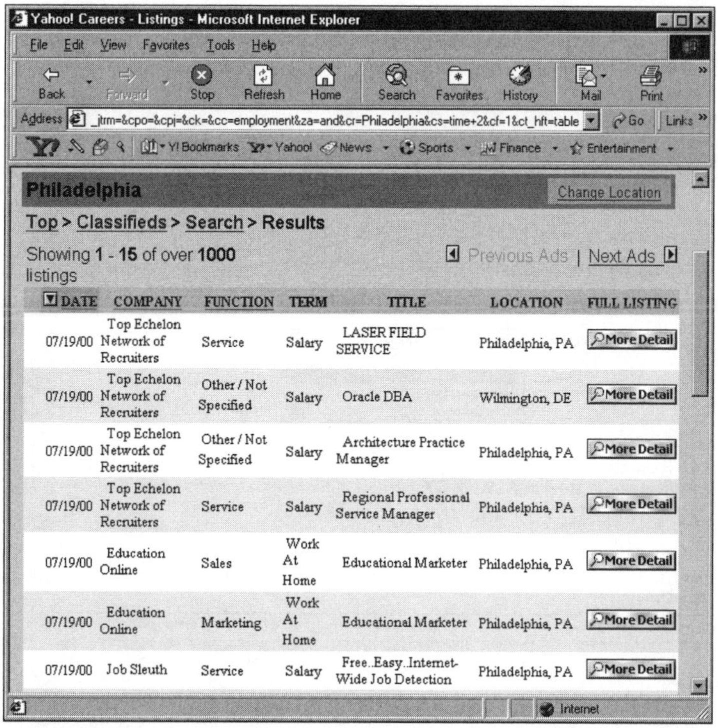

Figure 19-2: The Search Results page shows brief summaries of job listings.

Here's what to do:

1. **On the Yahoo! Careers page, click the <u>Resume</u> link.**

   The My Resumes page appears.

2. **Read the requirements and click the <u>Submit Your Resume Now</u> link.**

3. **On the Create/Edit Resume page, choose a Professional or Unstructured Template for your resume.**

   The Professional Template organizes your information for you. These steps follow the Professional Template path.

4. **On the Your Contact Information page, fill in all the information fields and then click the Submit button.**

   Only the URL field is optional.

5. **On the next Create-Edit Resume page, fill in the information fields and then click the Submit to Yahoo! Resume Pool button.**

   This page, which is shown in Figure 19-3, is where you enter your important resume information, including experience and the type of position you're seeking. Be sure to choose (with the radio buttons) whether you want the resume to be publicly available or remain private.

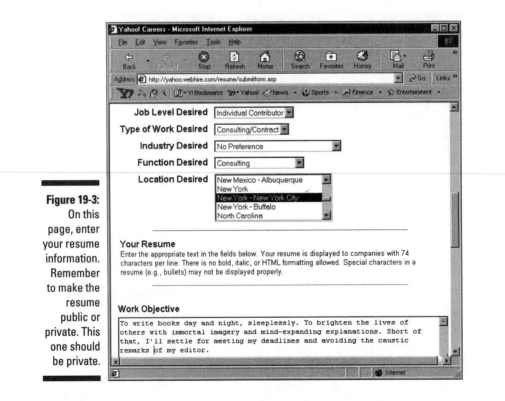

Figure 19-3: On this page, enter your resume information. Remember to make the resume public or private. This one should be private.

You can view your resume (or more than one — you're permitted to file up to three) by clicking the <u>Resumes</u> link on the Yahoo! Careers home page.

The remainder of the Yahoo! Careers home page is filled with links to helpful articles and a few interactive tools. One fun (and possibly depressing) gadget lurks behind the <u>Salary Comparison</u> link — it's a Salary Calculator for comparing your current salary (or salary requirement) in two cities. In other words, you learn the equivalent of your salary in, for example, New York or Nashville. It's an amusing catalyst for fantasies but also a useful tool if you're planning to relocate.

Gimme Shelter

Yahoo! Real Estate contributes to a growing trend of house buying and house selling over the Internet. With person-to-person contact becoming both more global and more precise, people are increasingly taking into their own hands what they used to entrust to professionals. At the grass roots level, Net-empowered individuals are buying and selling real estate as well as cars.

The Yahoo! Real Estate section contains articles and helpful educational readings. But the meat of the section consists of the listings themselves, part of the Yahoo! Classifieds system. I've separated real estate classifieds from other classifieds described in Chapter 23 because . . . well, because houses cost a heck of a lot more than other things people are selling. And because shopping for real estate is an online activity many people are particularly interested in.

The link for Yahoo! Real Estate is usually positioned near the bottom of the Yahoo! home page. You can also get started by surfing directly to this URL:

```
realestate.yahoo.com
```

The Yahoo! Real Estate home page, shown in Figure 19-4, presents home-buying news, help articles, and links to a search engine and directory of ads. You may browse or search, for both houses and apartments, either purchases or rentals.

If you're looking for a house to buy, here's the drill:

1. **On the Yahoo! Real Estate home page, click the <u>Buying</u> link.**

2. **Under the Buyer's Tools heading, click the <u>Search for a Home</u> link.**

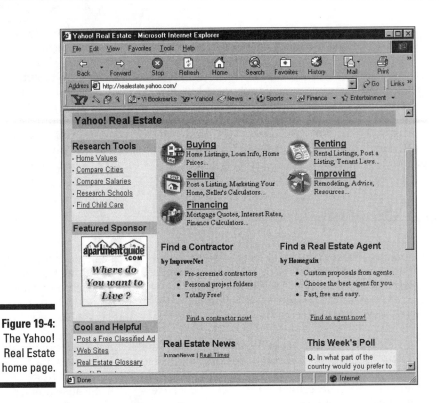

3. **On the Search Residential Real Estate Listings section of the next page, use the drop-down menus and text-entry fields to define what you're looking for.**

In this search form, if you don't fill in the City or Town field, you're likely to be steamrollered by an unmanageable number of results. Narrow them down with a city. Of the selections in the Property Type menu, Single Family Home is probably the most requested — Internet home shopping is all about connecting individuals and sidestepping realtors. On this page, if you decide you'd rather browse a directory than conduct a pinpoint search, scroll down to the Browse Residential Real Estate Listings section and click the regional link closest to your target location.

4. **Click the Search! button.**

5. **On the Search Results page, click a magnifying-glass icon next to any listing to see details and, in some cases, a photograph.**

The small camera icon indicates the presence of a photo on the details page. Note the links atop the four left columns. These DATE, PRICE, BEDS, AND BATHS links help you sort your search results by category — click any one to sort the list chronologically or numerically according to that category. If you want to change your search requirements, scroll down to the Modify Your Search table and enter new information. Remember that only fifteen matches are displayed on each page; click the <u>Next Ads</u> link to see more. Figure 19-5 shows a detailed listing.

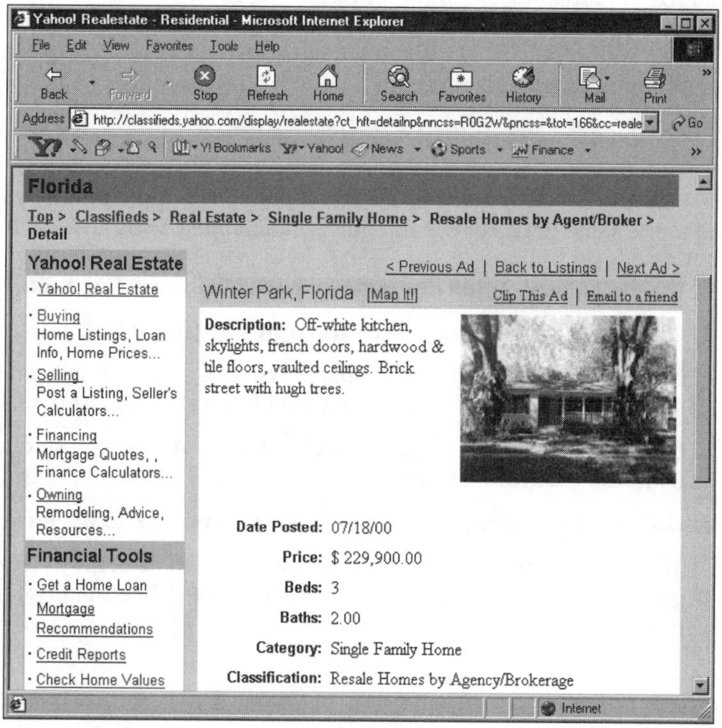

Figure 19-5: A detailed real estate listing with photo. Scroll down for contact information.

Apartments are nice, too. You can search for available rentals in your locality of choice, in much the same way as searching for houses. On the Yahoo! Real Estate home page, click the <u>Renting</u> link, and then click the <u>Search for Rentals</u> link on the next page.

Beyond the Tin Lizzie

If real estate is a hot Internet topic, car buying is blazing. Cars got a jump-start on homes in the frenzy to gain efficiency through the Internet. Cars are less expensive, of course, and the buyer-seller transaction is simpler than closing on a house. Furthermore, the brutal ritual of buying a car (in the United States, at least) was begging for improvement when the Web came along. In the last few years (since about 1997), the momentum of researching auto sales over the Net has grown to the point that almost everyone with any online experience knows you can get a better, probably friendlier, car deal online than offline.

Yahoo! Autos is partly about used cars and offers the same hook into Yahoo! Classifieds as the real estate and employment sections described earlier in this chapter. But Yahoo! Autos is also weighted toward researching new cars and obtaining financing. To this end, Yahoo! has licensed editorial content and research tools from around the Web, and the result is an impressive, well-rounded resource for car shoppers of all kinds.

To get to Yahoo! Autos, as shown in Figure 19-6, click the Autos link on Yahoo!'s home page or send your browser directly to this URL:

```
autos.yahoo.com
```

Yahoo! Autos provides a few ways to comparison-shop for new cars, but they all lead to the same data. Here is the quickest and most accurate way to get results:

1. **On the Yahoo! Autos home page, click the Buy A Car link.**

2. **On the Buy A Car page, click the New Car Guide link.**

   Or scroll down the page and select the types and brands of car you'd like to compare. This is a nifty service that I describe after this series of steps.

3. **On the New Car Guide page, click the link of any brand, class, or price from the category groups.**

4. **On the next page, click the car model you'd like to examine.**

   You may be shown one more winnowing-down directory page before you get to the final research page for a car model. Click the Photos & Specs link to see that page.

Used cars and figures and loans, oh my!

Yahoo! Autos is not only about researching new cars, though that's what most people use it for. Almost everything in the car-buying experience is represented at this site. If you're serious about buying a (new or used) car over the Net, you should explore every link on the home page. Here are some highlights:

✔ Click the Finance A Car link for a full range of loan calculators, credit assistance, and loan rate tables. You can actually get a car-loan quote in this section.

✔ The Buy A Car section covers used vehicles in addition to the new models. Click the Used Car Guide link for an overview of the pre-owned marketplace. The Classifieds section links you to the auto portion of Yahoo! Classifieds. Click Auctions to see what cars are on the block at Yahoo! Auctions.

✔ Go to the Maintain Cars section from the home page for repair guides and links to auto maintenance services.

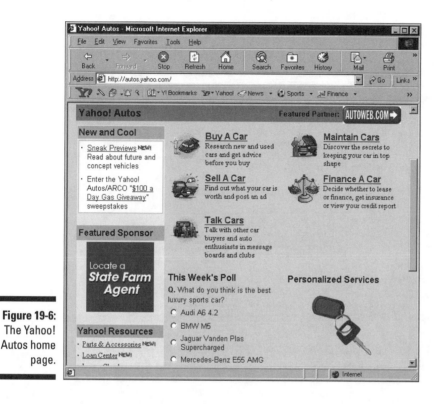

The information page for a car model presents a good overview of its equipment and specifications as well as links to more information from AutoSite, a Yahoo! partner. The information page, shown in Figure 19-7, has five main sections:

- ✔ **Top.** The upper portion of the page contains a photo and lists the base price and dealer invoice price (very good to know when negotiating). This section is a sticker overview, giving the engine type and fuel economy numbers. Click the picture to see a larger version.

- ✔ **Summary.** This paragraph is a brief summary, in plain English, of the car.

- ✔ **Equipment.** In text format, this portion describes the car's standard and optional features.

- ✔ **Specifications.** Presented as a table, this section details the engine type, interior dimensions, seating and cargo capacity, steering type, suspension type, brakes, and warranty information.

- ✔ **Other Resources.** These links all lead to AutoSite information pages.

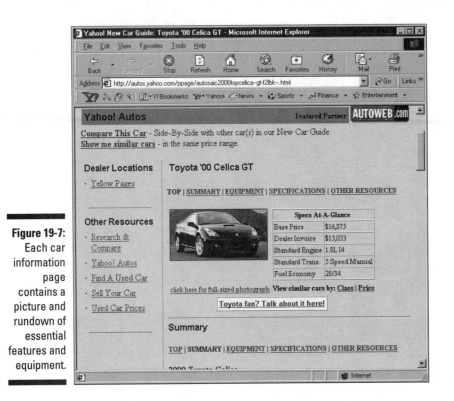

Figure 19-7:
Each car information page contains a picture and rundown of essential features and equipment.

One of the best features of Yahoo! Autos is the comparison tool. This database perk lets you put two car-information pages side by side on the browser page. Actually, you can put up more than two, but most monitors aren't wide enough to comfortably accommodate three or more cars being compared. Follow these steps to use the comparison feature:

1. **On the Yahoo! Autos home page, click the <u>Buy A Car</u> link.**

2. **On the Buy A Car page, scroll down to the Research and Compare New Vehicles section.**

3. **Check the boxes next to two (or more) car brands you want to compare.**

   Use the drop-down menu above the cars brand list to select the type of vehicle you're interested in — doing so saves a step later. If you're shopping in a price range, use the lower menus to specify that range.

4. **Click the Search & Compare button.**

5. **On the Vehicle Matches page, use the check boxes to select which two (or more) specific models you'd like to compare.**

   At this point, you may also click any <u>Photos & Specs</u> link to see an information page for that model, without comparing to another model.

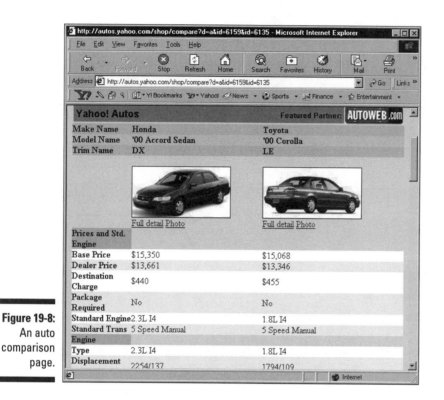

Figure 19-8:
An auto
comparison
page.

6. Click the COMPARE button.

The Vehicle Matches page appears, as shown in Figure 19-8. Each car is represented with a picture and a column of information. Scroll down the page to compare the details of each car's engine, pricing, dimensions, capacities, and much more.

Chapter 20

The Yahoo! Companion

*Y*ahoo! offers several compelling features and downloadable treats that aim to make the Yahoo! experience central to your entire Internet lifestyle. The Yahoo! Messenger (Chapter 15), My Yahoo! (Chapter 2), and Yahoo! Mail (Chapter 3) are effective, enjoyable, and useful anchors to the Yahoo! service. One other gizmo, the Yahoo! Companion, is designed to keep every important and customized portion of Yahoo! as close as a click in your Web browser.

Yahoo! Companion is a menu bar that attaches to your browser (version 4.0 and later of Internet Explorer or Navigator). This attachment tells you when you have Yahoo! e-mail and links to just about every portion of Yahoo!. Furthermore, you can use it to supplement (or replace) the Favorites system in Internet Explorer (or Bookmarks in Navigator).

I cannot overestimate the importance of Yahoo! Companion to the dedicated Yahoo! user and especially to the traveling user. The Companion stores your bookmarked Web destinations on the "server side" — that is, on Yahoo!'s computers — so you can access your favorites from any connected computer in the world. The Favorites (or Bookmarks) list is the heart of a person's online housekeeping, so the Companion's effortless portability is a tremendous benefit.

I use Yahoo! Companion constantly, at home and on the road. You may have noticed that the Companion is pictured in about half the figures in this book. I removed it from some figures to squeeze in more screen content, but in my daily Internet use, I never remove it. The Companion is an essential part of my Yahoo! toolkit — perhaps the most essential. Best of all it's free and easy to install. This chapter walks you through its features.

Activating the Companion

Yahoo! Companion is downloaded over the Net. Installing it is much easier than regular program downloads and doesn't require selecting a location on your hard drive or going through an involved installation procedure. You just activate it from a special Web page and wait for it to appear in your browser. Follow these steps to give it a try:

1. **Go to the Yahoo! Companion home page at the following URL:**

   `companion.yahoo.com`

2. **Click the Get Yahoo! Companion Now button.**

3. **If a window appears asking whether you want to download and install the Yahoo! Companion, do the following:**

   a. **Click the Yes button.**

   A new browser window appears displaying the Edit Yahoo! Companion page.

   b. **Close your old browser window.**

   The new window will, after completing the next step, incorporate the Companion. From that point on, every new browser window you open contains the Companion.

4. **On the Customize Yahoo! Companion page, which is shown in Figure 20-1, click the boxes next to the Yahoo! features you'd like to appear as buttons on the Companion toolbar.**

   Many of the selections result in buttons that drop down into a menu of destinations. Figure 20-2 shows how this menu system works with the News button, which drops down into many categories of news, each of which has its own Yahoo! home page.

5. **To alter the order in which the buttons appear on the Companion toolbar, use the Change Layout button.**

6. **When you're finished, click the Finished button.**

Yahoo! Companion appears below the links bar and above the radio bar of Internet Explorer version 5.0. If you disable those two bars, it appears directly under the address bar (as shown in Figure 20-2).

The Companion bar can't be removed in the standard Internet Explorer fashion, by right-clicking a bar and selecting one of the checked bars. In fact, the Companion isn't really optional as long as it's installed. The only way to remove it from your browser is to uninstall it, as follows:

1. **Click the Edit button of the Companion.**

2. **Select Uninstall.**

   A pop-up confirmation window appears.

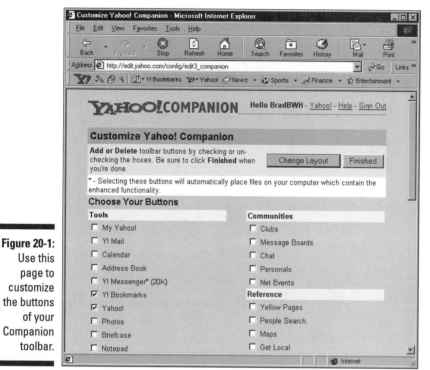

Figure 20-1:
Use this
page to
customize
the buttons
of your
Companion
toolbar.

3. **Click the Yes button.**

A pop-up window notifies you that Companion has been uninstalled.

4. **Click the OK button.**

You must close your browser and reboot for the Companion to disappear. You may activate it again at any time by following the first set of steps in this chapter.

Customizing the Companion

Like My Yahoo! (see Chapter 2) and Yahoo! Messenger (see Chapter 15), Yahoo! Companion comes to life when you customize it to your own preferences. You can revisit the Customize Yahoo! Companion page at any time:

1. **On the Companion, click the Edit button.**

The Edit button is on the left side of the Companion.

2. **Select Add/Edit buttons from the Edit menu.**

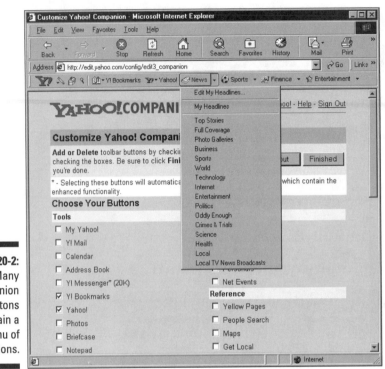

The Companion is like a glorified bookmark list for you browser, with most buttons dedicated to Yahoo! locations. (The Y! Bookmarks button houses links to outside sites, but I'll get to that a bit later.) Keep the following major points in mind when using Companion:

- Click the big red Y! button on the left edge of the Companion toolbar to display the Yahoo! home page.

- Click the magnifying-glass button to reveal a keyword search form. It operates just like the one in the main Yahoo! directory (see Chapter 5).

- An Alert button appears when you get e-mail or Yahoo! Personal mail. Click the button and select the alert you want to view. Click Refresh under the Edit button to reset your alerts.

- Click the More button on the right edge of the Companion to reveal your other selected buttons that don't fit on the toolbar. If you want different buttons on the toolbar, use the preceding instructions to change the toolbar layout.

- Some buttons have small arrows. Click the arrow to reveal specific Web page links for that button.

Y! Bookmarks (under the Tools section on the Customize Yahoo! Companion page) is a special button in three respects. First, it links to sites outside Yahoo!. Second, you can organize its links into folders. Third, the button is configurable and (in my opinion) improves the Favorites system of Internet Explorer.

Follow these steps to take advantage of the Y! Bookmarks button of the Companion:

1. **With the Yahoo! Companion installed, click the Edit button.**
2. **Click the Edit/Add buttons selection.**

   The Customize Yahoo! Companion page appears.
3. **Click the box next to Y! Bookmarks and then click the Finished button.**

The Stock Market Toolbar

Yahoo! Companion has added a companion since the first edition of this book. The Stock Market Toolbar is a corollary to the regular Companion toolbar. It gives you quick, one-click access to stock quotes, charts, investment news, research, and your Yahoo! portfolios (see Chapter 10). The Stock Market Toolbar is available from the regular Companion toolbar, under the Switch Toolbar button. Click that button and select Switch to Stock Market Toolbar. Companion takes a couple of seconds to communicate with Yahoo! and make the switch. The figure shows the Stock Market Toolbar in action.

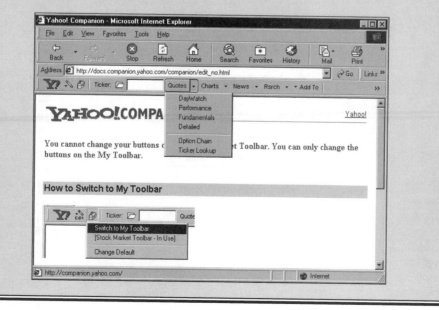

4. **On the Companion toolbar, click the Y! Bookmarks button.**

   A menu drops down with several default links.

5. **Click the Edit/Import Bookmarks selection.**

   The Edit your Bookmarks page appears.

6. **Click all boxes next to the default links that you want to remove from Y! Bookmarks and then click the Delete button.**

   You can check out the sites before deleting them from your Bookmarks list by clicking the site links.

7. **If you want to alter the Bookmarks listing of any link, click the Edit icon next to the link.**

   The Edit Bookmark page appears, as shown in Figure 20-3.

8. **Make the alterations you want and then click the Save button.**

   You can change the URL, the name of the link as it appears in your Bookmarks list, and any comment that you want to appear on the Edit your Bookmarks page. (Comments do not appear on the Y! Bookmarks list when you pull it down in the browser.)

9. **Create a new folder by clicking the New Folder link.**

   The Add Folder page appears.

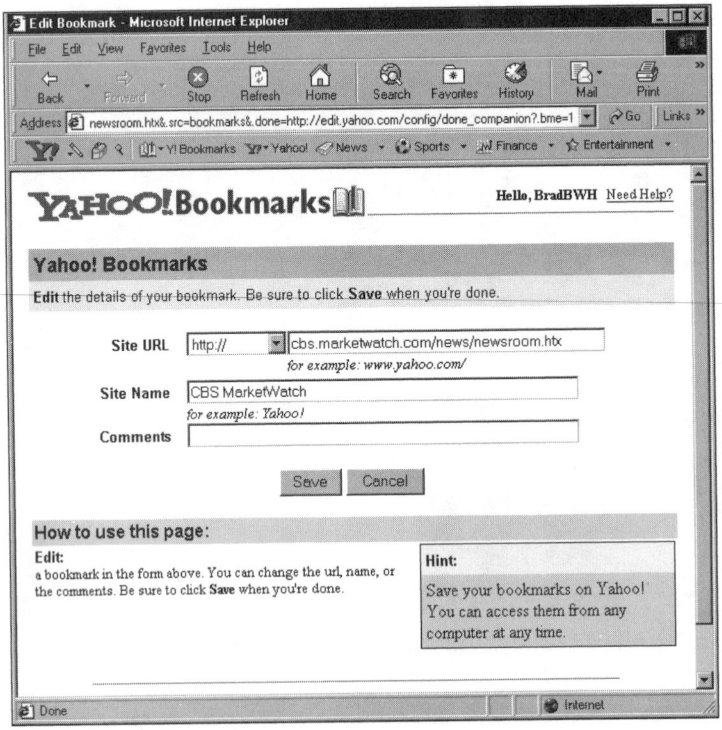

Figure 20-3:
Use this
page to
change how
your Y!
Bookmarks
appear on
your list.

10. **Type a folder name and any comments you want to attach to it. Then click the Save button, or click the Save & Add Another button if you want to create multiple folders.**

11. **Click the <u>Add Bookmark</u> link to add a single site link to the Y! Bookmarks list.**

12. **When you've finished making alterations to your Bookmarks, click the Finished button.**

Your Y! Bookmarks settings are saved on Yahoo!'s computers, not on your PC. This excellent feature makes it easy to access your bookmarks from any computer with an Internet connection. For anyone who travels, even to an office for work, having a Net-stored, completely portable bookmark system is a gigantic advantage over saving Favorites in your browser. The downside is that creating a new item is more cumbersome in the Y! Bookmark list than in Navigator or Internet Explorer. I use Y! Bookmarks for my *essential* bookmark sites, the ones I never want to be without.

The Yahoo! Companion responds to the sign-ins and sign-outs to and from Yahoo! through the browser. When you sign out of your Yahoo! ID while running Companion, a Sign in button appears on the Companion toolbar. That button takes your browser to the sign-in page but doesn't assume that you want to sign in with the ID that previously used the browser. Sign in with any Yahoo! ID and password. Your Companion settings are keyed to a single account password. If somebody else using the computer signs in with a different Yahoo! ID and password, the Companion stays attached to the browser in default format, ready to be edited. Your settings disappear until you sign in with your ID and password.

Part VI
Buying and Selling

The 5th Wave   By Rich Tennant

"SINCE WE BEGAN ON-LINE SHOPPING, I JUST DON'T KNOW WHERE THE MONEY'S GOING."

In this part . . .

Who doesn't like shopping? Especially from home!
Part VI explains how to best exercise your credit
card in Yahoo!, such as in the main shopping mall, Yahoo!
Auctions, and Yahoo! Classifieds.

Chapter 21

Shopping at the Yahoo! Mall

In This Chapter

▶ Browsing and searching the Yahoo! Shopping directory
▶ Using the shopping cart and buying things
▶ Personalizing with My Shopping

*I*t sometimes seems that the entire point of the Internet is to give consumers another way to shop. Is the visionary aspect of the Net dead? Once, futurists proclaimed a new era of planetary shrinkage, citizenry in the virtual global village, and equal self-expression for all. Now people speak of the unstoppable rise of e-commerce. Is the Utopian ideal nothing more than a dying ember in the human imagination? Heck, who cares, just give me a credit card and a secure online connection.

Actually, no vision of cyberspace society has been sacrificed to the gods of commerce. There's room for everything in a realm without boundaries. It's true, though, that the *convenience* of the Internet is emphasized strongly these days, and online shopping is a big part of saving time as we shift into the new millennium.

Let me speak personally. E-commerce has benefited my day-to-day life in any number of ways. Simple gift buying is greatly eased in many situations. Holiday shopping isn't nearly as grueling as it used to be. When planning a serious purchase, researching brands and prices has never been such a breeze, nor have so many stores been within easy reach. On the no-geography Net, all stores are a single click away, so merchants must compete by offering good prices and reliable service.

The modern Internet is a gravy train for consumers, for now at least. Online stores subsidize their businesses not only through sales but also through advertising on their sites. As a result, some e-commerce sites sell merchandise at or below wholesale to attract traffic, driving up their ad rates. Furthermore, Internet-only stores (called *e-tailers*) do not charge U.S. state sales tax. For the time being at least, we're in the midst of a golden age of Internet shopping.

Yahoo! contributes to consumer-friendly Internet mania in a unique way, and it is one of the major hosts for virtual stores. Although many Internet portals offer directory services to shopping around the Net, Yahoo! maintains its own mall, made up of stores that use its hosting and shopping-cart services. So, although Yahoo! provides a directory of online stores, they're all Yahoo! stores. This under-one-roof system has a few advantages:

✔ You can search for and locate specific products easily.

✔ Price comparisons are easy to see, though you are limited to Yahoo! stores as opposed to Net-wide price shopping. (Yahoo! helps you compare prices outside the Yahoo! collection of stores, too.)

✔ Buying stuff from multiple Yahoo! stores is simple, thanks to the universal on-screen shopping cart that links them together. You can put a music CD, a box of chocolate, and a computer mouse in a single shopping cart, though you buy the items separately. (Authors love receiving chocolate as a gift.)

✔ Yahoo! places hooks from the shopping area to Yahoo! Auctions (see Chapter 22) and Yahoo! Classified (see Chapter 23), so your shopping has other dimensions.

If the Yahoo! system has a downside, it's that visitors might get the impression that they are shopping the entire Internet, when in fact the experience is limited to Yahoo! stores. Fortunately, Yahoo! has a lot of stores. I have found the trade-off to be more than fair and definitely useful.

This chapter explains how to navigate through Yahoo! Shopping, from browsing to buying.

Hanging Out at the Mall

The fun begins on the Yahoo! Shopping home page. Go directly to this URL:

```
shopping.yahoo.com
```

The categories in the Yahoo! Shopping directory are displayed in the left sidebar of the home page. The center of the page is devoted to featured items. Yahoo! stores sell a broad range of stuff. If you know exactly what you're looking for, the search form is useful.

The search engine works best with specific queries as opposed to general ones. So *air conditioner* or *fruit basket* are better keywords than *appliance* or *gift*. Searching for authors and recording artists is productive when buying books and music CDs.

Browsing in the Yahoo! Shopping directory is like sailing along the rocky shoals of temptation. Not a directory page goes by that doesn't toss pictures and top-selling ideas in your face.

Each top-level directory category leads to a page of subcategories, helping you narrow your selections. Figure 21-1 shows the Chocolate directory page in the Desserts & Sweets portion of the Food and Beverages category, from which you can either proceed more deeply into the directory or go directly to any featured products (any one of which would be an appropriate gift to a hard-working author).

Whether you search with keywords or drill down into the directory, your goal is a product page. Figure 21-2 shows the Neckties page of the Men's Accessories section of the directory. Each necktie selection leads to a store — and the particular page of that store — selling ties. You can click the main product link, any of the necktie pictures, or the <u>matches</u> link below certain pictures. They all lead to a store page from which you can select merchandise, add it to your shopping cart, and eventually buy it. (Before buying, you can always remove items from your shopping cart or alter the quantity of any item.)

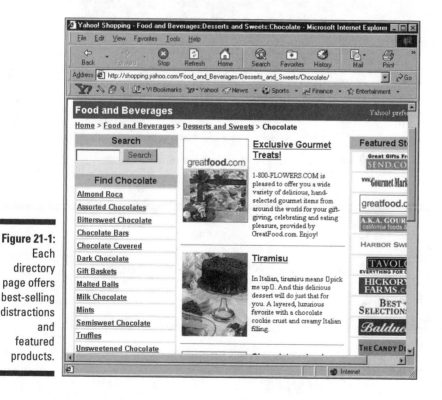

Figure 21-1:
Each
directory
page offers
best-selling
distractions
and
featured
products.

All Yahoo! stores look different but have identical shopping carts. In fact, it's really just one shopping cart (yours) that you carry around from one store to another, even though you don't see it most of the time. If you place something in your cart and then shop some more and eventually place a second item in your cart, both items appear in the cart. Your shopping cart continues to hold your items even if you sign out of Yahoo!, close your browser program, or turn your computer off.

Break out of the confines of Yahoo! Shopping with the <u>Compare Prices for this product on the Web</u> link at the bottom of some single-product comparison pages. Music and book products always have this link, enabling you to search outside Yahoo! to compare prices.

Speaking of searching, you can initiate a new search from any product page. Just scroll down to the search form at the bottom, choose a category with the drop-down menu, enter keywords, and click the Search button.

Figure 21-2:
A product
directory
page gives
you a
choice of
single
products
and stores.

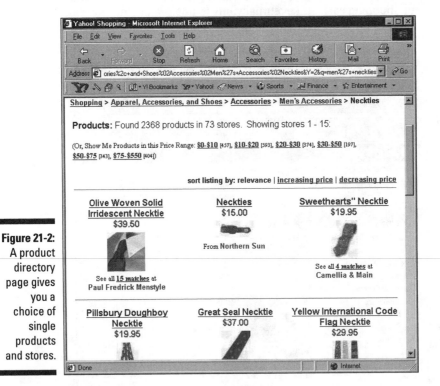

Shop Till You Drop

Time to get down to business. It's one of those days — you have to spend some money. Forget the mall with its teen throngs and Day-Glo ambience.

Bathe your face in the serene light of your monitor, place your credit card within easy reach of your quivering fingers, and log on to Yahoo! for some serious shopping.

The preceding section explains browsing and searching in Yahoo! Shopping. However you get there, at some point you find something you simply must own, and the consuming begins. Let's assume the object of your desire is a half-pound box of gourmet chocolates, so that *consuming* can take on a double meaning.

If you have a Yahoo! ID, it makes sense to sign on to Yahoo! with that ID before beginning your shopping. When you confirm your purchase, Yahoo! takes your address and plugs it into the on-screen order forms, saving you time. Otherwise, if you anonymously buy several items from different stores, each store needs to prompt you for shipping and billing information — it's a drag.

Figure 21-3 shows the purchase page for a certain gift box of chocolates. I show this not to tempt you unduly or to plant ideas of the perfect author's gift in your mind but to illustrate the Order buttons. (Honestly.) No matter what store you're in within Yahoo! Shopping, you always begin the buying process with that Order button. Following are the step-by-step instructions from any product purchase page.

Figure 21-3:
Click the Order button to place an item in your shopping cart.

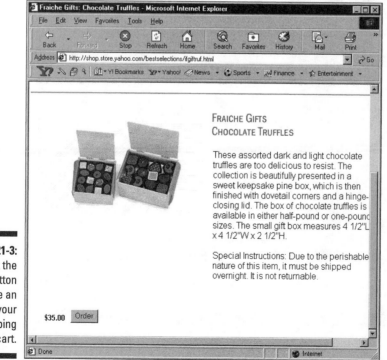

1. **On any product purchase page, click the Order button.**

   The Yahoo! Shopping Cart page appears and your item is placed in your shopping cart, as shown in Figure 21-4.

2. **Check the Item, Unit Price, and Quantity to make sure you selected the correct product.**

   The shopping cart doesn't make mistakes, but it's always possible that, in a chocoholic fever, your trembling hand clicked the wrong item. If you've made a mistake, change the quantity to 0 and click the Update Quantities button. Then back up to the order page and make the correct selection.

   In the Quantity field, enter the number of items you'd like or leave it alone to receive one item. (You might want to get one for yourself in addition to the one you're so generously sending to me.) If you do change the number in the Quantity field, click the Update Quantities button to update the price.

   Note that at this stage, shipping charges have not been added to your total. Each store adds its own shipping charges during the order confirmation process.

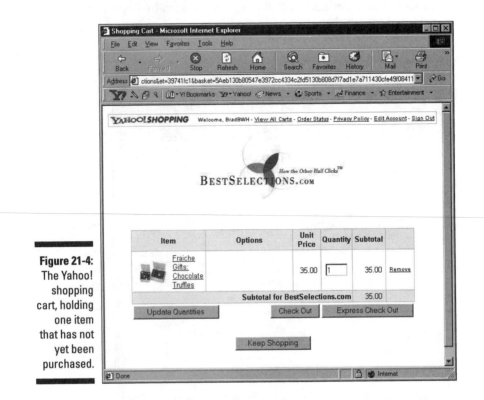

Figure 21-4: The Yahoo! shopping cart, holding one item that has not yet been purchased.

If you're using Yahoo! Shopping without signing in with your Yahoo! ID, an extra button appears on the Yahoo! Shopping Cart page called Place Order Without Registering. Yahoo! Shopping lets you proceed up to a certain point anonymously but then demands that you either sign in or start a new account.

3. **Click the Express Check Out button or the Keep Shopping button.**

   Use the Express Check Out button if you've finished shopping. (So soon?) If you'd like to keep the spirit of greed alive, click the Keep Shopping button. The Express Check Out button speeds the check-out process, but only if you're signed in to a Yahoo! ID. If so, the Express Check Out option takes your basic name and contact information so you don't have to enter it manually.

   This list proceeds with the assumption that you clicked the Express Check Out button.

4. **On the Shipping Information page, verify your shipping and billing addresses and then click the Continue button.**

5. **On the next Yahoo! Shopping Check Out page, fill in your credit card information.**

6. **Click the E-mail box to receive an order confirmation at your e-mail address.**

   Make sure the listed e-mail address is correct. If it isn't, replace it with a correct or preferred address.

7. **Click the SEND THIS ORDER button, unless you want to cancel your order.**

   You know what this means. This is the actual order page, and clicking that button sends the order to the Yahoo! Store. This page is your final chance to back out. If you want to cancel the order, click the Do Not Order button. Then, in good conscience, you must resign from the Frenzied Shoppers Guild.

As you receive order numbers for each item you buy, jot them down somewhere. You receive those numbers in an e-mail as long as you select the E-mail box in Step 6, but it doesn't hurt to have a handwritten note in case you accidentally delete the e-mail confirmation. (You can also use Send Page under the File menu of your browser to mail yourself a copy of the Web page.) You need that order number if you want to check the status of your order. To check an order, use the <u>Order Status</u> link on most Yahoo! Shopping pages.

As you're shopping, you can always view your shopping cart by clicking the <u>View Cart/Check Out</u> link on most Yahoo! Shopping pages. I've found it makes sense to pile stuff in the cart while browsing and sort it out later. You don't want to see something interesting, decide to buy it later, and then not be able to find it again. The Order button is not a purchase button, and it's impossible to get charged for clicking it. Because you can easily remove items from the shopping cart, placing things in the cart is a convenient way to organize your shopping.

Personal Shopping

Yahoo! is forever helping its users personalize their online experience. In the shopping realm, Yahoo! added a powerful customizing feature since the first edition of this book. This personalization tool is called My Shopping.

My Shopping is closely related to My Yahoo!, explained in finicky detail in Chapter 2. The basic operation of the two features is so similar — identical, really — that it makes little sense to describe them all over again here. Please refer to Chapter 2, which is all about one of the most important aspects of the entire Yahoo! service and which definitely deserves your rapt attention under any circumstances.

My Shopping applies the concept and design of My Yahoo! to various content modules related to shopping in the Yahoo! mall. One design expansion at My Shopping, compared to My Yahoo!, is that your page can have three columns instead of two, as shown in Figure 21-5.

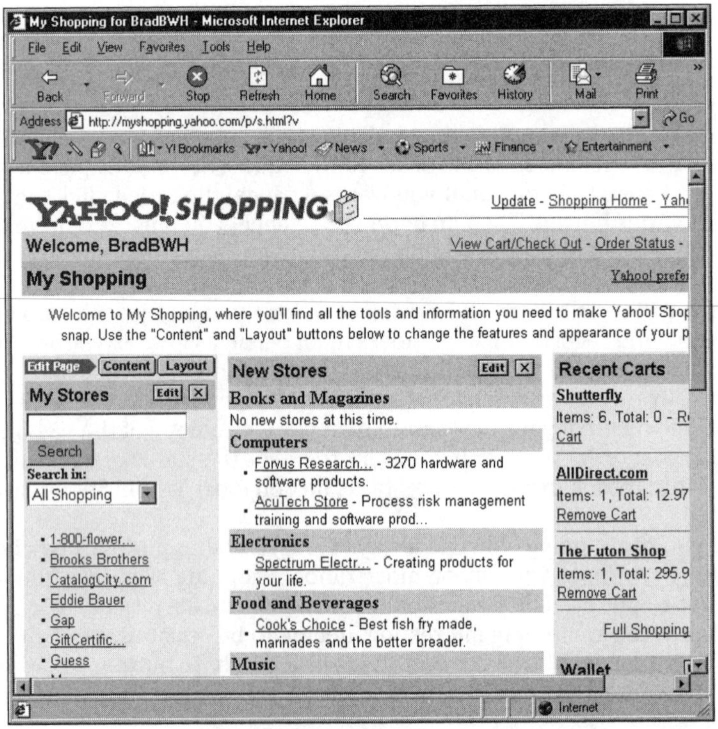

Figure 21-5:
My Shopping provides a personalized browsing and tracking page.

That extra column creates a center drop-down menu at the bottom of the page. This menu contains content choices that can be placed only in the center column. The right and left content menus are identical, so you have the same content choices for both the outer columns.

Chapter 22

Going Once . . . Going Twice . . .

In This Chapter

▶ Registering for Yahoo! Auctions

▶ Finding an auction and bidding

▶ Creating your own auction

Millions of people have discovered the odd, unique, exhilarating kick of winning an online auction.

When you think about it, it's strange that buying something through an auction is called *winning*. A sign of the sweepstakes-oriented, consumer-intensive culture? Certainly, buying through an auction can be a victory when you get a bargain. Some products sold in this fashion, though, don't have fixed prices, and in those cases it's not clear whether you've secured a bargain or participated in an expensive garage sale.

Two types of Internet auction sites are available. *House auctions* provide the merchandise and accept bids on it. These sites stock their own inventory, which can range from new products to second-run items, overstocked merchandise, and used or refurbished equipment. *User-to-user auctions* simply provide the cyberspace and the software for bidding and selling — the visitors supply the goods. Yahoo! Auctions is this second type of auction house. You can use it to buy from other individuals or sell your own stuff in an auction format.

In this chapter, I provide the details on registering for Yahoo! Auctions, bidding, and selling stuff in your own auction.

Finding Auctions and Bidding

The first step is to find the Yahoo! Auctions home page. Easy enough. Just click the <u>Auctions</u> link on the Yahoo! home page or go directly to

auctions.yahoo.com

You need a Yahoo! ID to buy or sell in Yahoo! Auctions.

Yahoo! Auctions is organized in directory fashion (no surprise), like most other portions of Yahoo!. The Yahoo! Auctions home page, which is shown in Figure 22-1, presents a directory of auction categories in the left sidebar. Featured auctions are shown in the center portion of the page. You get involved by either browsing or searching for an auction. If you're wandering around for the first time or are new to Internet auctions in general, you might want to take the directory route. Just click a main topic area to begin prowling around the directory.

Some directory topics extend several layers down before you see any auction listings. Subcategory pages get you close to specific types of objects being sold. Figure 22-2, the auction page for Indian-head American nickels, shows a seventh-level page of the auctions directory. Had you known you were looking for precisely such a numismatics auction, you could have used the search form with the keywords *indian head nickel*.

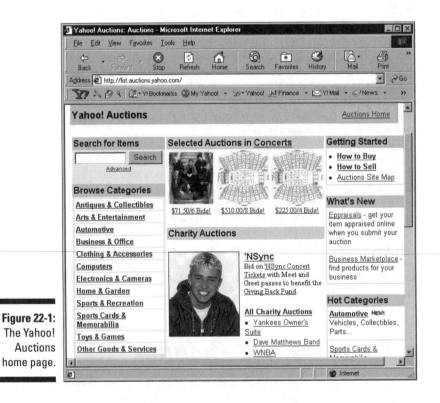

Figure 22-1:
The Yahoo!
Auctions
home page.

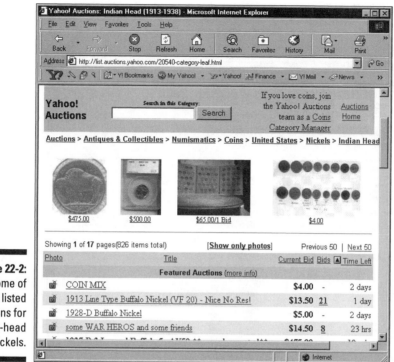

Figure 22-2:
Some of
the listed
auctions for
Indian-head
nickels.

Search forms are located on every directory page in Yahoo! Auctions. Use them to enter specific items you're looking to buy, such as _keyboard synthesizers, baby clothes,_ or _whitney houston cd._ (As you can see in these examples, you don't need to use capital letters when you search.) Be aware, though, that your keywords are matched against the descriptive text of the auction pages, not just the auction titles, and also that sometimes just one keyword is matched. I often search with the keywords _cd collections,_ hoping to scarf up lots of music from somebody liquidating his or her collection. Inevitably, the search results match with computer systems for sale with CD drives.

The auction directory pages (refer to Figure 22-2) show you the auction name, the current bid, the remaining time in the auction, and the number of bids if there's been any bidding at all. (Because Yahoo! Auctions holds so many auctions, many transpire without a single bid.) Lack of bids can indicate a too-high minimum price or a great bargain that has become lost in the crowd. To see an auction page in progress, click any auction title.

The auction page, shown in Figure 22-3, presents a bundle of information plus an opportunity to place a bid. Here are the major points to look for:

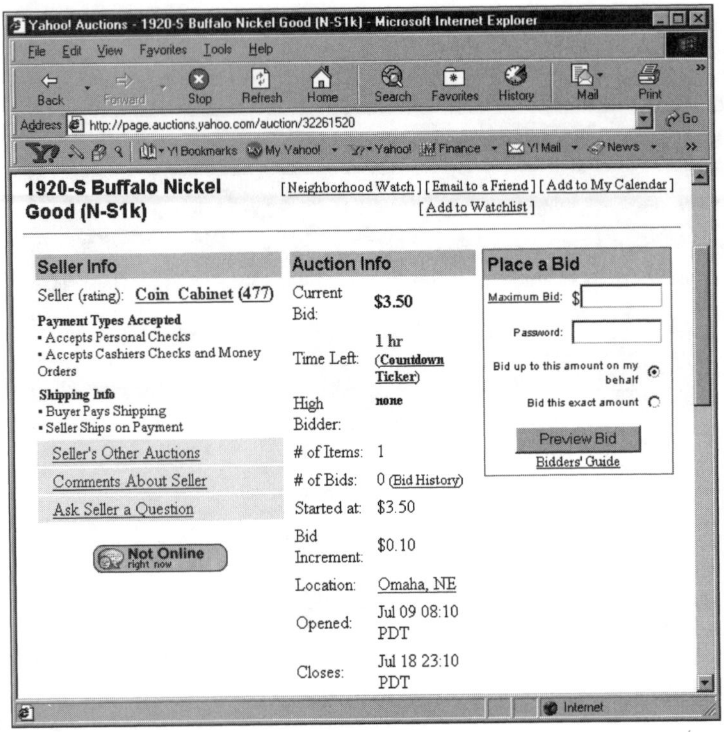

Figure 22-3:
An auction
page, where
you learn
about the
seller and
place a bid.

✔ Look at the left sidebar for type of payment accepted and shipping
information.

✔ Click the seller's name to read an auction profile (not a generic Yahoo! profile) describing the seller's background with auctions or business. (Many
sellers are auction dealers or other small-business people who have
migrated their retail operations to Yahoo! Auctions.) All of the seller's current auctions (some people have dozens going on at once) are listed on
the seller's page and linked. Every seller is ranked on a point system
based on buyer feedback at previous auctions. Figure 22-4 shows the ranking page of a Yahoo! Auction dealer with a long and flawless track record.

✔ Click the Bid History link to see a log of the bidding so far.

✔ Click the Question & Answer link to query the seller about the auction
item and read any previous dialogue that's been posted.

✔ Look at the right sidebar for the Place Bid Here section to participate in
the auction. Enter your maximum bid amount and your Yahoo! password. Use the radio buttons to determine whether Yahoo! should bid
you up to your maximum amount during the auction or simply bid the
exact amount your entered right away. When you're finished, click the
Preview Bid button.

Yahoo! Auctions - Microsoft Internet Explorer

File Edit View Favorites Tools Help

Back Forward Stop Refresh Home Search Favorites History Mail Print

Address http://ratings.auctions.yahoo.com/show/rating?userID=Coin_Cabinet

Y! YI Bookmarks My Yahoo! Yahoo! Finance Y! Mail News

Auctions Profile   Auctions Home
Coin_Cabinet (477)

Rating (477) | Auctions | About Me

477 ☀ - 0 🌧 = 477
Details   Details

Auctions with comments over time				
	Past Week	Past Month	Past 6 Months	Total
Good	15	59	327	857
Neutral	1	2	2	9
Bad	0	0	0	0
Total	16	61	329	866

- 857 auctions with positive comments by 477 unique users
- 0 auctions with negative comments by 0 unique users
- 9 auctions with neutral comments by 3 unique users
- More about ratings & feedback

All Comments Grouped by User

Showing **1** of **48** pages   Previous Page | Next Page

Rated a Excellent ☀ Seller by p1moon (6)
1955 Franklin Half Dollar PF-65 (Jul 09 23:49 PDT) $49.95
Buyer gives a Excellent Seller rating.
Comment:Very good description of coin, and extremely fast delivery. Would deal with this

Internet

Figure 22-4:
The ranking
page of an
experienced
seller at
Yahoo!
Auctions.

Yahoo! Auctions uses a system called Automatic Bidding. Yahoo! understands that if you enter a bid higher than $1 above the current winning bid, you want the system to manage your bidding for you. Yahoo! monitors the auction and bids up your figure to remain just above any new bids. Automatic Bidding continues in this fashion until your limit (the amount you typed in the Max Bid Amount field) is reached. Then, if someone tops your maximum amount, you're out of the auction. Until then, you are kept on top of the heap. With the system helping everyone in the same fashion, popular auctions reach the highest maximum bid quickly. You can always enter an auction again if you're pushed out by higher bids.

When you place a bid for the first time in Yahoo! Auctions, the system throws a long Terms of Service agreement on your screen. I've breezed past many of these agreements in other chapters of this book, but if you're going to read one of these legal documents fairly carefully, this should be the one. In it, Yahoo! describes exactly what its role is in the Auction process and what its responsibilities are and aren't. Yahoo! provides the auction space and under-lying software but has no involvement in actual transactions and money exchanges. Yahoo! doesn't warrant or endorse the sellers in any fashion. Basically, you're on your own and have no recourse to Yahoo! if you meet a shifty seller or don't get the item you paid for.

What happens if you win? Yahoo! brings you together with the seller and steps out of the picture. The seller contacts you by e-mail and arranges the details of your transaction. Each auction page (on the bottom left) indicates what forms of payment the seller accepts. Small-business sellers often take credit cards, but individuals running auctions as a hobby usually take check or money order and may implement precautions such as not shipping until the check clears. Each seller determines individual shipping and handling costs.

To see a list of all auctions in which you're participating, as a bidder or a seller or both, click the <u>My Auctions</u> link on the Yahoo! Auctions home page.

Selling Something in an Auction

Just as bidding is open to anyone in Yahoo! Auctions, so too is creating an auction. (The only requirement is that you have a valid credit card. However, I want to emphasize that creating an auction is free. The credit card is just for a verification procedure.)

The first thing you need to do is set up a Yahoo! Auctions account. Again, this is free, though you'll be asked for a credit card number. Follow these steps to set up an account:

1. **On the Yahoo! Auctions home page, click the <u>Submit Item</u> link.**

2. **On the category selection page, click a product category that best fits your item.**

   Some selections take you to subcategory pages. Continue selecting the niche most appropriate to your item.

3. **Read the Terms of Service Agreement and click the I Accept button.**

   The agreement relates to the auction portion of Yahoo!. The document spells out the rules of buying and selling and lists disallowed items — live animals, illegal items, food, cigarettes, guns, and a few others.

4. **Click the <u>Submit to this Category</u> link.**

5. **On the Instant Yahoo! Account Verification page, click the Secure Account Verification button.**

   You might wonder what this is all about. Yahoo! is about to ask you for credit card information. You can't put anything up for bidding in Yahoo! Auctions without a valid credit card. Your credit account is _not_ charged in this process. Selling something through Yahoo! Auctions is free.

6. **On the Secure Yahoo! Account Verification page, fill in the fields with your contact information, credit card number, and card expiration date, and then click the Finished button.**

7. **On the Yahoo! Account Verification — Complete page, click the <u>Continue to Yahoo Auctions</u> link.**

8. **On the Non-verified Email Address(es) page, verify your first e-mail address, add a second if you want, and then click the Send Verification button.**

   These are the addresses to which Yahoo! sends your account verification for starting auctions. Yahoo! sends that e-mail immediately, and you must receive it before proceeding with these steps. (You need the e-mail confirmation code contained in the message for the next step.)

9. **On the Yahoo! Account Information page, enter your Email Confirmation Code and your Yahoo! Password and then click the Verify button.**

   Copy the Confirmation Code from the account verification e-mail. You should already know your Yahoo! ID password.

   If you entered two e-mail addresses in Step 8, you need to verify both to hold auctions. Verify the first here and then, before continuing with Step 10, use the Back button to return here and verify the second address. If you're not overly concerned with the security risk of other people starting auctions in your name, use just one e-mail address to avoid this hassle.

10. **On the next page, click the <u>Continue using Yahoo!</u> link.**

    You are returned to the Yahoo! Auctions home page.

After you have an account, you can submit an auction. Yahoo! is extremely configurable in this department. You decide how long your auction lasts, whether a picture illustrates your item, how the auction is publicized, who pays shipping costs (you or the buyer), and more. To submit an auction, follow these steps:

1. **On the Yahoo! Auctions home page, click the <u>Submit Item</u> link.**

2. **On the next page, choose a category in which you want to hold your auction.**

   You may need to drill several levels into the auction directory to find just the right spot. If you're selling a music keyboard, for example, MIDI Gear might be the right niche. Eventually, the Submitting an Item page appears, as shown in Figure 22-5.

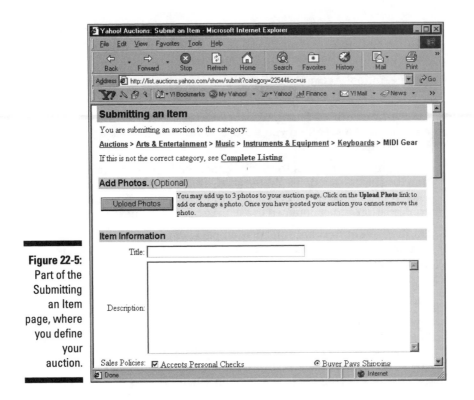

Figure 22-5:
Part of the
Submitting
an Item
page, where
you define
your
auction.

3. Fill in the information fields.

This page is where you name your auction and describe what it is you're selling. The Sales Policies boxes let you choose the kind of payment you accept and who pays shipping. (It's assumed you will not ship internationally, but a check box allows you to invite international orders.) In the Set up your auction preferences section, fill in your quantity of items, your starting price, and the length of the auction. (The system automatically rejects bids below the starting price.) The Additional Options are useful for configuring how your auction operates. You can control the minimum selling price (higher than the starting price) and a Sell Price at which the auction closes if bidding reaches that level. *Note:* You must enter at least a title, a description, and a starting price. If any of those fields are left blank, Yahoo! pesters you until you fill them in.

4. Click the Continue button.

The Preview Item Submission page appears, so you can check out how your auction will appear.

5. Check everything for accuracy and then click the Submit Auction button.

If you spot any mistakes or change your mind about any information, use the Back button of your browser to display the Submitting an Item page (refer to Figure 22-5) and adjust your information.

On the Thank You! page, under the View your Auction banner, click the URL to see your auction page. You can also use that URL to promote your auction around the Internet. E-mail it to friends, post it in relevant message boards, or promote it on your Web site.

You may add a photo to your auction page; doing so makes a big difference in attracting bids. If you have a digitized (scanned) photo of your item, follow these steps:

1. **On the Submitting an Item page (see Step 2 in the preceding list), click the Upload Photos button.**

   The Upload Photo(s) page appears, as shown in Figure 22-6.

2. **Click the Browse button.**

   At this point, your operating system prompts you to locate the graphics (photo) file on your hard drive, preparatory to uploading it to Yahoo!. I've written the next steps from the viewpoint of a Windows 95 user.

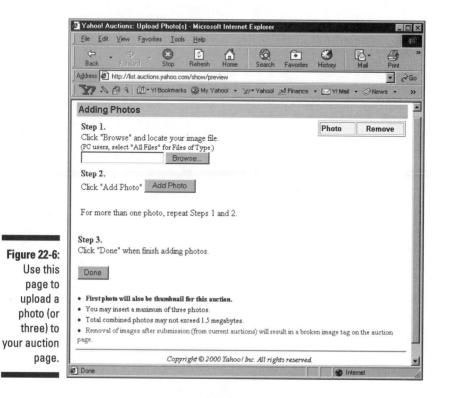

Figure 22-6:
Use this page to upload a photo (or three) to your auction page.

3. **In the Choose File window, locate your scanned photo, click it, and then click the Open button.**

4. **Click the Add Photo button.**

5. **If you have more than one photo to upload, repeat Steps 2 through 4.**

6. **Click the Done button.**

If you have a Web site and you want to avoid the Yahoo! upload process, which can be a little slow, simply post the photo to your site using whatever upload procedure you're accustomed to. Then, on the Submit an Item page, place the URL in the information that describes your item.

You are limited to three photos per auction and the cumulative file size can't exceed 1.5 megabytes. However, most photo files aren't that big.

Chapter 23

Yahoo! Classifieds: The Neighborly Way to Shop

. . . .

In This Chapter

▶ Navigating the Yahoo! Classifieds directory

▶ Posting your own classified ad

. . . .

*Y*ahoo! Classifieds is primarily about selling stuff. Yahoo! users can put up notices about any kind of product, item, or service — from a book to a house.

The Classifieds are more homegrown than Yahoo! Auctions (see Chapter 22), which is populated by dealers as well as individuals. Nevertheless, some stores advertise their wares in the Classifieds. In fact, the Autos & Motorcycles section of the Classifieds directory has a portion dedicated to new and used car dealer ads.

This chapter guides you through the Classifieds directory and explains how to post an ad of your own. I extracted three portions of the Classifieds (autos, real estate, and employment) and put them in Chapter 19. You can find out about the Personals in Chapter 17. It's fun how these explanations are scattered throughout the book, isn't it? There's nothing quite so enjoyable as an over-organized book.

Shopping the Ads

The starting point for browsing and placing ads is the Yahoo! Classifieds home page, shown in Figure 23-1. (When you visit the page while logged in to your ID, the page defaults to whatever city you listed in your Yahoo! profile.) Click the <u>Classifieds</u> link on the Yahoo! home page or go directly to this URL:

```
classifieds.yahoo.com
```

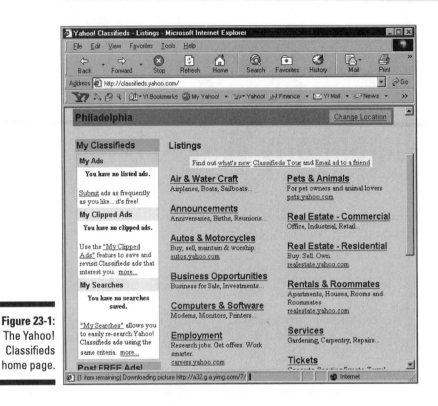

Figure 23-1:
The Yahoo!
Classifieds
home page.

Among the main topic headings in the Yahoo! Classifieds directory, the General Merchandise section (scroll down to see it) is probably the most packed with items and the directory portion is where most people turn to for general browsing. I'll use General Merchandise as an illustrative example of the other sections.

Note a couple of interesting and useful features in the left-hand sidebar of the Classifieds home page:

✔ **My Clipped Ads** is a feature that exists on every page that contains an ad. Use the Clip This Ad link to save any ad to a personalized clipping folder. (It's just a Web page, actually.) Then use the My Clipped Ads link to see everything you've saved.

✔ **My Searches** is a personalized way to save and reuse your search criteria. Search forms are located on each directory page except the top-level page (the Classifieds home page). On any search results page, click the Save this Search link to add the search to a special page. At any time, from any page in Yahoo! Classifieds, click the My Searches link to see your saved searches.

When you click any main directory heading, you get a second-level page with a merchandise directory (see Figure 23-2). Yahoo! automatically presents classifieds that correspond to your geographic area, assuming you log into the site after signing in to a Yahoo! ID. If not, you get a geographic directory first.

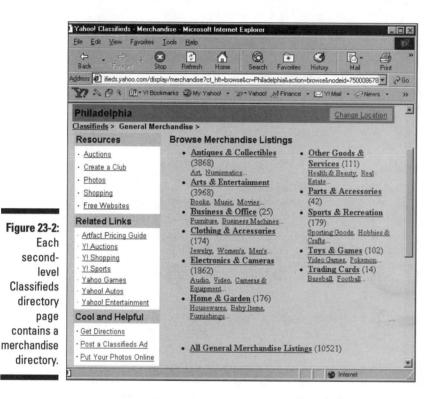

Figure 23-2:
Each second-level Classifieds directory page contains a merchandise directory.

The search engine (Figure 23-3) allows you to choose the location of the seller, the category of merchandise, and a date range (going back two weeks) in which the ad was posted. The Keyword form forces Yahoo! to display ads that match any word or group of words. Use the Photos check box to limit your search results to those ads with accompanying pictures, but be aware that doing so limits your results, sometimes drastically. You may need to scroll down the page to see the search form.

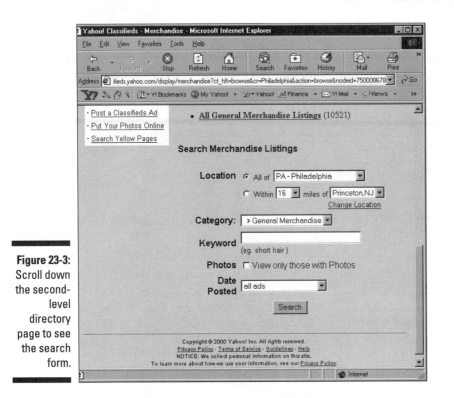

Figure 23-3:
Scroll down the second-level directory page to see the search form.

You have two basic choices on the second-level directory pages:

✔ Browse through the merchandise directory

✔ Search by keyword and geographic area for specific merchandise

Your goal is to eventually reach the actual classified ads. When you click through the directory, you eventually get to the bottom, most specific level of a topic. At that point Yahoo! displays a list of stuff for sale in that product, within your selected geographic area, as shown in Figure 23-4.

Note that the Classifieds listings are organized by date, category, and price — each a column on the page. The default display shows the ads by date, with recently posted ads at the top of the list, working back through time as you look down the list. That's a good idea, but you might also want to view the ads by price. Just click the <u>PRICE</u> link — the page reloads with the ads listed from cheapest to most pricey.

The little camera icon next to some ads indicates the presence of an accompanying photo.

Click any More Detail button to see a single classified ad. As you can see in Figure 23-5, ads contain a brief description of the item for sale, the date of posting, and the price.

The seller's e-mail address (not necessarily a Yahoo! Mail address) is usually listed, along with the seller's town and state. The seller sometimes includes an Additional Information link at the bottom of the ad to describe the item more completely.

Four notable links appear on each classified ad page:

- The Reply to this ad link brings up an e-mail page with which you can contact the seller for information or to buy.

- The Listings from *SellerName* link displays other ads placed by the same person. Of course, some people have only one listing.

✔ The <u>Map It!</u> link takes you to Yahoo! Maps (see Chapter 24) and draws a map of the seller's town or city.

✔ The <u>Clip This Ad</u> link is for saving the ad to your page of stored ads.

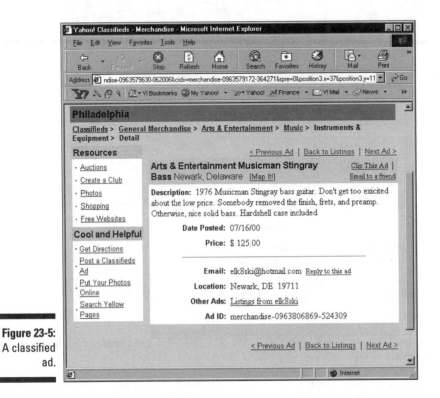

Figure 23-5:
A classified
ad.

Submitting an Ad

The flip side to buying somebody's old comic-book collection is posting your own ad. Want to unload that stack of psychedelic vinyl (LP records, to you youngsters) from the hazy days of your youth? You can either auction it off in Yahoo! Auctions or sell it through the Classifieds:

✔ Use Yahoo! Auctions (described in Chapter 22) when you're willing to accept a range of selling prices and when you're in the mood for the extra work of setting up the auction page.

✔ Use Yahoo! Classifieds when you have a non-negotiable price and crave the relative simplicity of posting an ad.

Here's how to proceed in Yahoo! Classifieds:

1. **On the Yahoo! Classifieds home page, click the <u>Post Ad</u> link.**

   The Submission page appears.

2. **Click any category.**

   Some category links lead to subcategory pages. Just continue selecting the best niche for your item.

3. **On the next page, fill in your ZIP code, a description of the item, and your contact information.**

   Only a few fields are required — the ones with asterisks next to them. Different categories have varying requirements. If you're selling something, you need to fill in at least one means of contact, such as your e-mail address. (You might not want to list your mailing address or phone number.)

4. **Click the Submit entry button.**

   Yahoo! shows you your ad. Your listing is automatically placed in the correct geographical location of the directory, according to your ZIP code.

If you are running multiple ads, you can view them by clicking the <u>My Ads</u> link on the Yahoo! Classifieds home page.

Part VII
The Part of Tens

The 5th Wave — By Rich Tennant

"IT'S JUST UNTIL WE GET BACK UP ON THE INTERNET."

In this part . . .

There's so much to Yahoo!, an entire book can barely do it justice. These two chapters gather together twenty services that didn't fit into the rest of the book.

Chapter 24

Ten Yahoo! Services You Need to Know About

*T*his chapter provides brief descriptions of Yahoo! services, many of which deserve their own dedicated chapter. In a crucial editorial meeting, we decided that the book could not feasibly contain forty-five chapters. Injury would result when lifting such a book. Lawsuits would ensue and people would sulk. Hence, this solution.

Yahoo! Wallet

wallet.yahoo.com

I've mentioned Yahoo! Wallet in various chapters, and this is where I deliver the goods on what it is, why it's useful, and how to get it. It's apparent from the name that the Wallet has something to do with money, and buying things, and online shopping. Exactly right.

The trick to using Yahoo! Wallet

Although the Wallet is a great feature, Yahoo! doesn't make using it as clear as could be. Some Yahoo! services, such as GeoPlus (Chapter 4) and Web hosting (Chapter 5), require the Yahoo! Wallet, so those sections are obvious. But Yahoo! stores do not necessarily make any mention of the Wallet on their order pages, leading to puzzled head scratchings among users who thought all Yahoo! stores accepted the Wallet. They all do. Nevertheless, you might find yourself staring at a shopping cart page of a Yahoo! store and seeing no mention of the Wallet. What to do? This to do:

1. **On any shopping cart page in Yahoo! Shopping, after selecting an item, click the View All Carts link at the top of the page.**

2. **Click the Express Check Out button corresponding to the item you want to purchase.**

3. **Confirm (and edit if you want) the Wallet Info appearing on the right side of the page.**

4. **Click the SEND THIS ORDER button.**

Nothing to it. The trick is to get out of an individual-store cart and into your general Yahoo! Shopping cart. There you see all the items you've selected (but not yet shipped) from Yahoo! Shopping stores. And that's where the Wallet comes into play, with that Express Check Out button.

By the way, not all advertising banners in Yahoo! Shopping relate to Yahoo! Stores. So if you shop in a store after clicking its ad, you might not be able to use Yahoo! Wallet.

Yahoo! Wallet is a secure online storage system for payment information. The virtual wallet holds your credit card data and shipping information. When you make an online purchase with Yahoo! Wallet, you enter your Wallet information instead of your credit card information. Yahoo! then completes the transaction with the merchant, using high-security connections to transmit your credit card number.

You can use the Yahoo! Wallet only in a Yahoo! store or when buying a Yahoo! service. You can't use it on eBay, or at Amazon.com, or any shopping haunt outside Yahoo!. The Wallet does work in every Yahoo! store, however, which means thousands of online merchants accept Wallet transactions.

Yahoo! Wallet provides a secure method of shopping online, and beyond the safety it offers, it also saves you time. No longer, when shopping at a Yahoo! store or buying a Yahoo! service, do you need to dig out your credit card, enter personal information, and type your shipping address. All of that is accomplished in the single quick step of entering your security key.

The security key is the . . . um, key to the whole Wallet. It's like the PIN of a bankcard. You enter the key whenever using the Wallet to buy goods or services from a Yahoo! page or merchant. The Wallet does the rest of the work.

Follow these steps to set up your Yahoo! Wallet:

1. **On the Yahoo! Wallet home page, click the Get Started Now! button.**

2. **Enter your Yahoo! password and then click the Submit button.**

    Obtain the Wallet for whatever Yahoo! ID you shop with.

3. **On the next page, fill in every information field and then click the Submit this form button.**

    Listen up, would-be Walleteers. This is where you set your Wallet preferences and, crucial to the whole deal, your security key. The security key is a second password for your Yahoo! account, a password that relates specifically to the Wallet functions. You make up the key yourself. It can't be the same as your Yahoo! ID name, and it can't contain your first or last name.

    Some of the fields on this page are filled in with information you entered in your Yahoo! profile — in particular, your billing and shipping addresses for work and home. You can change any of these four addresses (and phone numbers) by clicking the corresponding Edit button.

That's all there is to creating a Yahoo! Wallet. The three elements are in place: your credit card information (in the Wallet), your shipping and billing addresses (also in the Wallet), and your security key (in your hot, consumerist hand).

Yahoo! Alerts

    alerts.yahoo.com

Yahoo! has its hands in just about everything the Internet has to offer — news, community, real estate, sports, stocks, traffic . . . the whole shebang. (*Shebang* is a technical term.) The service provides several shortcuts for getting to the varied features, including Yahoo! Companion (see Chapter 20), My Yahoo! (Chapter 2), and Yahoo! Messenger (Chapter 15). But there's an even easier way to stay informed, and that's to let Yahoo! come to you.

Yahoo! Alerts is a service that pushes information to your e-mail address or mobile device, saving you the trouble of pulling it to your screen manually. (Some alerts may be delivered also to your Yahoo! Messenger.) Alerts are short bursts of information containing links to more information. The Yahoo! Alerts home page contains ten categories of alerts in the All Alerts table. Following are a few notes about how certain Alert categories work:

- Stock alerts come in two varieties: a Daily Alert and Price Alerts. The Daily Alert is available only to cell phones and pagers — not to e-mail addresses. Price Alerts are not limited in that way.

- Sports alerts are available only to cell phones and pagers. However, plenty of sports sources are listed in the News category, so you can create customized sports alerts by clicking the <u>News Alerts</u> link.

✔ As of this writing, Personal Digital Assistants (PDAs) can't be Alert destinations. The only supported mobile devices are cell phones and alphanumeric pagers.

✔ On the Yahoo! Alerts home page for your ID, you can turn alerts on and off by clicking the bell icon. When turned off, the alert appears in gray but is not deleted. You may turn it back on at any time. Change the settings of any alert by clicking the Edit icon and delete any alert by clicking the Delete icon.

✔ Most Alert categories allow you to select whether to receive alerts once a day, twice a day, or immediately when the alert is available. In many cases, you can choose between an HTML alert and a text alert. The text alerts contain live links.

✔ If you schedule alerts once or twice per day, they arrive punctually — but only if there is alert content that matches your configuration. If you have a news alert set up to send you stories about Bill Gates's hairdressing appointments, months may go by without receiving anything.

To give you an idea of how to set up alerts, the following steps walk you through configuring a News Alert. Other topics vary in the configuration options, of course.

1. **On the Yahoo! Alerts home page, click the <u>News Alerts</u> link.**

2. **On the Yahoo! News — Alerts page, click the <u>Create An Alert</u> link.**

3. **Configure your alert.**

   A portion of this page is shown in Figure 24-1. Assign a name to your alert — this name appears on your main Yahoo! Alerts home page when you're logged into your ID. Step 2 of this page is important, because that's where you assign words that must appear in the news article and words that must *not* appear. Put quotation marks around phrases if you don't want their words treated as individual keywords. Use the check boxes to select news sources to be searched.

4. **At the bottom of the page, select the alert destination and schedule.**

   You can send News Alerts to e-mail or Yahoo! Messenger. The drop-down menu holds the e-mail addresses in your Yahoo! profile. Select either one delivery per day or two. Select Immediate Delivery if the alerts must be fresh and you don't mind receiving a lot of mail.

5. **Click the Finished button.**

   Your alert now appears on the Yahoo! News — Alerts page with any other News Alerts you configure. The News Alerts and all other alerts appear on your Yahoo! Alerts home page.

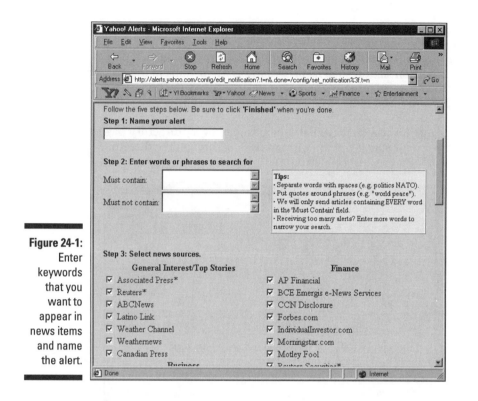

Figure 24-1:
Enter
keywords
that you
want to
appear in
news items
and name
the alert.

Business to Business Marketplace

b2b.yahoo.com

Yahoo! Business to Business Marketplace is relevant mostly to companies and small-business owners. Anyone running a home office can also benefit from this marketplace.

The Yahoo! Business to Business Marketplace operates as a used-product directory, for the most part. This portion of the Yahoo! service is an auction site, but Yahoo! does not provide the auction space. Instead, Yahoo! works with several B2B (that's the buzzword for business-to-business) online auction companies and links to their sites from the directory.

This system makes it easy for you, the visitor and hopeful shopper, to browse. Rather than visiting several auction sites, you can concentrate on the product type you want and then link to whatever site has the specific item of interest.

Figure 24-2 shows one directory page in the Business to Business Marketplace, this one listing computer hardware. As you can see, three outside destinations are listed as the hosts of these items. The Yahoo! page gives you crucial information such as price and time remaining in the auction, as well as the model number of the item. Click the item's link to visit the host site, learn more, and bid.

A search form is displayed at the bottom of every directory page. Search by keyword for specific items without drilling through the directory.

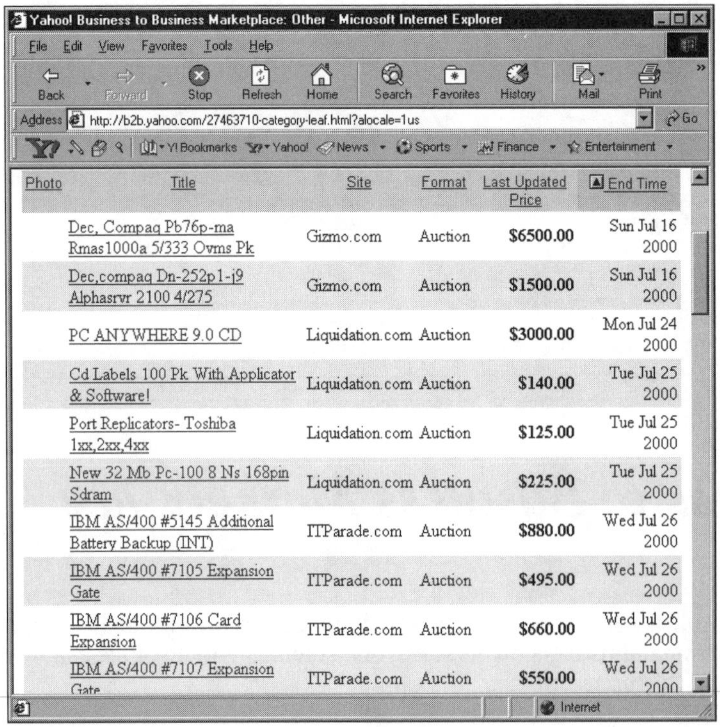
Yahoo! Business to Business Marketplace: Other - Microsoft Internet Explorer
File Edit View Favorites Tools Help
Back Forward Stop Refresh Home Search Favorites History Mail Print
Address http://b2b.yahoo.com/27463710-category-leaf.html?alocale=1us
Go
Y! Bookmarks Yahoo! News Sports Finance Entertainment
Photo Title Site Format Last Updated Price End Time
Dec, Compaq Pb76p-ma Rmas1000a 5/333 Ovms Pk Gizmo.com Auction $6500.00 Sun Jul 16 2000
Dec,compaq Dn-252p1-j9 Alphasrvr 2100 4/275 Gizmo.com Auction $1500.00 Sun Jul 16 2000
PC ANYWHERE 9.0 CD Liquidation.com Auction $3000.00 Mon Jul 24 2000
Cd Labels 100 Pk With Applicator & Software! Liquidation.com Auction $140.00 Tue Jul 25 2000
Port Replicators- Toshiba 1xx,2xx,4xx Liquidation.com Auction $125.00 Tue Jul 25 2000
New 32 Mb Pc-100 8 Ns 168pin Sdram Liquidation.com Auction $225.00 Tue Jul 25 2000
IBM AS/400 #5145 Additional Battery Backup (INT) ITParade.com Auction $880.00 Wed Jul 26 2000
IBM AS/400 #7105 Expansion Gate ITParade.com Auction $495.00 Wed Jul 26 2000
IBM AS/400 #7106 Card Expansion ITParade.com Auction $660.00 Wed Jul 26 2000
IBM AS/400 #7107 Expansion Gate ITParade.com Auction $550.00 Wed Jul 26 2000
Internet

Figure 24-2: The Yahoo! Business to Business Marketplace is a directory that links to other auction destinations.

Yahoo! Maps

`maps.yahoo.com`

It's too bad the Maps portion of Yahoo! can't be viewed in the car. It's probably only a matter of time before it can be. For now, we must settle for Yahoo! Maps over the computer.

Yahoo! Maps is a combination mapper and direction tool. You can view graphic maps and receive driving directions between two addresses.

Map anything

The best way to acquaint yourself with Yahoo! Maps is to map something. Anything. The service works with a specific street address or the name of a town. You can even put in the name of a state (in the United States) or an airport code, and get a map. Coverage is limited to the United States, Canada, and southern Icelandic fishing villages. (Two out of three, anyway.)

Get started on the Yahoo! Maps home page, shown in Figure 24-3, where you can enter an address, a city, a state, a ZIP code, an airport code, or an intersection. Click the Get Map button, and a map page appears showing your request. Figure 24-4 shows a map for a street, with no specific street number requested.

Handling the map

After you have a map on your screen, it's amazing what you can do with it. Fold it, put it in the glove compartment, use it to dry the dishes. Actually, you can do none of those things, but you *can* put it on the floor to paper-train your dog. Not really. Wrap fresh fish? No.

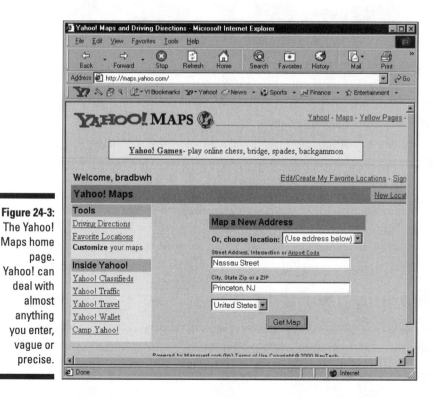

Figure 24-3:
The Yahoo! Maps home page. Yahoo! can deal with almost anything you enter, vague or precise.

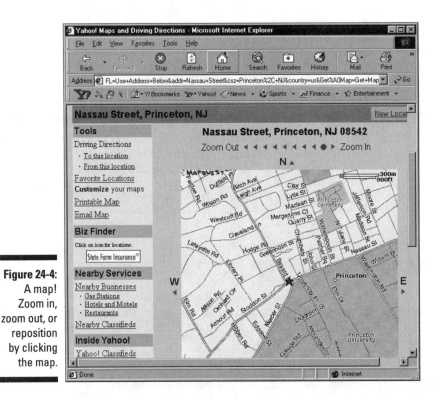

Figure 24-4:
A map!
Zoom in,
zoom out, or
reposition
by clicking
the map.

Here's what you can do:

- ✔ Click the Zoom In and Zoom Out arrows to change the map's scale. Each arrow is a link to a new page with a differently scaled map. Zooming in increases the map's detail.

- ✔ Click any of the four directional arrows to shift the map's orientation.

- ✔ Click anywhere on the map to create a new center point. You can continue with this reorientation indefinitely — the maps continue displaying new neighborhoods. Even with detailed neighborhood maps, you could move across the entire country this way by clicking on the edge of each map. Of course, it would take 7-bazillion clicks.

- ✔ Scroll down and use the Map a New Address fields to start over.

Finding your way

To be lost or not to be lost — that is the question. Yahoo! maps supplies driving directions between any two addresses. The more specific you can be in entering the address the better, but the system can cope with general starting and destination addresses. Here's how to proceed:

1. **On the Yahoo! Maps home page, click the <u>Driving Directions</u> link.**

2. **On the Yahoo! maps — Driving Directions page, which is shown in Figure 24-5, enter a starting address and a destination address.**

   Note the drop-down menus marked *(Use address below)*. If you're new to Yahoo! Maps, those menus contain nothing. In the next section, I explain how to put stuff in them.

3. **Click the Get Directions button.**

   The next page displays step-by-step, turn-by-turn driving directions. Each step is identified by its mileage duration. The heading above the directions summarizes the total distance and travel time. Click the <u>Reverse Driving Directions</u> to go back, saving yourself the time-honored struggle of reversing them in your head. Scroll down to see your route marked on a map.

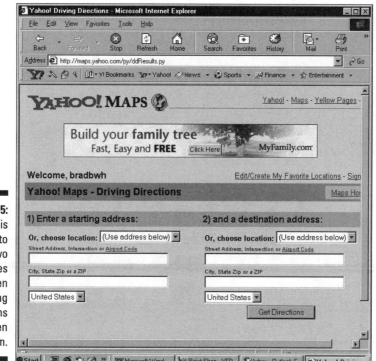

Figure 24-5:
Use this page to enter two addresses and then see driving directions between them.

Storing locations

One nifty feature of Yahoo! Maps lets you enter certain key addresses once and then select those locations from drop-down menus when requesting driving directions. Proceed with these steps:

1. On the Yahoo! maps home page, click the <u>Favorite Locations</u> link.

2. On the Your Favorite Locations page, enter the address and then click the Add Location button.

3. On any map or driving directions page, use the *(Use address below)* drop-down menu to select one of your stored addresses.

Yahooligans!

www.yahooligans.com

Yahooligans! (Figure 24-6) has for years been considered the preeminent children's directory to the Web. Following in the footsteps of the main Yahoo! directory, Yahooligans! consists of handpicked site links. The main criteria for inclusion are kid-friendliness and safety. You and your child can surf through Yahooligans! sites with some assurance that they won't present anything inappropriate.

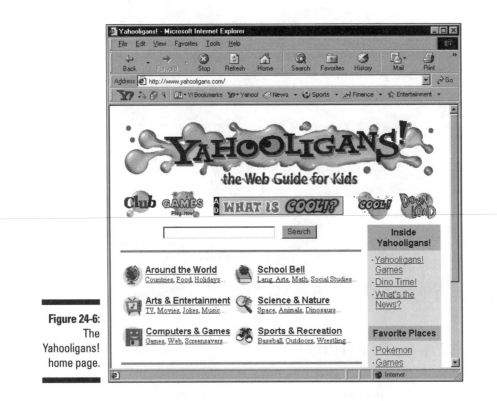

Figure 24-6:
The
Yahooligans!
home page.

In addition to the directory, Yahooligans! presents some special on-screen content such as a virtual club and online games. The Download section stocks child-suitable programs and multimedia clips.

Yahoo! Phone Booth

phonebooth.yahoo.com

The latest development in the fast-changing realm of *Internet telephony* is free long-distance phone calls. This may sound too good to be true, but amazingly, for once it's not. The Internet can be used to place a voice phone call from one PC to another or (far more popularly) from one PC to a regular phone. The cost of connecting a call by that means is lower than by the traditional phone network. It remains to be seen how long the Net-phone companies can continue giving away connection time, but for now the situation is great for consumers.

The one downside to free Internet phone calling is sound quality and connection reliability. I guess that's two downsides. Oh, and complexity. Three downsides. How many downsides would it take to dissuade you from getting unlimited *free* long-distance phone service in the United States? Yes, I thought so. Well, this section explains how to get started the Yahoo! way.

Yahoo! Phone Booth partners with two Net-phone companies, Deltathree.com and Net2Phone. Both offer free service, and the interfaces are quite different.

Using Deltathree.com

Deltathree.com is quicker to install than Net2Phone, but it can be argued that the set-up interfaces are more confusing. However, after you get it installed, subsequent uses are easy enough. Follow these steps to give it a try:

1. **On the Yahoo! Phone Booth home page, click the <u>PC to Phone Call</u> link.**

2. **In the pop-up window, enter your name and e-mail address and then click the Sign Up and Call! Button.**

3. **In the next pop-up window, fill in the required fields and then click the Submit button.**

   If you don't like giving your mailing address, quit now. In this form, your phone number is optional.

4. **On the second page of the second pop-up window, click the Close Window button.**

   Nothing like a useful page, huh? An e-mail is sent with your user ID and password.

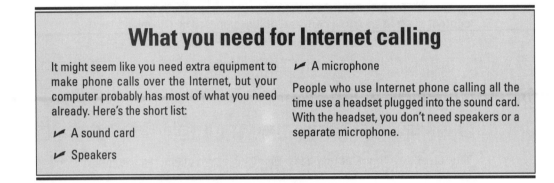

What you need for Internet calling

It might seem like you need extra equipment to make phone calls over the Internet, but your computer probably has most of what you need already. Here's the short list:

✔ A sound card

✔ Speakers

✔ A microphone

People who use Internet phone calling all the time use a headset plugged into the sound card. With the headset, you don't need speakers or a separate microphone.

5. **In the first pop-up window, enter the phone number you want to call and then click the CALL button.**

A browser plug-in automatically downloads and installs. Figure 24-7 shows the call window.

Although the on-screen instruction says to "enter your Phone Number," making it seem as if you should enter your personal phone number in that space, it really means you should enter the number you want to dial.

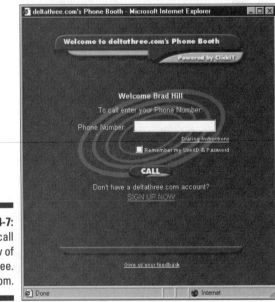

Figure 24-7: The call window of Deltathree. com.

6. **On the next page (still in the pop-up window), click the Make the call button.**

The page asks if you'd like to add funds to your account. You don't need any funds if you're a United States resident calling anywhere in the U.S. or Canada. This screen appears only the first time you use Deltathree.com.

The call is made, and you hear the destination phone ringing through your computer's speakers. Remember to hook a microphone or headset to your computer, or you'll be at a loss for words when somebody answers at the other end.

Using Net2Phone

Net2Phone is a popular Internet phone company that normally charges a penny per minute for domestic (U.S.) calls. In cooperation with Yahoo! Phone Booth, Net2Phone is (as of this writing) offering free domestic calling to Yahoo! users. The service also offers low international rates. Follow these steps to set up the program:

1. **On the Net2Phone page, click the Click Here to Download icon.**

2. **On the download page, fill in the fields and then click the Click Here to Download! button.**

You may see a Security Warning dialog box — if so, click the Yes button. Installation proceeds automatically, and the Net2Phone panel appears on your screen.

3. **On the Confirmation panel, click the Yes button.**

This step starts your registration, which is necessary to use the service. A registration form appears in your browser window.

4. **Fill in all required fields of the registration form and then click the Submit Form button.**

This page collects basic identifying information.

5. **On the next page, fill in all required fields and then click the Submit This Form button.**

Giving up personal information is always the price you pay on the Internet for free or very cheap service.

6. **Copy down your account number from the pop-up Net2Phone Registration Form and then click the OK button.**

Now you're ready to make a call. Use the mouse to enter a number on the Net2Phone panel or, easier yet, use your keyboard's number pad. Then press the Enter key to place the call.

The VoiceEmail feature is for sending a recorded message to an Internet e-mail address.

Yahoo! Invitations

invites.yahoo.com

Sometimes I think the whole purpose of cyberspace is to replace paper. The intent of Yahoo! Invitations is to replace paper invites with an online party management system. Invitations are sent through e-mail, and the recipients respond by means of an interactive Web page linked to the e-mail.

The Yahoo! Invitations home page presents several possibilities, but the truth is they all lead to the same form that you use to set out the details of your invitation. On that form, you determine what and when the occasion is and also enter the e-mail addresses of the folks you're inviting.

On the receiving end, each invitee gets an e-mail with a link to a more elaborate notice that appears in a browser window. That invitation lets the recipient respond and see who else is attending and who was invited (by e-mail address, not name).

To send an invitation, follow these steps:

1. **On the Yahoo! Invitations home page, click an invitation type.**

   Scroll down to see a complete list. In truth, it doesn't matter which you choose — you can change the invitation type later.

2. **On the Create Invite page, fill in the fields and make all selections with the drop-down menus.**

   The Title appears in the e-mail header received by your invitees. Whatever you put in the Invitation Notes box appears in the body of the e-mail.

3. **Click the Preview and Customize button to see how the Web version of your invitation looks.**

   On the Preview page, use the links in the left navigation bar to edit the details and colors of the invitation.

4. **Click the Send Now button.**

   At this point, your invitation is sent to every address on your invitee list. Recipients receive an abbreviated invitation as shows in Figure 24-8. Recipients then click the e-mail link to see you Web invitation, similar to that shown in Figure 24-9. As they respond with Yes, Maybe, and No, your invitation updates automatically, showing how your event is shaping up.

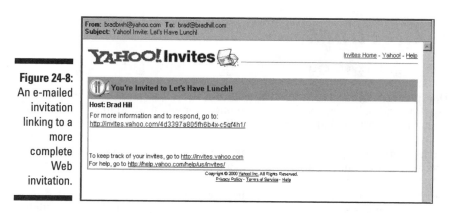

Figure 24-8:
An e-mailed
invitation
linking to a
more
complete
Web
invitation.

A very nice feature is positioned at the bottom of each Web invitation, under
the Message Board heading. There, invitees can start discussion threads
about the event or about anything they want, including the questionable
snacks at your last party.

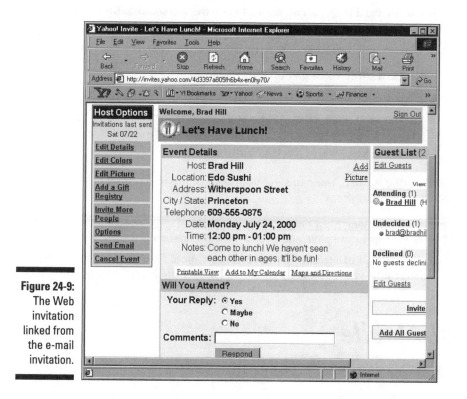

Figure 24-9:
The Web
invitation
linked from
the e-mail
invitation.

Yahoo! Greetings

greetings.yahoo.com

Hardly anything has taken the Net by storm to such a degree as electronic greeting cards. Perhaps you've gotten one yourself, nestled into your e-mail box. If not, start the ball rolling yourself with a trip to Yahoo! Greetings.

Each greeting is a picture and a message. It appears in the recipients e-mail box as a simple link, leading to the card itself displayed in a browser window.

Sending a greeting could hardly be simpler. The service is set up like a directory. When you settle on a card, you fill in a few information fields and click a button. Follow these steps:

1. **On the Yahoo! Greetings home page, click any occasion or type of greeting.**

2. **On the next page, click any thumbnail image of a card.**

3. **On the card page, scroll down to see the personalization form.**

   Fill in all the fields — the Optional Message field is, naturally, optional. Choose a delivery date from the drop-down menu. Click the Add Voice box if you have a microphone attached to your computer and you want to add a short voice greeting.

4. **Click the PREVIEW YOUR GREETING button.**

5. **On the next page, click the Make More Changes button to edit your card, if you want.**

6. **Click the Send This Greeting button.**

One terrific feature: You can send your own photo as a greeting. You can do this in three ways:

- ✔ Click the Send Your Own Photos As Online Cards link from the Yahoo! Greetings home page and then follow the instructions.

- ✔ Upload a photo (or more than one) to Yahoo! Photos (see Chapter 6). After uploading, click any photo and select the Send Greeting link.

Yahoo! Mobile

mobile.yahoo.com

Yahoo! Mobile is a young, evolving service that remains on the forefront of mobile computing. Nearly every mobile service provider features Yahoo! as one of its premium services. This section of Yahoo! summarizes all your possibilities for taking Yahoo! out on the street.

Mobile computing is accomplished with three types of devices:

   ✔ Cell phones with associated e-mail addresses
   ✔ Alphanumeric pagers logged to the Internet
   ✔ Personal Digital Assistants (PDAs), also known as palmtop computers

To most observers, PDAs represent the future of portable Internet access, to a greater degree than cell phones or pagers.

Yahoo! Mobile is partly focused on delivering Yahoo! service portably and also concentrates on helping you shop for a mobile device and download programs for whatever device you have. You can learn a lot from Yahoo! Mobile, even if you aren't yet equipped for portable online access.

Yahoo! Picture Gallery

`gallery.yahoo.com`

Yahoo! Picture Gallery is an online repository for free photographs. Every picture in the Gallery is either in the public domain or licensed by Yahoo! for your unlimited online use.

Three Yahoo! services make good use of photos from the Picture Gallery:

   ✔ The Yahoo! Photo Album (see Chapter 6)
   ✔ Yahoo! Greetings, described earlier in this chapter
   ✔ PageBuilder at Yahoo! GeoCities (see Chapter 4)

Conveniently, Yahoo! Picture Gallery links effortlessly to all three services. The Gallery is set up like a directory. Simply browse your way through the photo categories (you can find everything from musical instruments to historic photos), eventually clicking a specific photo. On that photo's page, click any of the three links that interface with the Photo Album, Yahoo! Greetings, and PageBuilder.

Chapter 25

Ten More Yahoo! Services You Need to Know About

*J*ust one more time. Chapter 24 didn't quite do the trick. Here are ten more services stuffed into the nooks and crannies of the sprawling Yahoo! empire.

Yahoo! Calendar

`calendar.yahoo.com`

The preceding URL displays your main calendar page when you're signed in to your Yahoo! ID. You're likely to bump into your own calendar while roaming around the expanse of Yahoo!, because it hooks into Yahoo! Clubs and Yahoo! Net Events, as well as other portions of the service.

The Calendar service has been evolving for years and has become fairly complex and extremely useful. You can view it by day, week, month, or year. Adding events to the calendar is a simple matter of filling in a form — or, in several parts of Yahoo!, by clicking the <u>Add to Calendar</u> links that you see next to scheduled events of information. Those with advanced cell phones can link their calendar to their phone. Yahoo! Calendar is most slick when scheduling online events, but you can use it for anything, including offline chores and appointments.

Yahoo! FinanceVision

`financevision.yahoo.com`

It was a big day when Yahoo! announced its FinanceVision Webcasting feature (see Figure 25-1). Yahoo! is brilliant at gathering content from all over the Internet and presenting it in easily navigable pages. Only rarely does the service create its own content, as is the case with Finance Vision. This feature is an audio and video streaming console that netcasts financial programming 24 hours a day (except during some holidays).

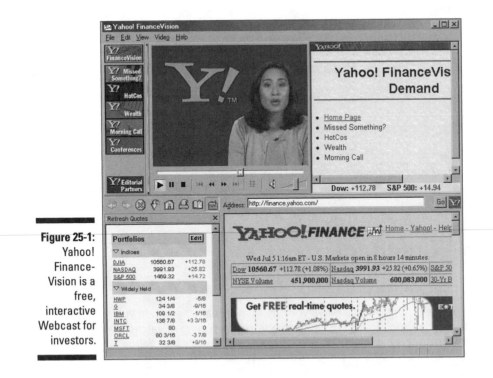

Figure 25-1:
Yahoo!
Finance-
Vision is a
free,
interactive
Webcast for
investors.

You can click the <u>Yahoo! FinanceVision</u> link from the main Yahoo! Finance page. To see the feature, try the <u>Click to Watch FinanceVision</u> link. (You may be prompted to add one or two plug-ins — click the Yes button on those panels.) Doing so initiates a browser-based Webcast.

The full-featured download creates an interactive viewing environment that invites you to search for past programs, check your own stocks, rummage through Yahoo! Finance (or any other Web site) in an integrated browser window, and view the schedule of upcoming events. Programming features market-hours commentary and plenty of interviews with guest investing experts.

Yahoo! Pets

pets.yahoo.com

A resource for animal lovers and pet owners, Yahoo! Pets, shown in Figure 25-2, links to articles from other pet-expert sites. Certain animals — dogs, cats, horses, fish — enjoy their own home pages and resource guides. Yahoo! Pets links aggressively into Yahoo! Classifieds for finding pets, Yahoo! Messages and Chat for discussing pets, and Yahoo! Greetings for sending electronic greeting cards with pictures of animals.

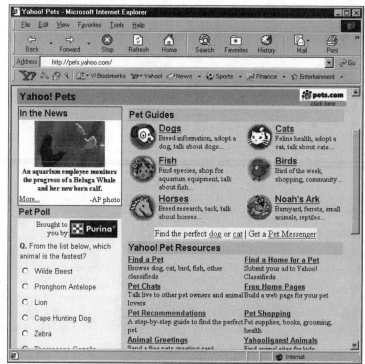

Figure 25-2: The Yahoo! Pets home page.

Yahoo! Bill Pay

bills.yahoo.com

Internet bill paying is an increasingly popular service in online personal finance. Offered by traditional banks, Internet banks, and third-part bill-paying services, all these competing systems liberate the user to some extent from the tyranny of writing checks and sending them through the mail. Online bill-paying services let you enter the names, account numbers, and mailing addresses of your bills. Then, either according to a regular schedule or on demand, the service issues a check for a certain amount and mails it to the payee. For this to work, you must give the bill-paying service access to at least one checking account — which is why the service works so well when supplied by the bank itself.

Yahoo! has created an extremely clear and intuitive bill-paying service. (See Figure 25-3 for a glimpse of what it looks like.) Inexpensive, too. Yahoo! Bill Pay can handle electronic payments (no checks) to companies that accept them.

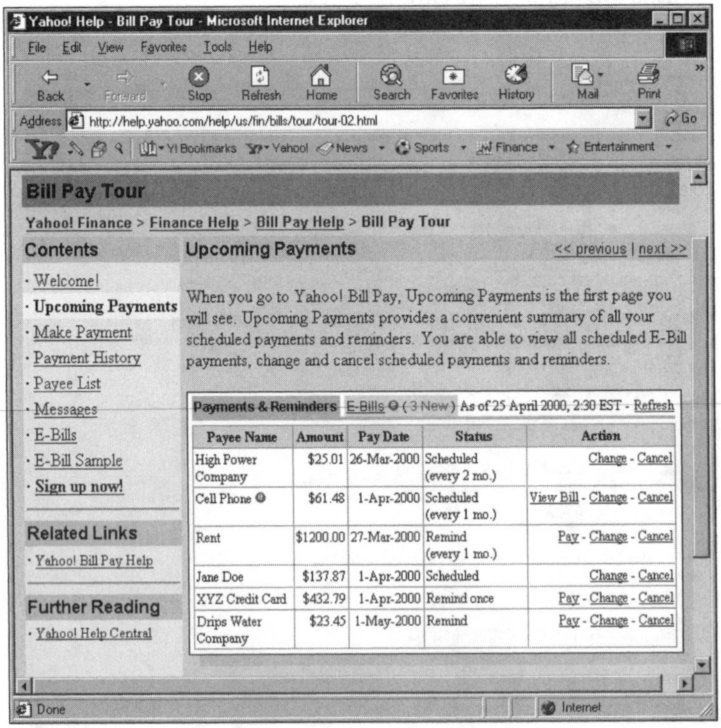

Figure 25-3: An example of the scheduled payments screen in Yahoo! Bill Pay.

Yahoo! Family Accounts

`family.yahoo.com`

Parents are right to be concerned about exposing their kids to the Internet. The entire range of human experience and behavior is represented online, and a child's explorations should be monitored. The Yahoo! Family Account is a master household account to which children can be added. Each child gets his or her own Yahoo! ID, but the parents control the password and features of the account.

Family Accounts contain automatic controls of what kids of certain ages can and can't do. Children under the age of thirteen are restricted most severely in the Family Account — they're unable to start a Yahoo! Club, add an address or phone number to their account information, participate in sweepstakes, register in People Search, create a public Yahoo! profile, participate in Yahoo! Auctions, post a Yahoo! Personals ad, or view any Yahoo! Adult area.

Yahoo! Notepad

`notepad.yahoo.com`

Yahoo! Notepad is a simple, surprisingly useful, little feature. Notepad is an on-screen version of a pad of stick-notes. Jot down thoughts, musings, appointments, and click the Save button. Your notes are stored in folders of your own creation (you're given a default folder to start), and a search engine helps you find notes if you develop a big stack of them.

Yahoo! Points

`points.yahoo.com`

Yahoo! Points is a reward system for shopping in Yahoo! Stores. Click the Enroll Me Now! button to sign up. There's no registration form; Yahoo! signs your ID right into the system. After you're signed in, the Yahoo! Points home page displays special points-earning purchases. Points are redeemable for gift certificates in Yahoo! Stores. Please note that points are not awarded for *every* purchase in Yahoo! Shopping. The yellow star icon shown on the home page (see Figure 25-4) indicates a points opportunity throughout Yahoo!. Your Points balance is always displayed in the left sidebar of the Yahoo! Points home page.

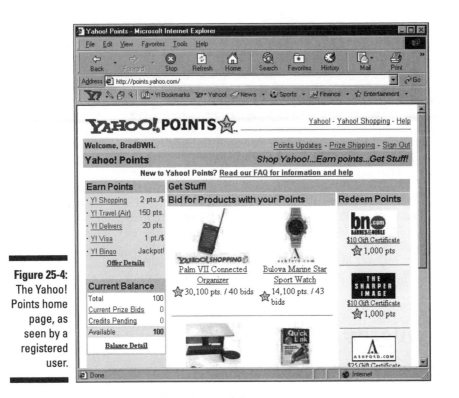

Yahoo! How-To

howto.yahoo.com

A general tutorial for Internet newcomers, Yahoo! How-To does a good job separating objective information from Yahoo! promotion. Two broad divisions split the Yahoo! How-To home page: Learn About the Internet, and Learn About Yahoo!. Both are useful, though the latter can't compare to the book you're holding right now, if I do say so. The first section presents a nice overview of surfing, searching, getting news, and joining online communities.

Yahoo! Domains

domains.yahoo.com

Yahoo! Domains is somewhat connected to Yahoo! Website Services, described in Chapter 5. Finding and buying a domain (the heart of a Web address) is part of the Website Services but also stands on its own as a dedicated service. Use

Yahoo! Domains to search for and reserve a domain even if you decide not to host that domain's Web site with Yahoo! Website Services. If you're a little confused about what domains are and how they work, please consult Chapter 5.

Yahoo! Gear

www.store.yahoo.com/yahoogear

Insert Yahoo! T-shirts? A Yahoo! watch? Duffel bag? Oh no — not a Yahoo! slinky? Yes, it's all true, and more. Figure 25-5 shows where you can shop online to load up on Yahoo! wearables. I'm not going to buy the watch, but the fleece pullover is nice. Of course, for the money (plus shipping) you could buy two more copies of this book as wedding presents.

Figure 25-5:
Yes, you can purchase a Yahoo! Slinky. What's stopping you?

Index

Notes

Notes

Notes

WWW.DUMMIES.COM

YOUR ONLINE RESOURCE

Discover Dummies Online!

The Dummies Web Site is your fun and friendly online resource for the latest information about *For Dummies®* books and your favorite topics. The Web site is the place to communicate with us, exchange ideas with other *For Dummies* readers, chat with authors, and have fun!

Ten Fun and Useful Things You Can Do at www.dummies.com

1. Win free *For Dummies* books and more!
2. Register your book and be entered in a prize drawing.
3. Meet your favorite authors through the IDG Books Worldwide Author Chat Series.
4. Exchange helpful information with other *For Dummies* readers.
5. Discover other great *For Dummies* books you must have!
6. Purchase Dummieswear® exclusively from our Web site.
7. Buy *For Dummies* books online.
8. Talk to us. Make comments, ask questions, get answers!
9. Download free software.
10. Find additional useful resources from authors.

Link directly to these ten fun and useful things at
http://www.dummies.com/10useful

For other technology titles from IDG Books Worldwide, go to
www.idgbooks.com

Not on the Web yet? It's easy to get started with *Dummies 101®: The Internet For Windows® 98* or *The Internet For Dummies®* at local retailers everywhere.

Find other *For Dummies* books on these topics:
Business • Career • Databases • Food & Beverage • Games • Gardening • Graphics • Hardware
Health & Fitness • Internet and the World Wide Web • Networking • Office Suites
Operating Systems • Personal Finance • Pets • Programming • Recreation • Sports
Spreadsheets • Teacher Resources • Test Prep • Word Processing

IDG BOOKS WORLDWIDE
BOOK REGISTRATION

Register This Book and Win!

We want to hear from you!

Visit **http://my2cents.dummies.com** to register this book and tell us how you liked it!

- ✔ Get entered in our monthly prize giveaway.

- ✔ Give us feedback about this book — tell us what you like best, what you like least, or maybe what you'd like to ask the author and us to change!

- ✔ Let us know any other *For Dummies*® topics that interest you.

Your feedback helps us determine what books to publish, tells us what coverage to add as we revise our books, and lets us know whether we're meeting your needs as a *For Dummies* reader. You're our most valuable resource, and what you have to say is important to us!

Not on the Web yet? It's easy to get started with *Dummies 101*®: *The Internet For Windows*® *98* or *The Internet For Dummies*® at local retailers everywhere.

Or let us know what you think by sending us a letter at the following address:

For Dummies Book Registration
Dummies Press
10475 Crosspoint Blvd.
Indianapolis, IN 46256

™

...FOR DUMMIES

BESTSELLING BOOK SERIES